Calixthe Beyala
Performances of Migration

Contemporary French and Francophone Cultures 5

Contemporary French and Francophone Cultures

Series Editors
EDMUND SMYTH
Manchester Metropolitan University
CHARLES FORSDICK
University of Liverpool

Editorial Board
LYNN A. HIGGINS
Dartmouth College
MIREILLE ROSELLO
Northwestern University
MICHAEL SHERINGHAM
University of Oxford
DAVID WALKER
University of Sheffield

This series aims to provide a forum for new research on modern and contemporary French and francophone cultures and writing. The books published in *Contemporary French and Francophone Cultures* reflect a wide variety of critical practices and theoretical approaches, in harmony with the intellectual, cultural and social developments which have taken place over the past few decades. All manifestations of contemporary French and francophone culture and expression are considered, including literature, cinema, popular culture, theory. The volumes in the series will participate in the wider debate on key aspects of contemporary culture.

1 Chris Tinker, *Georges Brassens and Jacques Brel: Personal and Social Narratives in Post-war Chanson* (0-85323-758-1 cloth, 0-85323-768-9 paper)

2 Debra Kelly, *Autobiography and Independence: Selfhood and Creativity in Postcolonial African Writing in French* (0-85323-659-3 cloth)

3 Matthew Screech, *Masters of the Ninth Art: Bandes dessinées and Franco-Belgian Identity* (0-85323-938-X cloth)

4 Akane Kawakami, *Travellers' Visions: French Literary Encounters with Japan, 1881–2004*

NICKI HITCHCOTT

Calixthe Beyala
Performances of Migration

LIVERPOOL UNIVERSITY PRESS

First published 2006 by
Liverpool University Press
4 Cambridge Street
Liverpool L69 7ZU

Copyright © 2006 Nicki Hitchcott

The right of Nicki Hitchcott to be identified as the author
of this work has been asserted by her in accordance
with the Copyright, Designs and Patents Act, 1988

All rights reserved.
No part of this book may be reproduced,
stored in a retrieval system, or transmitted,
in any form or by any means, electronic, mechanical,
photocopying, recording, or otherwise,
without the prior written permission of the publisher.

British Library Cataloguing-in-Publication data
A British Library CIP record is available

ISBN 1-84631-028-8 cased
ISBN-13 978-1-84631-028-7 cased

Typeset in Sabon by Koinonia, Manchester
Printed and bound in the European Union by
Biddles Ltd, King's Lynn

Contents

	Acknowledgements	vi
	Abbreviations	vii
	Introduction: A Postcolonial Phenomenon	1
1	Calixthe Beyala Incorporated?	15
2	Invented Authenticities	39
3	Migrating Subjectivities	66
4	'Afro-française': In-Between or Out of Sync?	89
5	Performing Identities	112
	Conclusion: Survival in a Post-Exotic Age	137
	Notes	151
	Bibliography of Works Cited	171
	Index	181

Acknowledgements

A number of people and institutions have offered me support during the production of this book. I particular, I would like to thank the AHRC and the University of Nottingham for providing me with an extended period of research leave to complete the manuscript in 2004–2005. Alec Hargreaves and Dominic Thomas have supported this project from its inception and I have had the privilege to enjoy their intellectual companionship along the way. Robin Bloxsidge, Anthony Cond, Andrew Kirk and Ed Smyth at Liverpool University Press have been a pleasure to work with, and my sincere thanks go to Charles Forsdick for suggesting that I place my book in this series. I would also like to acknowledge the good advice and encouragement I received from the following colleagues, family members and friends: Rosemary Chapman, Elizabeth and Peter Coates, Sam Haigh, Anna Hitchcott, Margaret-Anne Hutton, Laïla Ibnlfassi, Diana Knight, Marie-France Malonga, David Murphy and Mireille Rosello.

Most of all, I would like thank Richard Matthews for so much that would be lost in translation. This book is dedicated to him.

January 2006

Abbreviations

AA	*Assèze l'Africaine*
APE	*Les Arbres en parlent encore*
AS	*Amours sauvages*
CCMA	*Comment cuisiner son mari à l'africaine*
CSB	*C'est le soleil qui m'a brûlée*
FNFN	*Femme nue, femme noire*
HP	*Les Honneurs perdus*
LAFC	*Lettre d'une Afro-française à ses compatriotes*
LASO	*Lettre d'une Africaine à ses soeurs occidentales*
LP	*La Plantation*
LPPB	*Loukoum: the 'Little Prince' of Belleville*
MAA	*Maman a un amant*
PFR	*La petite fille du réverbère*
PPB	*Le petit prince de Belleville*
SDS	*Seul le Diable le savait*
SHL	*The Sun Hath Looked Upon Me*
TTT	*Tu t'appelleras Tanga*
YNT	*Your Name will be Tanga*

INTRODUCTION
A Postcolonial Phenomenon

> Calixthe Beyala a fait de l'écriture une profession à part entière.[1]
>
> [Calixthe Beyala has made writing a fully fledged profession.]

In 1994 Calixthe Beyala's sixth novel, *Assèze l'Africaine*, appeared in bookshops with the red and white publicity wrapper connoting a best-selling or canonical author in France. Calixthe Beyala had become a name that sells. In 2005 her most recent novel, *La Plantation* went straight into the bestseller lists, ranked seventeenth by *L'Express*/RTL in its first month of publication.[2] Beyala is one of the few francophone African authors to make her living from writing fiction, receiving advances from her publisher, Albin Michel, of more than £100,000 per novel.[3] The author of thirteen novels and two essays to date, Beyala is undoubtedly the most famous woman writer from francophone sub-Saharan Africa. Born in 1960 in Douala, Cameroon, she migrated to Europe in her twenties and has been living in Paris for many years. Her work has been awarded numerous literary prizes, including the prestigious Grand Prix du Roman de l'Académie Française in 1996. However, Beyala's image as a writer has been tarnished by two high-profile allegations of plagiarism, one of which led to her conviction in 1996 in the High Court in Paris. Often appearing in the media, Beyala also has the reputation of being something of a loudmouth; she has been 'critiquée pour ses interventions médiatiques tonitruantes et ses coups de gueule réguliers' [criticized for her thundering media interventions and her regular rantings].[4] Beyala is, then, an extremely controversial figure in France and in Africa. On the one hand, she is something of a postcolonial celebrity: a prolific and successful author who is regularly invited to contribute to television talk shows. On the other, she is reviled as a literary fraud who lacks a sense of propriety.

Yet despite (or indeed because of) the controversy surrounding her, Beyala continues to publish and be widely read not only in

France and the francophone world but also, in French and in English translation, in Britain and North America. The fact that her novels are produced by prominent French publishers (Stock, Le Pré aux Clercs and, since 1992, Albin Michel) immediately distinguishes her from other francophone African women writers who are published either in African publishing houses such as Les Nouvelles Editions Africaines, with short print runs and limited marketing, or with small specialist publishers in Paris, such as L'Harmattan and Présence Africaine.[5] By contrast, eleven of Beyala's thirteen novels have been reprinted in a low-priced, pocket paperback format produced by Editions J'ai Lu. Three of her novels have been translated into English and published by Heinemann in the prestigious – but now regrettably defunct – African Writers Series.[6] Whereas only 2000 copies of her debut novel, *C'est le soleil qui m'a brûlée* were produced in the first print run, Beyala now sells over 150,000 copies of every novel (300,000 including the cheap paperback and book club editions).[7]

Surprisingly, given her unprecedented success, no book-length study of Beyala has previously been published in English. While a considerable number of academic articles have appeared on various aspects of her work, there is, to date, only one monograph on Beyala's fiction: Rangira Béatrice Gallimore's *L'Oeuvre romanesque de Calixthe Beyala*.[8] Published as it was in 1997, this book is only able to discuss half of Beyala's fictional production, stopping at *Maman a un amant* (1993) and focusing mainly on the first two novels, *C'est le soleil qui m'a brûlée* and *Tu t'appelleras Tanga*. Chapters on selected novels by Beyala have appeared in more general studies of African women's writing but, like Gallimore, the authors of these books tend to limit their discussions to the early texts. Irène Assiba D'Almeida, for example, provides a detailed analysis of *Tu t'appelleras Tanga*; Juliana Makuchi Nfah-Abbenyi discusses only the first two novels.[9] Those critics who do include a wider selection of novels, such as Odile Cazenave and Kenneth Harrow, include Beyala's novels among a wide range of texts by African women writers.[10] As such, none of the published works considers the entirety of Beyala's oeuvre, a gap this book attempts to fill. Moreover, Beyala criticism tends to read her as an African rather than a migrant writer, despite the fact that she has lived in Paris for around half her life and has published all her books there. This is not to suggest that to identify Beyala as an African writer is wrong, but rather to emphasize what I consider to be one of the defining features of her profile as an author.

This book analyses the phenomenon that is Calixthe Beyala through two main routes, the first of which begins by considering her problematic status in France, where her attempts to be taken seriously as a writer have been consistently undermined by the media's campaign to expose her as a fraud. Led by the satirical magazine *Le Canard enchaîné*, as well as publisher and editor Pierre Assouline, the media created what became known as 'l'Affaire Beyala' [the Beyala Affair]. In the light of this 'Affair', I discuss the ambivalent reception of Beyala and her writing in France and also in Africa, both in terms of reviews of her work by critics and journalists as well as through analysis of her appearances on TV and radio. The contradictions that emerge in Beyala's reception and representation epitomize the ambivalence of the space that she occupies in France. Is this ambivalence simply a result of all the controversy that surrounds her, or is it rather a consequence of the fact that she is both an African migrant and a woman? This book will attempt to unpack the ways in which Beyala draws on her ambivalence, consciously performing her own marginality in a strategic attempt to reappropriate exoticism for her own ends.

As a migrant writer who is well established in France, Beyala is exotic but at the same time familiar. Herein, according to Elleke Boehmer, lies the key to her success. Boehmer notes that migrant writers are especially popular with readers and critics in European metropolises because 'although bearing all the attractions of the exotic, the magical, the Other, they also participate reassuringly in [familiar] aesthetic languages'.[11] In other words, the migrant text combines what Spivak calls 'new orientalism'[12] with an appeal to Gilroy's notion of 'cultural insiderism'.[13] Like its author, the migrant text is simultaneously located inside and outside the majority culture of the host nation, in this case metropolitan France. It is no surprise that Beyala's most successful novels are her novels of migration, particularly the 'Loukoum' novels, which combine the exotic otherness of African characters with the familiar landscape of Paris.[14] As Boehmer notes, 'postcolonial writers who retain a more national focus, who don't straddle worlds, or translate as well, do not rank as high in the West as do their migrant fellows'.[15] In terms of reception, Calixthe Beyala and her novels are incorporated into French culture in the form of literary prizes and critical acclaim, and yet at the same time they are marginalized as exotic and/or illegitimate. Just as Beyala is both incorporated and marginalized in relation to France, she is also simultaneously inside and outside her geographical home in Africa. The complexity of this geographical (dis)location generates ambivalence not only in the migrant author but also among her readers. In this book I consider Beyala's ambivalent relationships with both France and Africa, an ambivalence that, I will argue, is symptomatic of the experience of migration and one that she advocates using to one's own advantage.

The second focus of the book is on critical readings of Beyala's texts. I discuss Beyala's oeuvre in terms of 'migrant writing', analysing the ways in which experiences of migration (both literal and fictional) manifest themselves in her writing on the levels of both content and form. I trace the fictional migration of Beyala's settings from the African continent in the early texts to Paris in those published in the early 1990s, and then between Africa and Paris in her more recent novels. In particular, I consider the ways in which identities are transformed by, and renegotiated through, the experience of migration in Beyala's fiction. What emerges is an emphasis on the performativity of migrant identity such that it only exists in the moment of its articulation and, like Beyala herself, is constantly being reinvented.

As a migrant author, Beyala is what geographers King, Connell and White describe as 'the critical participant-observer into his/her own condition' and for this reason Beyala's texts will not be discussed in isolation from their author.[16] In my analysis of Beyala as both migrant writer and postcolonial phenomenon, I take as my starting point a question posed by Françoise Lionnet in her essay, 'Logiques métisses: Cultural Appropriation and Postcolonial Representations', that is: 'how does she [the 'other' woman] articulate her relationship to a global system (of knowledge, of representation, of capital) within which her narratives are inevitably inscribed, yet not fully contained?'[17] In other words, I compare the ways in which the migrant author is positioned – and positions herself – with the articulation of these positions in her fictional writings. The book attempts to draw together Beyala's fictional politics of positioning with the 'real life' positioning of Beyala herself by the ethnic majority in France. What emerges is Beyala's self-conscious staging of identity in response to her positioning in the global marketplace, confirming Graham Huggan's claim that 'ostensibly *anti*-colonial writers/thinkers are all working, some of them conspicuously, within the *neo*colonial context of global commodity culture'.[18]

Using what can broadly be defined as a postcolonial approach, this book will draw on research in the fields of literary criticism and cultural studies. The limitations of what has become known as postcolonial criticism have been well documented and I do not intend to re-rehearse the arguments here.[19] It is enough to draw attention to the fact that, as Nicholas Harrison reminds us, 'postcolonial theory is not an identifiable "type" of theory' but is rather a 'response to political and historical issues of vast importance and scope', which draws on research in a number of different fields.[20] My aim, then, is not to produce yet another critique of the 'post(-)colonial'; rather, I want to use theories of identity and culture to analyse the formation of migrant subjectivities in the writings of Calixthe Beyala. Following Carole Boyce Davies in *Black Women, Writing and Identity*, this book adopts what she calls a 'visitor theory' approach, that is 'a kind of critical relationality in which various theoretical positions are interrogated for their specific applicability to Black women's experiences and textualities and negotiated within a particular inquiry with a necessary eclectism'.[21] A pluralist approach reflects the syncretic nature of postcolonial migrant subjectivities. It also reflects the comparative and interdisciplinary nature of postcolonial studies and responds to recent calls for more relational approaches to postcolonial texts. The aim of a multiplicity of perspectives is, as Murdoch and Donadey explain, 'to subvert the hegemonic hold of theory' and to consider what they term the 'productive intersections' between different schools of thought.[22]

Despite an increasingly large corpus of postcolonial writing in France, particularly from the second-generation Maghrebian population, French literary critics have tended to shy away from postcolonial theory. One of the best-known critics of migrant literature in France is Michel Laronde who, in a collection of essays on first- and second-generation immigrant writers, includes Beyala as an example of what he calls 'écriture décentrée' [decentred writing], that is, 'une Ecriture qui, par rapport à une Langue et une Culture centripètes, produit un Texte qui maintient des décalages linguistiques et idéologiques' [a Writing that, in relation to a centripetal Language and Culture, produces a Text that maintains linguistic and ideological gaps].[23] Despite the postcolonial connotations of the title of his collection, Laronde's introduction to 'de-centred writing' makes no mention of postcolonialism. Familiar markers of postcolonial texts such as creolization and hybridity are ambiguously presented as signifiers of 'l'évolution de réalités linguistiques et culturelles' [the evolution of linguistic and cultural realities] (p. 8). In this respect, Laronde's study is typical of what a number of British and American critics have identified as a French resistance to postcolonial theory.[24] Only recently has Laronde begun to address an explicitly postcolonial perspective, notably in his essay published in Murdoch and Donadey's volume, *Postcolonial Theory and Francophone Literary Studies*. I would suggest that it is not without significance that this particular essay is published in English in the United States rather than in France.[25] Regrettably, Laronde's essay remains trapped in the now well-worn 'post-colonial' versus 'postcolonial' debate, further demonstrating the lack of dialogue between postcolonialists in France and those in Britain and North America.[26] Unlike Laronde, fellow French critic Jean-Marc Moura has embraced postcolonial theory for quite some time, but his work often remains at a fairly descriptive level.[27] Moura's book, *Littératures francophones et théorie postcoloniale*, does, as its title suggests, set out to discuss postcolonial theory but, as Celia Britton and Michael Syrotinski rightly point out, it is ultimately 'rather introductory, and taxonomic' in nature.[28] Even as a catalogue of postcolonial francophone literature, Moura's book is far from comprehensive since it fails to include Calixthe Beyala among the authors it lists.

The lack of sustained engagement with postcolonial theory in France leads me to draw largely on what the French would call an 'Anglo-Saxon' theoretical framework. This includes work by critics aligned with another British and American stronghold, that of cultural studies. Often marginalized as a discipline, cultural studies' usefulness for postcolonial theory is underlined in an article by James Procter who reminds us that 'cultural studies has been recognised as an essentially postcolonial discourse intimately bound up with the decline of empire and post-war migrations between "centre" and "periphery"'.[29] Given this book's emphasis on the representation and performance of cultural identities, an important frame of reference is found in the work of cultural theorist Stuart Hall. Hall's conceptualization of cultural identity as a production is central to my analysis of Beyala and her texts. In his essay, 'Cultural Identity and Diaspora', Hall suggests that:

> Perhaps instead of thinking of identity as an already accomplished fact, which the new cultural practices then represent, we should think, instead, of identity as a 'production', which is never complete, always in process, and always constituted within, not outside

representation. This view problematizes the very authority and authenticity to which the term, 'cultural identity', lays claim.[30]

Hall's problematizing of authority and authenticity in relation to cultural identity are reflected in Beyala's writings, not least through her engagement with the philosophy of Negritude.[31] As a francophone author, Beyala cannot ignore Negritude's influence on the construction of 'African identity', and so Senghor is an important intertext throughout her fictional works. Yet at the same time as she acknowledges its historical importance, Beyala undermines the ideological basis of Negritude, reducing the concept of an African 'essence' to that of an 'invented authenticity' that fixes Africa and its peoples in a mythological past and refuses to address the ways in which identities are reconfigured in response to changing contexts and situations (see Chapter 2).

What distinguishes cultural studies thinkers from those distinctly labelled 'postcolonial' is, then, an emphasis on the material contexts of postcolonial production. For Hall, diasporic identities and cultural productions are always positioned and contextualized. In other words, cultural studies helps to align the circumstances of a particular writer with their work or, as Edward Said puts it, helps us 'to read the work *and* its worldly situation'.[32] This emphasis on position and context underlies my analysis of Beyala as an exotic commodity in postcolonial France. So, while I do draw on the work of what Charles Forsdick among others refers to as the 'Holy Trinity of Postcolonial Thought' (Edward Said, Homi Bhabha and Gayatri Spivak),[33] the writings of Stuart Hall and, more recently, Graham Huggan offer particularly useful models for the analysis of the representation of postcolonial identities within the context of global market forces, and are thus a stronger influence on my readings of Beyala and her work. Indeed, Huggan's book, *The Postcolonial Exotic: Marketing the Margins*, is central to my analysis since his emphasis on reading postcolonial literatures as cultural commodities leads me to suggest that Beyala cannot be read independently of her ambivalent status as a writer. Furthermore, Huggan's observation that there are 'varying degrees of complicity between local oppositional discourses and the global late-capitalist system in which these discourses circulate and are contained' helps explain the mixed reception Beyala experiences in Africa and in France.[34] For Mongo Beti, in particular, Beyala is very much a product of the publishing marketplace in France, a marketplace she chooses not to challenge in her pursuit of literary success.[35]

This book considers Beyala's complicity in her own commodification. It analyses the ways in which Beyala and her characters perform their identities in what will emerge as an ambivalent strategy for survival in postcolonial, late-capitalist France.

A strategy of performing identities emerges as a key to understanding Beyala's representations of migrant identity, particularly those of displaced African women in France. For this reason, Judith Butler's theory of the performativity of gender identity provides a useful route for thinking about migrant femininity in Chapter 5. Butler's influential analysis of identity in her best-known book, *Gender Trouble*, has found many applications in the relatively new academic fields of performance studies, queer theory and cultural studies. However, Butler is rarely cited in postcolonial criticism, despite the fact that, as Huggan notes, 'the increasing body of work emerging from an intersection of postcolonial and queer theory suggests, however, that performativity may yet become a central concept for the understanding both of colonial strategies of physical oppression/ regimentation, and postcolonial identity formation'.[36] While in the field of African literature Butler's work tends only to be mobilized in feminist critique, her emphasis on identity as a performance can, I argue, be usefully applied to Beyala's fiction.[37] For Butler, 'gender is an act which has been rehearsed, much as a script survives the particular actors who make use of it, but which requires individual actors in order to be actualized and reproduced as a reality once again'.[38] The same applies to an identifiably 'African' or even 'exotic' identity. This book considers to what extent Beyala and her novels re-enact the script of 'African identity'. Does the migrant perform different versions of myths of Africanness? How does she stage her identity against the script of majority ethnic culture? I suggest that where Beyala's approach differs from that of Butler is in the question of volition. In Butler's analysis, performativity is read as 'not the act by which a subject brings into being what she/he names but rather as that reiterative power of discourse to produce the phenomena that it regulates and constrains'.[39] While Beyala acknowledges the role that discourse plays in the performance of migrant identities, her novels nevertheless point to a certain degree of choice or intentionality, albeit within the constraints of social and economic circumstance.

Metaphors of performance do appear in discussions of migrant writing, but without specific reference to Butler's work. In particular, Paul White's description of migrant subjectivity presents migrants with a choice of different interpretations of themselves. According to White, the migrant chooses to perform his or her ethnic identity in one of a number of ways: by maintaining his or her ethnic difference (possibly by emphasizing symbolic or ritualistic manifestations of that difference); by demonstrating a willingness to integrate completely into the culture of the host country (in this case, to become 'French'); by creating a new identity independently both of the culture of origin and the receiving culture; or by accepting the pluralism of migrant identities, which White describes as '[living] in a number of worlds, and [moving] between them on a daily, annual or seasonal rhythm'.[40] Beyala's novels stage these various versions of migrant identity, reflecting the different ways in which migrants represent themselves in the unfamiliar context of postcolonial France.

Beginning in real or imagined nations in Africa, the settings of Beyala's novels journey to France and back again, the first mention of migration taking place at the end of the third novel, *Seul le diable le savait,* when the protagonist, Mégri, decides to leave for Paris in search of a better life. While Ayo Abiétou Coly is right to suggest that the early novels reflect Beyala's personal migration from Cameroon to Paris, Coly's analysis of this dislocation is limited to the four best-known texts.[41] It is not the case that Beyala's fiction migrates definitively to France. Rather, almost relentlessly negative images of Africa in the texts published in the late 1980s are followed by representations of migrants' experiences in Paris in the 1990s' novels (see Chapters 3 and 4). In 1998 Beyala's fiction returns briefly to Africa with the publication of *La petite fille du réverbère*, a novel which is in part a response to the negative positioning of Beyala as a plagiarist in 1996. The most recent novels, *Les Arbres en parlent encore, Femme nue, femme noire* and *La Plantation*, published in 2002, 2003 and 2005 respectively, constitute an ambiguous return to Africa. The first challenges the reification of African authenticity through what appears to be a 'traditional' African tale (see Chapter 2). *Femme nue, femme noire* is Beyala's first 'erotic novel' and, as will be discussed later in this book, has been condemned by some readers as porn. In *La Plantation*, the third-person narrative focalizes a family of white Zimbabwean farmers being forced from their land as a result of Robert Mugabe's land reforms.

Switching as it does between Africa and France and back again, Beyala's oeuvre straddles the two geographical spaces she inhabits just as the migrant writer simultaneously experiences two cultural spheres. As this book will demonstrate, the ever-shifting focus of her narratives mirrors the difficulty migrants face in locating themselves: 'home' is both 'here' and 'there', yet at the same time it is neither 'here' nor 'there'. This is a difficulty that is also manifest in Beyala's self-representation: Chapter 4 considers the implications of her shifting identification from African to sometimes French through the ambiguous hyphenated identity of the 'Afro-française' [Afro-French]. Beyala's fiction deconstructs the very concept of 'home', confirming King, Connell and White's suggestion that 'once a migration takes place, the migrant may never be quite sure where home is, ever again. What ensues is a permanent mobility of the mind, if not the body, a constant dual or multiple perspective on place.'[42] This uncertainty about where home is generates an ambivalence that, I will argue, is symptomatic of the experience of transculturation. As a migrant, Beyala begins to view 'home' through the eyes of the traveller but at the same time becomes alert to the fraudulent nature of that gaze. The ambivalent nature of Beyala's relationship with Africa is immediately established in her first two novels: *C'est le soleil qui m'a brûlée* and *Tu t'appelleras Tanga*, published in the late 1980s. Both present an unremittingly pessimistic vision of fictional African societies characterized by violence and oppression and a lack of willingness to change. Such bleak representations of the African continent have generated much criticism of Beyala as an African writer. In Chapter 2, however, I reassess the negativity of these images as a challenge to the exoticist clichés perpetuated by touristic and anthropological discourses. I consider them as part of a more complex strategy of rejection and recuperation of stereotypes which forms the basis of Beyala's personal and fictional agendas.

Seul le diable le savait (1990) is also critical of Africa and its peoples but, perhaps because of its fantastical nature, has been less subject to criticism than its predecessors. In fact, this novel has largely been ignored in Beyala scholarship, an omission that is rather surprising given the considerable attention that all the other novels of the late 1980s and early 1990s have received. As mentioned above, *Seul le diable le savait* marks the beginning of a narrative relocation from Africa to Europe. It also acts as a novel of transition between the angry novels of the 1980s and the more moderate tones of those that followed. Critics of Beyala's writing have noted the switch in tone as Beyala's settings migrate from Cameroon to France. Denise Brahimi, for example, draws attention to fact that the later novels (post-1990) are less brutal than the more hard-hitting yet lyrical style of the first two texts.[43] This view is confirmed by Beyala herself who, in an interview on the publication of *Les Honneurs perdus*, offers an explanation for her more subdued writing style:

> Un écrivain vieillit aussi. Je prends maintenant le monde dans sa globalité. J'ai fait une psychanalyse. La révolte est toujours là, mais elle est devenue compréhensive. Avant, je disais: 'Un homme est égoïste'. Maintenant, je dis: 'Un homme est égoïste parce que...' Je trouve des explications.[44]

> [Writers grow up too. Now I take the world in its globality. I've had psychoanalysis. My revolt is still there but it's become comprehensive. Before I would say, 'Men are selfish'. Now I say, 'Men are selfish because...' I find explanations.]

By emphasizing her personal and authorial maturity, Beyala avoids any suggestions that she has in any way 'sold out' to the demands of her majority ethnic audience. However, it is also worth noting that, although critics tend to consider *C'est le soleil qui m'a brûlée* and *Tu t'appelleras Tanga* as Beyala's greatest literary works, neither of these novels has been consecrated by the publishing world. Beyala has been awarded a large number of literary prizes but only for those novels deemed less shocking in terms of content and style. There are two possible explanations for this apparent contradiction: first, Beyala switched in 1992 to the highly commercial publishing house, Albin Michel, whose marketing department has sufficient resources to push novels onto shortlists; but secondly, perhaps, the members of prize committees may be more receptive to a 'palatable' version of exoticism. The extent to which Beyala plays to the exoticist desires of her readership is directly addressed in Chapter 1 as well as in the conclusion of this book. Indeed, it underpins all my readings of Beyala's performances of migration.

While the later novels may present less brutal and less explicitly disturbing analyses of societies, the outspokenness of Beyala's early novels does not completely disappear. Traces remain throughout her fiction, particularly in characters' dialogues and in vulgar, sometimes graphic descriptions of sexual acts. Beyala also finds an outlet for her anger at social injustice in her two published essays, *Lettre d'une Africaine à ses soeurs occidentales* (1995) and *Lettre d'une Afro-française à ses compatriotes* (2000), produced by lesser-known publishers, Spengler and Mango. Neither essay received much critical acclaim but both shed some light on Beyala's fiction and in particular on questions of displacement and belonging in relation to the identities of African women immigrants in France. Both are fairly personalized open letters ostensibly addressed to sympathetic French readers; both are written in a colloquial style that is always direct, sometimes vulgar and often ironic, packed with rhetorical questions and exclamation marks. Beyala's motive in writing these essays is to draw the French public's attention to the oppression of women and black people in the world. It is fair to say that neither essay is particularly well crafted; neither displays the originality of Beyala's fictional work. As she explains, 'ce qui compte c'est l'écrit, c'est le cri' [what counts is writing, what counts is shouting] (*LASO*, p. 10), implying a less controlled, more instinctive way of writing.

In *Lettre d'une Africaine à ses soeurs occidentales* Beyala writes about feminism. The essay is, she claims, a call for solidarity in an individualistic world (p. 13). Here she also outlines her philosophy of 'féminitude', a rather loosely formulated version of African feminism (see Chapter 1). Largely autobiographical, this published letter makes a number of connections with Beyala's fictional writings. For example, we are told that Beyala's mother informed her that she would be handicapped without a man (p. 37), a point that is echoed by a number of the unsympathetic women characters in her novels. This is not to suggest that all Beyala's novels are autobiographical but rather to reinforce the importance of situating the author in relation to her work. She describes herself as 'femme africaine, vivant à cheval sur les deux continents' [an African woman straddling the two continents] (p. 61), an image of hybridity that is analysed and challenged through Beyala's representations of African migrants in France discussed in Chapters 3 and 4.

Beyala also uses this letter to condemn social structures and practices that oppress African women. Taboos such as female genital mutilation, dowries, polygamy and arranged marriages are criticized as systems that allow the control of women by men. In particular, Beyala challenges the perpetuation of such practices in the name of 'Tradition'. This critical engagement with what Beyala exposes as the myth of 'Tradition' is a strong thread in her fictional writings (see Chapter 2). Migrants who are unable to adapt to the new demands of their host culture often retreat into what they see as the safe space of 'Tradition'. Beyala's fiction reveals this to be a largely unsuccessful means of negotiating migration.

The second published letter focuses on racism in France and can be read as a manifesto of the black rights movement, Collectif Egalité, founded in 1998 with Beyala as its president.⁴⁵ At the end of the twentieth century, the Collectif began an active campaign, focusing in particular on the representation of what they termed 'les minorités visibles' [visible minorities] on French television. In 1999, refusing to pay their TV licence fee, members of the Collectif approached French government ministers as well as the national broadcasting regulatory body, the Conseil Supérieur de l'Audiovisuel (CSA), about the lack of 'visible minorities' on terrestrial TV. Hervé Bourges, then president of the CSA, was receptive to the Collectif's position and, in 1999, agreed to commission a review of the French terrestrial channel remits. In recognition of the need for television to reflect the multicultural contemporary French nation, a revision of these remits was subsequently approved on 16 May 2000.⁴⁶ At the time of the CSA study, the Collectif Egalité was beginning to acquire a certain level of notoriety in the French media with its proposal for a system of quotas for TV performers based on racial criteria. Beyala explains that, 'on pourrait imaginer la mise en oeuvre des quotas à durée déterminée – Q.D.D. – qui permettrait de débloquer une situation particulièrement difficile, héritée de notre passé colonial et esclavagiste' [we could imagine the establishment of fixed term quotas (QDD) which would help unblock a particularly difficult situation that we have inherited from our history of colonization and slavery] (*LAFC*, p. 90). In *Lettre d'une Afro-française*, Beyala makes ironic reference to the very negative response this proposal received from different sectors of French society, including anti-racist groups such as Intégration France (e.g. p. 79). The Collectif Egalité achieved further notoriety on 19 February 2000 when they decided to gatecrash the twenty-fifth annual César ceremony. Accompanied by Guadeloupean actor/director, Luc Saint-Eloi, Beyala walked onto the stage during the performance and read a public statement to then Minister of Culture, Catherine Trautmann, about the lack of black actors in French cinema. She and Saint-Eloi also awarded a posthumous 'unofficial César' to Darling Legitimus, star of Euzhan Palcy's film *Rue cases-nègres*.⁴⁷ The text of part of the Collectif's statement is reproduced in *Lettre d'une Afro-française* (pp. 70–71).

To a certain extent, Beyala's political activities under the aegis of Collectif Egalité are reflected in her fiction of that period. *Amours sauvages* and *Comment cuisiner son mari à l'africaine*, published in

1999 and 2000, both address the difficulties faced by African immigrants in France. Indeed, with the exception of *La petite fille du réverbère*, each of the texts published in the 1990s deals with the ways in which African women experience and negotiate migration. In other words, Beyala's essays offer a perspective on migrant identity that complements her fiction. As descriptions of and reactions to the treatment of minority groups in France and in Africa, they contextualize the novels and provide a socio-political narrative against which Beyala's fictional subjectivities can be read. In this book I have chosen to focus on the performance of migrant identities – by both Beyala herself and her fictional characters – and, as such, I take the novels rather than the essays as the principal textual bases of my argument. Beyala's public manifestations will also make an important contribution to my discussion, for her political activities along with her TV and radio performances all inflect her (self-)positioning as migrant woman writer in France.

CHAPTER ONE

Calixthe Beyala Incorporated?

Je ne suis pas une partisane de l'assimilation à tout prix.[1]

[I'm not in favour of assimilation at any cost].

In May 1996 Beyala was charged with having partially plagiarized Howard Buten's novel, *Burt*, in her novel, *Le petit prince de Belleville* [*Loukoum: the Little Prince of Belleville*], and was ordered to pay Buten and his publisher substantial damages plus costs. In November 1996 Pierre Assouline, editor of the literary magazine *Lire*, publicly accused Beyala of having plagiarized Ben Okri's *The Famished Road* in *Les Honneurs perdus*.[2] Ironically, the latter novel had been awarded the prestigious Grand Prix du Roman de l'Académie Française exactly one month earlier, on 24 October 1996. What the paradox of 1996 exemplifies is the very mixed reception of Beyala and her writing in her adopted country, France. It also points to what will emerge in this book as the ever-shifting positioning of Calixthe Beyala by readers on the one hand and by Beyala herself on the other. This chapter will consider the unique status of Beyala as a famous black African woman writer living in France. Beginning with a discussion of the reception of her work, not just in France but also in Africa, I shall evaluate the ways in which Beyala has become something of an icon of black femininity in France through her fictional writings, her polemical public statements and her TV and radio appearances. An analysis of the reception and representation of Beyala and her writing will consider the extent to which she has been incorporated into majority ethnic culture in France. It will also begin to trace the effects of a French politics of positioning on the postcolonial phenomenon that is Calixthe Beyala. Taking as its starting point the influential work of Graham Huggan, this chapter will evaluate the commodification of Beyala in France as a symptom of the 'postcolonial exotic'.[3]

In terms of marketing, Beyala's fiction fits the category of what Huggan describes as the 'anthropological exotic' which 'allows for a reading of African literature as the more or less transparent window onto a richly detailed and culturally specific, but still somehow homogeneous – and of course readily marketable – African world'.[4] The anthropological exotic is sufficiently strange and yet also reassuringly familiar to the Euro-American consumer. Herein lies its appeal. It is no coincidence, then, that the promotion of Beyala's fiction is marked by an attempt to situate the author in relation to both Africa and metropolitan France. On the back of the low-priced paperback J'ai Lu editions, Beyala's personal itinerary and her novels are described in the following terms: 'Née au Cameroun, elle a fait ses études en Afrique et en Europe, puis s'est installée à Paris. Ses romans nous racontent avec brio le continent africain et la France.' [Born in Cameroon, she studied in Africa and Europe before settling in Paris. Her novels brilliantly describe the African continent and France.] By initially referring to her birthplace in Africa, the publishers seem to be emphasizing the exoticism of this migrant writer but at the same time they point to her close proximity in the familiar space of Paris. The familiarity of Parisian Beyala is then shaken up once more with the juxtaposition of Africa and France in the final sentence stressing geographical separation rather than interpenetration. For the French reader, Beyala represents both (Parisian) self and (African) other. A geographical distinction is also made in the title of Jean-Marie Volet's article, which identifies Beyala as 'a Cameroonian woman living in Paris', an epithet that emphasizes the strange over the temporarily familiar.[5] In other words, the reception and promotion of Beyala's writing point to the dichotomous position of the postcolonial writer, simultaneously located inside and outside the national culture of, in this case, France. Yet whereas her publishers and critics such as Volet highlight her African roots, other French readers de-emphasize these roots, focusing only on the fact that Beyala is now resident in their capital. The most glaring example of this emerges when Sylvie Genevoix, writing for *Madame Figaro*, describes Beyala as 'Parisienne jusqu'au bout des ongles' [Parisian right down to her toes].[6]

Whether she is located inside or outside the geographical space of France, Calixthe Beyala has been incorporated into the literary world of Paris and is now identified in relation to it. This kind of identification is ideologically problematic in a postcolonial context since Beyala represents a minority francophone artist who has been incorporated into mainstream French culture. Recalling the French colonial mission to create 'French Africans' through a policy of assimilation, literary incorporation denies cultural difference and suggests a neocolonization of postcolonial writing by publishers in France. The incorporation of Beyala is a symptom of the way in which the cultural field of African literature is controlled and defined by publishers and associated bodies in the former colonial centres. In Beyala's case, her neocolonial incorporation is symbolized not only in the packaging of her novels but also in the notorious prize she was awarded by the Académie Française, the self-appointed bastion of high culture in France.[7]

As a prize-winning, media-friendly author, Beyala has achieved what Pierre Bourdieu calls 'literary legitimacy' or 'consecration', which culminates in the authority to bestow legitimacy on others.[8] In 2003 the French translation of Choga Regina Egbeme's best-selling story of her life in a Nigerian harem was published with a preface by 'Calixthe Beyala, auteur de *Les Honneurs perdus*, Grand Prix du Roman de l'Académie Française'.[9] On the back cover of *Je suis née au harem*, a quotation from Beyala legitimizes Egbeme's text with the words, 'Jamais je n'ai perçu avec autant d'acuité la souffrance et la force morale de la femme noire' [Never before have I felt so intensely the suffering and the moral strength of the black woman].[10] This quotation is intriguing since it seems to suggest – to the unfamiliar reader – that Beyala is white: the suffering of 'the black woman' is positioned at a distance from the consecrated author, safe in her own legitimization by the Académie Française. Of course, Beyala's quotation has been selected by Egbeme's publisher from the preface to the novel and indeed the preface is less of a piece of cultural tourism than the isolated quotation suggests. What the quotation demonstrates, however, is the way in which Beyala's Africanness is negotiated by the French book industry: she can confer authority on another African woman writer to promote sales of that writer's books, but at the same time cannot be identified as too much of an African woman writer herself. Futhermore, Beyala's assessment of *Je suis née au harem* emphasizes the troubled otherness of its narrator and in so doing confers, as Timothy Brennan suggests, authority on Egbeme as a 'minority writer'. Writing about cosmopolitanism, Brennan describes the careful balancing of ethnic identity that marks the promotion of authors from India, Latin America or Africa:

> Being from 'there' in this sense is primarily a kind of literary passport that identifies the artist as being from a region of underdevelopment and pain. Literary sophistication against this troubled backdrop,

then, is doubly authoritative because it is proof of overcoming *that* to join *this*.[11]

Although Beyala herself, as we have seen, is also identified as being 'from there' by her publishers, what distinguishes her from other 'cosmopolitan' writers from the developing world is her apparent willingness to join *this* at the expense of leaving *that* behind. It is this aspect of the 'Beyala phenomenon' that some writers and critics find rather difficult to digest.

In his unforgiving article, 'L'Affaire Calixthe Beyala ou comment sortir du néocolonialisme en littérature', fellow Cameroonian author Mongo Beti unequivocally condemns Beyala as an ambitious networker. According to Beti, Beyala is rejected by Africans as a neocolonial servant and seen by the French as a friend of France:

> La percée de Calixthe Beyala, qui n'est pas seulement concrétisée par le Grand Prix de l'Académie Française, mais s'est aussi manifestée par une vente sans précédent de son roman pour un auteur africain, frisant des records jusqu'à la bombe du plagiat, s'explique par la conjonction de cette réalité qu'on peut qualifier de sociologique et de la présence au pouvoir d'une droite néo-gaulliste, attachée, à sa manière, à l'Afrique, à laquelle C. Beyala a su se rendre sympathique dès son arrivée en France.[12]

> [Calixthe Beyala's breakthrough, evidenced not only by the French Academy's Grand Prix but also by the sales of her novels which are unprecedented for an African author – almost record breaking until the plagiarism bombshell – can be explained by the conjunction of what we might call a sociological reality and a neo-gaullist right-wing government with a particular kind of relationship with Africa, and which C. Beyala knew how to win over as soon as she arrived in France.]

At the same time as he accuses her of pandering to the RPR leadership in France, Mongo Beti criticizes Beyala's failure to contribute to the national liberation struggle in her birth country, Cameroon. He also views her many appearances on state-controlled national television in Cameroon as evidence of her implicit support of President Paul Biya's politically intolerant regime.[13] Beyala, on the other hand, indirectly justifies and challenges Mongo Beti's characterization of her, claiming France as a place of freedom of expression, unlike Cameroon. She tells Emmanuel Matateyou:

> Si j'habitais le Cameroun, je n'aurais pas droit à la parole. L'exil me donne la liberté qui m'est refusée, l'exil me donne la parole qui m'est refusée, l'exil est ma survie. Je ne dirai pas vie, mais survie. Car si j'habitais le Cameroun aurais-je pu écrire et avoir cet impact international?[14]

> [If I lived in Cameroon, I wouldn't have the right of free speech. Exile gives me the freedom that I'm denied. Exile gives me the speech that I'm denied. Exile is my survival. I wouldn't say it's my life, but it's my survival. For, if I lived in Cameroon, would I have been able to write and have this international impact?]

Here, it seems, Beyala is beginning to distance herself from her geographical home in Africa and reposition herself as a writer in exile with an international readership. The fact that Mongo Beti himself spent the majority of his own career in political exile in France confirms Beyala's point about exile offering a safe place to speak. What is more interesting is his assertion that Beyala has 'sold out' to France and created an intellectual distance between herself and Cameroon.

Mongo Beti is not the only author to criticize Beyala in this way. Other African writers also identify a marked distance between Calixthe Beyala and her African roots. Senegalese woman writer Aminata Sow Fall condemns Beyala's fiction as 'inspirée par une vision très pessimiste de l'Afrique et des Africains. Ce n'est pas la mienne' [inspired by a very pessimistic vision of Africa and Africans. This is not my vision].[15] This Afro-pessimism is not something that Beyala denies. On the contrary, she herself makes a very similar point when, in an interview with Emmanuel Matateyou, she reacts to the interviewer's remark that some readers are shocked by her writing:

> Je choque certains Africains, j'en suis consciente. Mais ceux-là ne m'intéressent pas, car ce sont eux qui ont conduit ce continent au bord du gouffre [...] Je choque beaucoup plus les Africains [que les Européens] puisque ce message s'adresse d'abord à eux.[16]

> [I shock some Africans, I know that. But those people don't interest me because they're the ones who have dragged this continent to the edge of the abyss [...] I shock Africans more than Europeans because, first and foremost, this message is intended for them.]

It is not only Beyala's writing that some readers find shocking; the media circus that surrounds her has also led to criticisms. While at the time professing his affection and admiration for Beyala, Guinean author Tierno Monénembo advises her to step back from the spotlight, warning that 'le battage médiatique risque de l'ensevelir avant qu'elle n'ait fini de produire son œuvre. Ah! Les lumières de Paris...' [she is in danger of being buried under her own publicity before she has even finished writing. Oh! The bright lights of Paris...].[17] Unusually, Monénembo is here positioning Beyala as a kind of ingénue, seduced by the bright lights of the French capital. Unlike Mongo Beti, Monénembo fails to consider Beyala as a more-than-willing participant in her own commodification.

Like the paradox of 1996, what is becoming evident here is the ambivalent reception of Calixthe Beyala, particularly in Africa. While she resists the suggestion that she is writing for a primarily European audience, the reality is that Beyala's books are far less well known in Africa than in Europe and North America (see Chapter 4). Such is the hegemony of North America in the global book industry that Beyala's publishers, Albin Michel, quote her popularity there as evidence of her canonicity, presenting her on their web pages as 'de plus en plus médiatisée et connue à l'étranger, notamment aux États-Unis où elle va régulièrement faire des conférences et où son œuvre est étudiée dans plusieurs universités. Elle est considérée comme l'un des auteurs majeurs de la francophonie' [more and more media friendly, especially in the United States where she regularly gives talks and where her works are studied in several universities. She is considered one of the major francophone authors].[18] The fact that Beyala's status as a major 'francophone' author should be defined by her success in the United States is another unsettling example of the impact of globalization on African cultural production. More specifically, as a 'francophone' author Beyala has become de-Africanized by her editors and assimilated into the nebulous concept of 'la Francophonie'. Although 'francophone' in the French language tends to exclude metropolitan France, its connotations further contain Beyala within a neocolonial French-owned space.

Further evidence of the incorporation of Beyala into the Euro-American canon can be found in the tendency among critics to focus on the Paris-based novels, especially the 'Loukoum' diptych and *Les Honneurs perdus*. This leads critics to approach and define Beyala's fiction in its relation to metropolitan France and, in particular, to Paris. In *Black Paris: the African Writers' Landscape*, Bennetta Jules-Rosette aligns Beyala with what she terms the 'Parisianism' movement. According to Jules-Rosette, the genre of 'Parisianism' in African literature was reborn in the 1980s, in the light of changing attitudes to immigration in contemporary France. Tracing it back to Bernard Dadié's 1959 novel, *Un Nègre à Paris*, Jules-Rosette defines 'Parisianism' as referring to 'a literary interest in Paris as the social context for the author's works, the subject matter of their writings, and the source of their focal audience'.[19] Although, in the interview with Matateyou, Beyala claims that the 'message' of her novels is primarily aimed at an African audience, sales of her novels confirm Jules-Rosette's conclusion that Beyala's target audience is, in fact, Parisian.

Not only are Beyala's novels published in France by the highly successful, commercial French publisher Albin Michel, but three of them have appeared in English translation in Heinemann's prestigious African Writers Series (AWS). This series, according to former AWS literature editor Becky Clarke, has become 'the standard bearer – the canon' of African literature.[20] Together with Beyala, only six authors from francophone Africa are included in the series and, of them, only two are women (Mariama Bâ and Véronique Tadjo).[21] For the anglophone reader, then, Beyala is now ranked alongside such canonical figures of African literature as Chinua Achebe and Ngugi Wa Thiong'o. Moreover, the places on the AWS list will remain forever uncontested as, for commercial reasons, the series stopped commissioning new material in 2003.

In his analysis of the African Writers Series, Graham Huggan makes the important point that the lack of a local publishing infrastructure in Africa is symptomatic of what he calls a 'neocolonial knowledge industry', which persuades African writers and readers that 'cultural value, as well as economic power, is located and arbitrated elsewhere'.[22] Accusing the AWS of contributing to the perpetuation of the 'anthropological exotic', Huggan emphasizes and interrogates what he presents as the Series' virtual monopoly over publishing in Africa.[23] This monopoly was confirmed and rewarded at a high-profile awards ceremony, held in Cape Town in 2002, to celebrate 'Africa's 100 Best Books of the Twentieth Century'. During the ceremony Heinemann Educational Publishers received a prize for publishing the top twelve books on the list. Alastair Niven, representing Arts Council, England, applauded Heinemann's success with the words, 'Heinemann's is a unique achievement in the history of publishing and anyone who cares for Africa will want to celebrate what they have done over the past forty years'.[24] The notion of 'caring for Africa' smacks of neo-imperialist rhetoric and positions the role of AWS as one of benevolent intervention and control rather than the enabling collaboration that Becky Clarke describes.[25]

Launched by the Zimbabwe International Book Fair in 2000, the 'Africa's 100 Best Books' project was organized in collaboration with the African Publishers' Network, the Pan-African Booksellers Association and African writers' associations, book development councils, and library associations. It was conceived in response to the 1998 American '100 Best Books' list, which did not contain a single African title. The African '100 Best' included four francophone women writers from sub-Saharan Africa: Mariama Bâ, Ken Bugul, Aminata Sow Fall and Véronique Tadjo. Calixthe Beyala was conspicuous by her absence.[26] The fact that none of Beyala's novels was among the winners supports the view that, despite the canonizing power of the AWS – and despite Beyala's commercial success in Europe and North America – her fiction does not, in fact, appeal to an African readership. Ambroise Kom substantiates this conclusion:

> En vedette dans certaines grandes surfaces en France, les romans de Beyala ont également réussi à se hisser au hit-parade des textes cités dans nombre d'universités occidentales, singulièrement nord-américaines, et même dans les colloques scientifiques où il est question d'études africaines et/ou du tiers monde. Mais, assez étonnamment, le grand public africain et le monde universitaire du continent noir ignorent Beyala.[27]
>
> [On sale in some hypermarkets in France, Beyala's novels have also succeeded in making the charts for works quoted in many universities in the West, particularly in North America, and even in academic conferences on African or Third-World studies. Astonishingly, however, the African general public and the university world on the dark continent know nothing about Beyala.]

By foregrounding Beyala's success in terms of sales in French hypermarkets, Kom seems to be suggesting that Beyala is not viewed as a serious or 'great' writer in France.[28] Furthermore, his presentation of North American academic interest in her work as belonging to African or 'Third World' (rather than literary) studies supports the view that her texts have been received as exotic objects in the West, and confirms Huggan's hypothesis that 'the Africa [AWS] has promoted by way of its talented protégés has been subjected to a self-empowering, implicitly neocolonialist "anthropological gaze"'.[29]

It might then be argued that the rejection of Beyala by her fellow African writers and readers can be read as a backlash against the way in which her novels have been lauded by critics in the Western Academy and incorporated into the global canon. Whereas Mongo Beti condemns Beyala as an author who cannot write and who is more interested in the quantity of her sales than the quality of her literature,[30] US-based critics such as Sonja Darlington heap praise on Beyala's writing style. In her recently published analysis of *Tu t'appelleras Tanga*, Darlington describes the novel as 'a new form of fiction that bears the stamp of African genius, experiments with new language and images, and does not need to be named by someone else'.[31] Although Darlington is right to warn of the dangers of classification, she inevitably falls into the exoticist trap herself, claiming Beyala as an 'African genius' and – fifteen years after its publication – presenting *TTT* as if it were a text that had not been 'discovered' before.

Whether she is received as a genius or a charlatan, Beyala, as we have seen, tends not to leave critics indifferent to her work. In the ambivalent reception Beyala's fiction has received, three areas in particular have generated most controversy: the narratives' political ideology (and specifically what is perceived to be their feminist agenda); their sexually explicit content; and Beyala's writing style which Denise Brahimi, like Mongo Beti, suggests is marked by an 'absence d'écriture' [lack of writing].[32] Describing women as 'les fesses' [arses] and men as 'la crasse' [filth], Beyala's writing is designed to shock; her narratives are packed with expletives, slang and sexually graphic vocabulary. In particular, Beyala uses explicit descriptions of sexual violence between women and men to expose the oppression of women in what she presents as inherently violent societies. Such scenes demonstrate the way in which relationships in Beyala's fictional world are characterized by abuse and a struggle for power. While the language is violent and crude, it is necessarily so to convey the brutality of the situation. However, failing to acknowledge the appropriateness – and the power – of Beyala's narrative style, critics repeatedly single out her use of language as excessive and uncouth. Beyala answers this charge by saying:

> Je n'ai pas un discours violent. J'ai un discours inattendu. [...] Et ma langue, c'est celle de Douala. Je ne parle pas un français de Paris. Je ne vais pas dans les milieux où l'on va exiger que j'emploie l'imparfait du subjonctif. Je viens de la rue et je n'ai pas quitté la rue.[33]

[My writing is not violent. I have an unexpected way of writing. [...] And my language is the language of Douala. I don't speak Parisian French. I don't spend time with people who use the imperfect subjunctive. I come from the streets and I haven't left the streets.]

By referring to her origins in the back streets of the Cameroonian city of Douala, Beyala is here adopting what will emerge in this chapter as a strategic pattern of self-defence. When faced with external criticism she retreats into the safe space of her foreignness and thus prevents any challenge from those without the relevant cultural capital. Interestingly, in defending her writing style, she chooses not to foreground her gender, perhaps because sympathetic female critics in Europe and North America often emphasize the fact that she is a woman. For example, in a discussion of Beyala's writing style, French critic Madeleine Borgomano concludes:

> Il est vrai qu'il s'agit d'une écriture brutale, volontiers provocante, qui adopte la truculence du langage parlé et même surenchérit souvent. Ces audaces choquent d'autant plus que l'écrivain est une femme et que les femmes écrivains africaines adoptent le plus souvent une écriture sage, conforme à la norme, voire conformiste, se pliant aux lois scolaires apprises du beau langage. Calixthe Beyala, elle, refuse les conformismes linguistiques, signes fréquents d'acceptation des règles. Elle ne respecte pas la loi du silence: elle écrit ce qu'il ne faut pas dire.[34]

> [It is true that this writing is brutal, deliberately provocative. It adopts the verve of spoken language and often even exaggerates it. This effrontery is all the more shocking because the writer is a woman, and African women writers tend to adopt a sober writing style which conforms to the norm, is conformist even, bowing to the rules of French they have learnt at school. Calixthe Beyala refuses such signs of accepting the rules of linguistic conformity. She does not respect the law of silence: she writes what should not be said.]

Borgomano's point is, of course, pertinent: a male writer such as Sony Labou Tansi is not criticized for his similarly excessive language but rather praised as a lexical innovator and a great African writer, part of a recent trend in African francophone writing that 'makes the *unspeakable* readable'.[35] Calixthe Beyala, on the other hand, is condemned as a vulgar extremist lacking in talent. Unlike established canonical figures such as Mariama Bâ, Beyala is an African woman writer who confounds the expectations of many readers – Western and African – by refusing to play by the rules of patriarchy and (neo)colonialism.

What shocks readers, as Borgomano acknowledges, is the fact that Beyala is an African woman. While an emphasis on Beyala's gender is important for understanding her sometimes negative reception, it can also be problematic when, as I shall suggest later in this chapter, it becomes part of a (re)appropriated exoticism for commercial ends.

Focusing as it does on gender issues, Beyala's fiction is often categorized as feminist. This is particularly the case in studies of the early novels set in Africa, but also applies to the fiction published from the 1990s onwards. As a feminist writer, Beyala opens herself up to challenges of ideological incorporation since feminism is traditionally viewed as inappropriate in an African context. Writing about feminist discourse in Beyala's fiction, Ambroise Têko-Agbo explains that:

> les femmes du continent africain ont accueilli toute cette agitation autour du Mouvement de libération de la femme, sinon de façon mitigée, du moins avec beaucoup de scepticisme et de méfiance. Car elles trouvaient le concept, d'obédience occidentale, quelque peu éloigné de leur vécu quotidien.³⁶

> [the women of the African continent responded to all the fuss around the women's liberation movement, if not with mixed feelings, then at least with much scepticism and mistrust. For they found the notion to be too close to the West and somewhat removed from their daily lives.]

Têko-Agbo's qualification of feminism as 'd'obédience occidentale' [too close to the West] highlights the way in which feminism in former colonies is often rejected as an imperial force, a view that has famously been echoed in the writings of postcolonial women critics such as Chandra Mohanty and Trinh T. Minh-ha.³⁷ Têko-Agbo's criticism of Beyala's early novels is ostensibly based on what he sees as her one-dimensional characterization and legitimization of violence, both of which he equates with Beyala's aim to denounce phallocratic power. Indeed, Têko-Agbo's view of feminist writing in Africa is revealed when he appropriates for himself the words of Tanga's abusive lover, Hassan, declaring that 'la "femme-plume" [...] a volé la gloire à la Femme' [the 'woman of letters' has stolen Woman's glory].³⁸ Underlying Têko-Agbo's analysis seems to be an aversion to an African woman writer who disregards tradition and creates a radical female narrative voice.

On the other hand, critics such as Adèle King and Madeleine

Borgomano interpret the ideology of Beyala's fiction as more complex than the anti-feminist critics suggest. Ironically, King initially chooses to align Beyala with the Cameroonian literary tradition and with her toughest critic, Mongo Beti, but ultimately concludes that 'la tradition camerounaise est radicalisée dans le fond et la forme des romans de Beyala, qui ne sont typiques ni de la littérature africaine ni du féminisme occidental' [Cameroonian tradition is made more radical in the content and the form of Beyala's novels which are not typical of African literature nor of Western feminism].[39] While King's analysis of feminism is not very rigorous, her refusal to pigeonhole Beyala in terms of 'African' or 'Western' traditions is refreshing. Likewise, Borgomano also resists the binary trap in her reading of Beyala, coining instead the term 'déplacé' [displaced] to describe both the writer and her writing.[40] Indeed, Beyala's own version of feminism, as articulated in *Lettre d'une Africaine à ses soeurs occidentales*, is closer to King's and Borgomano's interpretations than to the antifeminist reading of Têko-Agbo. Beyala promotes what she calls 'féminitude', an international solidarity movement that is 'très proche du féminisme mais divergente dans la mesure où elle ne prône pas l'égalité entre l'homme et la femme, mais la différence-égalitaire entre l'homme et la femme' [very close to feminism but different in the sense that it does not claim equality between men and women but rather difference-equality between men and women].[41] Acknowledging debts to both feminism and Negritude, Beyala's 'féminitude' suggests a blending that defies the overly simplistic rejection of her writing as feminist and therefore anti-African. In an interview with Jean-Bernard Gervais, Beyala explains the etymological roots of the term:

> Vous n'êtes pas sans savoir que le mouvement de la négritude a placé sur un piédestal la femme africaine. En sublimant l'Africaine, des poètes comme Senghor ont en fait voulu glorifier le passé antécolonial africain. La féminitude serait pour moi un mélange de féminisme et de négritude. Avec ce nouveau concept, je cherche à montrer en quoi la femme noire est supérieure. Je veux affirmer la suprématie de la femme noire sur l'homme noir.[42]

> [You know, of course, that the Negritude movement placed the African woman on a pedestal. In fact, by elevating the African woman, poets like Senghor tried to glorify Africa's anti-colonial history. Feminitude, for me, is a mix of feminism and Negritude. With this new concept I hope to show in what ways the black

woman is superior. I want to affirm the supremacy of the black woman over the black man.]

In her attempts to fictionalize what she claims to be the supremacy of black women over black men, Beyala presents relationships between women in her novels as the antidote to the negativity and violence of contemporary life in Africa and in France. A number of critics view these female friendships as promoting gay relationships between women. In particular, what some have interpreted as the lesbian relationship between Ateba and Irène in *C'est le soleil qui m'a brûlée* has, as Nfah-Abbenyi notes, been the focus of much controversy.[43] Just as Saïda in *Les Honneurs perdus* has 'pensées indignes' [shameful thoughts] (*HP*, p. 386) about her landlady, Ngaremba, so Ateba fantasizes about her close friend, Irène. The much-quoted scene in which Ateba wants to put her hand on Irène's leg (*CSB*, p. 158; *SHL*, p. 107) has led some critics – particularly African men – to condemn Beyala's representation of what they see as a homosexual relationship between the two women.[44] Beyala, however, is quick to dismiss such readings as both inaccurate and culturally inappropriate:

> Je pense que ceux qui voient du lesbianisme dans mes écrits sont tout simplement des pervertis car la tendresse entre femmes n'implique pas forcément le lesbianisme. Comment expliquer aux Occidentaux qu'en Afrique traditionnelle les rapports intimes entre personnes du même sexe ne se définissent pas en termes d'homosexualité?[45]

> [I think that those who see lesbianism in my writings are quite simply perverted since tenderness between women doesn't necessarily imply lesbianism. How can we explain to Westerners that in traditional Africa, intimate relations between persons of the same sex are not defined as homosexual?]

Beyala's rejection of those 'perverted' critics who have identified lesbianism in her fiction is disingenuous since she assumes them to be Western and thus culturally incompetent. Elsewhere, as we have seen, Beyala claims her intended readership to be African, and indeed much of the criticism of Beyala's 'lesbian' relationships has come from readers originating from Africa. On this occasion, though, it is convenient for Beyala to position her readers outside her text as uninitiated strangers or tourists enjoying the erotic-exotic thrill of a cultural concept they allegedly do not understand.

It is interesting that both Beyala and her critics rely on a notion of

African authenticity in their attempts to defend or attack her writing: Beyala claims that Western readers do not understand relationships in 'Afrique traditionnelle' [traditional Africa]; conversely, some African critics condemn Beyala's ideological framework as 'd'obédience occidentale' [too close to the West]. What both sides are attempting to do is fix a myth of 'real' Africa and turn this myth to their own advantage. The myth of authenticity is central to understanding Calixthe Beyala not only as an African writer living in France but also as a postcolonial phenomenon. She is forever being positioned – and positioning herself – in relation to what ultimately emerges as an 'invented authenticity' (see Chapter 2). Much of the ambivalence that characterizes Beyala's reception is generated, I would suggest, by readers' differing expectations of what constitutes an 'authentic' African woman writer. It is Beyala's ability to understand these different expectations and to reinvent herself accordingly that is undoubtedly the key to her success.

For some, the antithesis of the 'authentic' African author is the one who is perceived to have sold out to her Western readership. Those who, like Nigerian critic Tunde Fatunde, accuse Beyala of producing discourse that is 'broadly provocative, raw and "pornographic"' appear to hold this view.[46] It is true that Beyala's fiction presents a vast range of sexual behaviours, including masturbation, homosexuality, incest, rape, fellatio and orgies. The suggestion, though, that her writing is not fiction but pornography implies a self-conscious exoticism in which the representation of sexual relationships is not part of a socio-political agenda, but is rather a form of touristic pleasure for what is, by implication, identified as a Euro-American readership. As evidence of what he also sees as Beyala's 'pornographic writing', Ambroise Kom chooses a passage from *Seul le Diable le savait* in which the protagonist, Mégri, recalls playing 'mummies and daddies' with her childhood sweetheart, Erwing.[47] Kom quotes the lines, '[Erwing] avait envie de me pétrir, de m'investir, de me dévorer presque' [Erwing wanted to mould me, to besiege me, almost to consume me] (*SDS*, p. 48), words which, from the memory of a child are surely anything but erotic. Here I would suggest that Beyala is demonstrating the way in which young boys have already been indoctrinated into seeing girls as objects to be manipulated ('pétrir'), attacked ('investir') and overcome ('dévorer'). Following his misreading, Kom makes a telling point when he concludes that 'l'on peut comprendre que des critiques n'hésitent pas à accuser Beyala de s'adonner passionnément à une écriture pornographique, technique destinée à accrocher un public en quête d'érotisme et d'exotisme bon marché' [we can understand why critics do not hesitate in accusing Beyala of passionately giving herself over to pornographic writing, a technique intended to attract a readership looking for cheap eroticism and exoticism].[48] Ironically, his own interpretation reflects the tendency among critics to (mis)read the sex scenes in Beyala's fiction as erotic titillation rather than political statements, a tendency encouraged by the book industry's promotion of Calixthe Beyala as an erotic-exotic object in France.

While sex in the early novels serves a political agenda, more recent publications have begun to confirm the condemnations of Beyala as a pornographer. In 2003 Beyala published *Femme nue, femme noire*, a novel that declares itself to be 'un roman érotique africain'. Ten years earlier, Beyala published a relatively unknown erotic short story, 'La Sonnette', in a collection entitled *Troubles de femmes*.[49] *Femme nue, femme noire* is, as *Jeune Afrique* journalist Dominique Mataillet confirms, the very first erotic novel by a writer from francophone Africa.[50] This novel, largely devoid of plot, describes the sexual adventures of Irène, a young kleptomaniac, whose insatiable sexual appetite leads her to become a healer since it is believed that she must be mad, and that having sex with a mad woman will cure all ills. The novel overflows with graphic descriptions of sexual intercourse in all its forms and is, in fact, as Mataillet suggests, better classified as pornography than erotic fiction. In terms of reception, *Femme nue, femme noire* resembles Catherine Millet's controversial bestseller, *La Vie sexuelle de Catherine M.*[51] Both are written by women with relatively high profiles in French cultural life; and both generated something of a furore among readers in France. In an internet forum dedicated to discussing Beyala's novel, one reader condemns it as a 'torchon d'assimilation et vice' [filthy rag of assimilation and vice] whereas another responds that the book is 'loin d'être un torchon, c'est même presque une seule et unique tirade, un cri, un chant, un film, un opéra...' [far from being a filthy rag, it's a singular and unique tirade, a cry, a chant, a film, an opera...].[52] Such polarized reactions are, of course, very good for book sales. Furthermore, Beyala's decision to publish this text at a time when 'le porno féminin' is the latest trend in France is undoubtedly a strategic decision.[53]

Where Beyala's novel differs from Millet's is, of course, in its African setting. This then is a novel that is both erotic and exotic.

The erotic-exotic tag is, as Kom implies above, an extremely useful marketing ploy and one which, I shall suggest later, Beyala learns to use to her own advantage. Indeed, the exotic appeal of sexually explicit fiction written by an African woman has not gone unnoticed by Beyala's publishers, Albin Michel. *Femme nue, femme noire* presents the reader with photographs of two beautiful black women: one on the front cover, naked but heavily made up, carrying a large bunch of erotically suggestive white calla lilies covering her genitals but allowing a glimpse of her breasts; the other Beyala herself, smiling provocatively on the back. This, however, is by no means the first time that Beyala's work has been promoted as erotic-exotic. Even the publisher's blurb for Beyala's first novel, *C'est le soleil qui m'a brûlée*, promotes the 'touches, très pudiques et tendres, d'érotisme qu'elle pose ça et là' [discreet and tender touches of eroticism here and there], claiming that, 'avec elle [Beyala], un écrivain, authentiquement africain, authentiquement femme, se révèle' [in Beyala a writer who is authentically African and authentically woman is revealed].[54] Eroticism, this blurb suggests, is 'authentically' African. Thus, from the very beginning of her career, Beyala is contained within a framework of colonial desire, her work deemed 'authentic' because it combines Africa with sex.

As such a famous – and infamous - black African woman writer living in France, Calixthe Beyala is unique. Only Marie Ndiaye has experienced anything close to comparable commercial success with her novels published by the prestigious Editions de Minuit, the most famous of which, *Rosie Carpe*, won the Prix Femina in 2001. However, born in France of a French mother and a Senegalese father, Ndiaye has never been represented (nor represented herself) as a black African writer; indeed, she is keen to reject any suggestion that she is 'francophone' rather than 'French'. It is perhaps Beyala's unprecedented and seemingly privileged position as an economically successful African woman writer in France that explains her ambivalent reception in the land of the 'civilizing mission'. Does the very spectacle of Beyala's success rekindle the imperialist need to constantly justify the cultural superiority of (white) metropolitan France? Certainly, Beyala herself has condemned the way in which she has been treated by the French press in terms of racial persecution. Philippe Cusin, writing in *Le Figaro* on 25 November 1996 (the day after Pierre Assouline publicly accused Beyala of plagiarizing Okri), quotes Beyala saying:

> Ce que je comprends aujourd'hui, c'est je gêne les journalistes de gauche, je n'entre pas dans leur cadre en tant que femme et en tant que Noire. Je gâche leur fonds de commerce. C'est de la malveillance et de la méchanté, de la haine raciale! J'en ai assez! [...] Ils essaient de me casser, c'est de la persécution.⁵⁵

> [What I now understand is that I make left-wing journalists uncomfortable; as a woman and a Black woman, I don't fit in with them. I spoil things for them. It's malicious and nasty. It's racial hatred! I've had enough! [...] They're trying to break me. It's persecution.]

By 'left-wing journalists', Beyala is presumably referring not only to Pierre Assouline, editor of *Lire*, but also to the satirical magazine, *Le Canard enchaîné*, in which the first allegations of Beyala's plagiarism appeared in 1995.⁵⁶ It was *Le Canard enchaîné* that initially exposed the similarities between *Le petit prince de Belleville* and the French translation of Howard Buten's novel, *Burt*, similarities which ultimately led a judge to rule that 'Il apparaît incontestable que Mme Beyala s'est largement inspirée de l'œuvre de M. Buten' [It appears indisputable that Mme Beyala drew considerable inspiration from Mr Buten's work].⁵⁷

The *petit prince de Belleville* judgement was, of course, only the beginning of what has become known as 'l'Affaire Beyala'. It was the second allegation of plagiarism, launched by Assouline in relation to the prize-wining novel *Les Honneurs perdus*, that caused the greater scandal in the European press. Assouline's claim that Beyala had plagiarized Ben Okri's *The Famished Road* generated debates around textual ownership not just in France but also across the Channel. In February 1997 Assouline published a four-page article in *Lire* in which he claimed that Beyala's fiction is 'truffée de plagiats' [peppered with plagiarism].⁵⁸ Here, he presents a sample of passages from novels by Romain Gary, Paule Constant, Alice Walker and Ben Okri alongside passages from three of Beyala's novels in which, he claims, she has plagiarized. The story provoked much media frenzy in France and in Britain. For the first time a photograph of a francophone African woman writer appeared on the pages of British broadsheet newspaper, *The Guardian*, in a half-page spread entitled 'Famished Road Feeds French Book Fever'.⁵⁹

Apart from the ensuing media circus, the 'Beyala Affair' raises three key issues concerning the reception of African literature in France: racism, orality, and intertexuality. These issues are analysed in Véronique Porra's pertinent analysis of Beyala's defence. Each of these three concepts was cited by Beyala in her responses to Assouline, most notably in the statement, published in *Le Figaro* in January 1997, that forms the basis of Porra's discussion.⁶⁰ What interests me in Beyala's response to Assouline's campaign is the way in which she chooses to play the 'authenticity' card. By strategically placing herself first as victim of racism because of her alterity, then as oral storyteller because of her African roots, Beyala attempts to reappropriate and then manipulate the French public's image of her. *The Guardian* quotes her saying 'I know Ben Okri well. We lived in the same world and come from the same poor background.' Having attacked the press for its persecution of her, Beyala turns to the intertextual nature of the African storytelling tradition, claiming that, 'borrowings were common in African literature'.⁶¹ Ben Okri, however, counters each of Beyala's claims, retorting, 'I don't buy that. It's not part of the literary tradition... I want people to read me, but I don't want people to steal from my work.' Furthermore, he concludes with the categorical statement that 'It's nothing to do with race'.⁶² Apparently oblivious to Okri's reponse made two months earlier, Beyala continued to foreground her racial origins and the stereotypes associated with them in her open letter to *Le Figaro*.⁶³ She ends her statement of defence by ironically positioning herself as an impoverished immigrant in France, exclaiming, 'Merci encore à la France qui m'a acceuillie, qui m'a donné mon pain, un toit pour mes enfants' [Thanks again to France for welcoming me, giving me food and a roof over my children's heads].⁶⁴

In the case of the alleged similarities between *Les Honneurs perdus* and *The Famished Road*, Assouline's efforts were largely in vain: Ben Okri and his French publisher, Julliard, decided not to pursue the claim.⁶⁵ However, Assouline did not fail to remind readers that this was not the first time that Beyala had been accused and that she had in fact been charged with plagiarism earlier that year in the High Court in Paris. Readers of *Lire* were invited to speculate as to how a convicted plagiarist came to be nominated for – and indeed awarded – one of the top literary prizes in France. Was the Académie Française oblivious to the widely discussed case of *Le petit prince de Belleville*?⁶⁶ How was it that Paule Constant, author of *White Spirit* and member of the jury that awarded the Prix Tropique to Beyala's novel, *Assèze l'Africaine*, did not spot Beyala's plagiarism of her own novel in that same text, as alleged by Assouline in his article?⁶⁷ When she was later prompted by Assouline to review *Assèze l'Africaine,* Paule Constant was struck by the similarities with her own novel, remarking that 'ça m'a sauté au visage!' [it leapt off the page!].[68] If nothing else, the 'Beyala Affair' exposes the illegitimacy of the institution of literary prizes in France. It also begs the question as to whether Beyala was in fact right to play the authenticity card in her reaction to the French press: not that, as she claimed, she was the victim of racism or misogyny but rather that she is a tokenistic symbol of the alleged success of integration and 'Francophonie'. As Marilyn Randall notes, Beyala is all too aware of the fact that 'as a Black African woman writer she is not a "neutral," or even a natural, choice'.[69]

In some ways, the 'Beyala Affair' in the 1990s echoes the discrediting of another famous African writer, Prix Renaudot winner Yambo Ouologuem, in the 1970s. The two cases are not, however, completely identical.[70] What is perhaps most striking about the differences between them are the reactions by the two authors and the subsequent effects on their publishing careers. Whereas, despite protests of innocence, Ouologuem's novel was withdrawn from sale for thirty years and the author retreated into literary silence,[71] Calixthe Beyala continued to make the bestseller lists for her five subsequent novels, and has become something of a minor celebrity on French TV and radio. In fact, Beyala's unmasking as a fraud did absolutely no damage to her marketability: *Les Honneurs perdus* sold 120,000 copies in its first three months of sale, despite the allegations of plagiarism made earlier that year.[72]

As we have seen, when the October 1996 allegations were launched, Beyala immediately claimed her place as a victim of racism and misogyny, taking refuge in her otherness and relying on the current climate of political correctness to protect her from further defamation. She dedicated the Grand Prix du Roman de l'Académie Française to African women, telling the members of the Academy, 'Vous ne pouvez pas savoir le plaisir que vous faites à toutes les femmes d'Afrique' [You cannot know how happy you have made all the women of Africa].[73] A couple of months later, Beyala remarked in an interview about the alleged plagiarism that 'Même blanche et blonde, une femme jeune et belle aurait été accusée de tous les maux par les mêmes' [Those people would accuse any young, beautiful woman of all kinds of things, even if she was white and blonde], a comment that she then qualifies with the words, 'peut-être moins violemment' [perhaps a bit less nastily].[74] While on one level Beyala is maintaining her assumed position of victim as a black woman immigrant in France, these last remarks also reveal her awareness of her own physical beauty (Beyala is a former model) and of how beauty can sometimes be a stumbling block to a woman writer who wants to be taken seriously. More explicitly, she tells Narcisse Mouellé Kombi in an earlier interview in *Amina* magazine that 'le phantasme érotique relié à la femme noire n'arrange pas toujours les choses. J'en fais quotidiennement l'expérience en tant qu'écrivain' [the erotic fantasy associated with the black woman doesn't really help. As a writer I put up with this on a daily basis].[75]

On the other hand, Calixthe Beyala is also very well aware of the advantages that physical beauty can bring. Regularly appearing on French television as well as in a range of newspapers and magazines, Beyala is, as Congolese writer Caya Makhélé explains, 'la réussite littéraire africaine la plus médiatisée de ces dix dernières années. On l'invite à parler aussi bien de politique que de cuisine et de dessous féminins' [the most media-hyped African literary success of the last ten years. She is invited to talk as much about politics as about cooking and ladies' underwear].[76] Indeed, Beyala's success as a minor media star is as unprecedented as her literary career. In spite of the fact that only 11% of French television guests are of black, Maghrebian or Asian origin,[77] Calixthe Beyala herself is no stranger to the small screen. Indeed, she has been described in *Elle* magazine as 'pleine de [...] télégénie' [extremely telegenic].[78] In the paradoxical year that was 1996, Beyala appeared at least twelve times on terrestrial television in France.[79] As invited TV guest or 'expert', Beyala has voiced her opinions on a range of subjects, including whether women can live without men, Brigitte Bardot's memoirs, retirement homes and chocolate. While it is true that her television appearances are generally motivated by the promotion of her books, Beyala has at the same time become something of an icon of African femininity in France. Interviewers draw attention to her physical appearance; camera operators often focus on her legs; and even in discussions of her fiction, such distinguished television presenters as Patrick Poivre d'Arvor single out the erotic qualities of her writing.[80] Beyala herself never openly challenges the ways in which she is constantly constructed as an exotic object of beauty; on the contrary, she often flirts with male presenters, reminding them that her given name, Calixthe, means 'la plus jolie' [the prettiest] in Greek.

In 1988 Beyala appeared for the second time on Antenne 2's

morning magazine programme, 'Matin Bonheur', with Thierry Becarro. During this programme, Becarro mispronounces Beyala's name no less than ten times in forty-five minutes. When Becarro eventually realizes his mistake and apologizes to Beyala, she laughs. The apology follows a sexually charged interaction during which Becarro reacts to the news of Beyala's advanced pregnancy by telling her, 'C'est bien! Vous êtes superbe! Je me permets de vous le dire' [That's great! May I say that you look fantastic!] The show culminates in a cookery demonstration. Here Beyala comments, 'Je suis tellement gourmande que j'ai envie de sauter dessus!' [I'm such a foodie that I feel like jumping on it!][81] Thus, from an early stage in her television career, Beyala seems prepared to accept and also to reinforce the media's positioning of her as the exotic-erotic other, despite the fact that, as president of Collectif Egalité, her intention is to draw the French public's attention to the racist representation of black people in the media. Of course, stereotypes of African women as both exotically beautiful and sexually voracious hark back to the colonial era, the epitome being Saartje Baartman, nicknamed 'The Hottentot Venus'. It is initially surprising, then, that a woman such as Beyala, who wishes to challenge the representation of blacks on French TV, should appear to implicitly legitimize her own mystification by the media and at the same time allow the perpetuation of the discourse of colonial fantasy.

Even after several television appearances in which the question of the representation of ethnic minorities was her main talking point, Beyala's media image remains fixed in the stereotype created for her in the late 1980s. Fellow guests on the late-night magazine programme, 'On a tout essayé!', broadcast in October 2000, make numerous comments on Beyala's physical appearance, including 'Vous êtes plutôt une belle femme!' [You really are a beautiful woman!] and 'Elle est ravissante' [She is ravishing]. Beyala had been invited onto the programme to present her novel, *Comment cuisiner son mari à l'africaine*, which is described in condescending terms as 'un petit peu de l'Afrique folklore, mais c'est bien écrit' [a little bit of African folklore, but it's well written].[37] What these television programmes demonstrate is the French media's attempt to fix Calixthe Beyala within two colonial models: the exotic beauty and the savage. Writing about cinema, Homi Bhabha has famously argued that 'an important feature of colonial discourse is its dependence on the concept of "fixity" in the ideological construction of otherness'.[82] French television is thus perpetuating a colonial discourse in its representation of black celebrities such as Beyala, and simultaneously forestalling any notion of a multicultural France.

As an erotic-exotic object, the image of Beyala on TV can be read as a continued attempt by the French to justify the 'mission civilisatrice' of their colonial endeavour. It is, however, difficult to reconcile Beyala's apparently willing participation in this normalization of colonial discourse with either her fictional writings or her role as prominent campaigner for equality of representation. On the one hand, Beyala's TV performances could be read as nothing more than a strategic quest for stardom. Indeed, her different incarnations reveal her to be a competent performer, playing to the images created for her by the French media. However, such a game could have very serious implications for the representation of ethnic minorities – and black women in particular – on television in France. On the other hand, Beyala's protean media image could be read as a sign of her uncertainty about how to position herself in the French public eye and, by extension, within the French nation-state. According to Blanchard and Bancel, the politics of integration in France has generated two models of identity for immigrants from the former empire: the 'assimilated' or the 'rebel'.[83] What Beyala's media career reveals is a woman attempting to position herself between these poles, sometimes as assimilated, sometimes as rebel, sometimes as neither, sometimes as both. Moreover, this book will suggest that what might have begun as Beyala's uncertainty about where and how to position herself develops into a complex game of strategic negotiation.

At the same time as she attempts to challenge racist representations of people from the African diaspora in France, Beyala is also subject to the pressure of the global marketplace in France. Indeed, the contradictory nature of Beyala's public image is symptomatic of what Graham Huggan calls the 'postcolonial exotic':

> The postcolonial exotic [...] occupies a site of discursive conflict between a local assemblage of more or less related oppositional practices and a global apparatus of assimilative institutional/ commercial codes. More specifically, it marks the intersection between contending regimes of value: one regime – postcolonialism – that posits itself as anticolonial, and that works toward the dissolution of imperial epistemologies and institutional structures; and another – postcoloniality – that is more closely tied to the global market, and that capitalises both on the widespread circulation of

ideas about cultural otherness and on the worldwide trafficking of culturally 'othered' artifacts and goods.[84]

Calixthe Beyala's success precisely emanates from her position at the intersection Huggan describes. As an outspoken political activist and writer she challenges colonialism and its legacies; as a product manufactured by the French book industry she reaps the benefits of her own exoticism, self-consciously promoting herself as a 'postcolonial exotic' commodity. While she may appear to be passively complicit in the process of her own objectification, Beyala in fact understands very well the uniqueness of her position in France and manipulates what she experiences as a neocolonial fear of – and desire for – exotic otherness. The tensions that emerge between the postcolonial commodity that is Calixthe Beyala and the expectations of her consumers are revealing of the enduring nature of colonial ideology: she is expected to write and behave as an 'authentic' African woman on anybody's terms but her own. Beyala, however, is all too aware of these expectations, which from the safety of her incorporation into the canon of 'la Francophonie' she is able to play with and ultimately undermine.

This chapter has suggested that the consecration of Beyala as a major francophone author is largely the result of the symbolic capital she has acquired as an exotic object rather than a great writer. As we have seen, her symbolic recognition has often taken the form of negative and/or racist criticism. Deliberately provocative and controversial, however, Beyala plays the media at their own game, becoming what Huggan calls a 'cultural celebrity' a self-conscious participant in the mediatizing process.[85] As Huggan remarks of Canadian writer Margaret Atwood, Beyala is 'highly aware of herself, and of her writing, as a commodity; and she is conscious, too, of the roles she plays in the image-making industry that surrounds her work'.[86] Huggan's concept of 'staged controversiality' can be applied to both Atwood and Beyala. However, whereas Atwood fulfils what Said defined as one of the tasks of the oppositional intellectual, that is 'to break down the stereotypes and reductive categories that are so limiting to human thought and communication',[87] Beyala's cultural celebrity relies, to a certain extent, on the preservation of those categories. Huggan accuses Atwood of playing to her audience; the same can be said of Calixthe Beyala. The difference lies in the fact that Atwood's relationship with her readership is measured in terms of sameness (white, middle-class, female, feminist) whereas Beyala is always positioned by her reader as other. In order to maintain her celebrity status, Calixthe Beyala needs to preserve a degree of otherness, to challenge the fixity of the colonial gaze only to confirm its legitimacy once more. What emerges, then, is a complex game of resistance and (re)incorporation in which Beyala endeavours to stay one step ahead. This game gives Beyala a kind of deliberate slipperiness or unlocatability. Paradoxically, it is precisely Beyala's unlocatability that compels readers to attempt to locate her: as exotic beauty, as troublemaker, as prize-winning writer, as plagiarist, perhaps, but always as black African woman in France.

CHAPTER TWO

Invented Authenticities

> Elle recherchait le peuple, celui qui n'a pas inventé le poudre, l'idiot qui n'a pas distillé le souffle du canon. [...]Elle trouva le peuple d'Ousmane. [...] Aujourd'hui, la vie s'effondre. Le peuple d'Ousmane N'EXISTE PAS.[1]
>
> [She did research on those people who had not invented gunpowder; the blockhead who had not distilled the cannon's blast. [...] She found Ousmane's people. [...] Today her life is falling apart. Ousmane's people DO NOT EXIST].[2]

When, as discussed in the previous chapter, Beyala faced the allegations of plagiarism that became known as the 'Beyala Affair', her chief accuser, Pierre Assouline, subjected her novels to detective-like scrutiny in an attempt to expose her as a fraud. This dissection of Beyala's novels was not dissimilar to the attempts at cultural deciphering that are made by anthropologists and ethnologists, or 'tourist-explorers' in Africa.[3] Just as ethnological studies were used to confirm the assumed inferiority of African cultures and so justify France's 'civilizing mission', so Assouline's mission led him to the conclusion that Beyala's work is not prize-worthy but fake. Like tourists who have paid a high price for a purportedly 'authentic' African mask, only to find that the mask is nothing more than a copy, the French book industry (represented by Assouline) felt betrayed and disappointed by Beyala's prize-winning novel, while at the same time happy to congratulate themselves on having their suspicions about the inferiority of African cultural production confirmed. In the 1970s, when Malian writer Yambo Ouologuem's novel *Le Devoir de violence* was the focus of a similar controversy, Eric Sellin wrote about what was then dubbed the 'Ouologuem Affair': 'many authentic good things have come out of Africa and this novel [*Le Devoir de violence*] appeared to be one of the finest, whence my great disappointment'.[4] What both 'affairs' reveal is the French (and American) readership's desire for the consumption of 'authenticity': suddenly Beyala, like Ouologuem, was no longer identified as an 'authentic African author', and so became invalidated – temporarily in her case – by the collectors of African culture.[5]

Two years after the events of the 'Beyala Affair', Beyala published *La petite fille du réverbère* which includes as an epigraph a quotation from Maupassant's *Etude sur le roman*: 'Qui peut se vanter, parmi nous, d'avoir écrit une page, une phrase qui ne se trouve déjà, à peu près pareille, quelque part?' [Who among us can pride themselves on having written a page or even a sentence that does not already exist in a very similar form somewhere else?] Through this thinly veiled reference to the plagiarism charges made against her, Beyala expresses her contempt for those who might have imagined that the events of 1996 would see the end of her literary career. The novel ends with a parodical sketch of Pierre Assouline, his name anagrammatically rewritten as 'Riene Poussalire' [Nothing Makeshimread]:

> Je revins sur mes pas, pour alimenter les Missiés Riene Poussalire, ces critiques envieux, et leur permettre de continuer une carrière infertile qui, selon Alexandre Dumas, n'apporte au monde littéraire que ces couronnes de ronces qu'ils ont tressées et qu'ils enfoncent en riant sur la tête du poète vainqueur ou vaincu.
>
> [I retraced my steps to give food for thought to those Mister Nothing Makeshimreads, those jealous critics, and to allow them to carry on their sterile careers which, as Alexandre Dumas said, bring nothing to the literary world apart from the crowns of thorns they've woven to push deep onto the head of the conquering or conquered poet, laughing as they go.] (*PFR*, p. 233)[6]

So this novel begins and ends with references to Beyala's alleged plagiarism. By framing in this way a text that is marketed by its publisher as 'largement autobiographique' [largely autobiographical] and '[le roman] le plus intime et le plus émouvant que l'auteur [...] ait jamais écrit' [the most intimate and moving novel the author [...] has ever written], Beyala not only keeps fanning the flames of the 'Beyala Affair' but also does so in the context of what is purportedly her most autobiographical novel. In other words, this novel flaunts Beyala's history of plagiarism, while at the same time promoting its textual 'authenticity' (by stressing both authorship and autobiography). The term 'authenticity' is, of course, extremely controversial and increasingly meaningless since, as Iain Chambers writes, it attempts to 'subtract a culture, a history, a language, an identity, from the wider transforming currents of the increasingly metropolitan world'.[7] Nonetheless it is constantly bandied about in discussions of African literature and culture both inside and outside the African continent.

In her study of African migrant writing in Paris, Bennetta Jules-Rosette identifies three images of Africa that recur in this fiction: '(1) natural or untouched Africa (*Afrique nature*); (2) scientific Africa; and (3) Africa in combat'.[8] In fact, the first and second images are closely linked since the discourse of what Jules-Rosette calls 'scientific Africa' often promotes a vision of Africa as 'natural or untouched', uncontaminated by 'civilization' which, for many, is synonymous with Western culture. This chapter takes as its starting point the discourse of 'scientific Africa'; in other words, images that recall the exoticist representations of the so-called 'primitive' continent made by ethnologists such as Marcel Griaule and the founders of the Palais du Trocadéro in Paris. The representations made by these collectors of cultures have all contributed to the myth of African 'authenticity', according to which Africa is characterized as a 'pure state of humanity from which modern civilization has deviated'.[9] In metropolitan France, the first public manifestations of 'scientific Africa' appeared in the colonial exhibitions of the late nineteenth and early twentieth centuries at which, as Elizabeth Ezra notes, 'crowds gathered to watch imperial subjects displayed like living museum exhibits in their "natural habitats", or French-designed reconstructions of native villages'.[10] Such exhibitions served a dual purpose: confirming exoticist stereotypes of Africa as a primitive place, and providing justification for France's mission to 'civilize' these 'primitive' peoples.[11] According to Jules-Rosette, the search for a pre-civilized 'Other' that underlies exoticism provokes two types of response among African writers in France: narratives of longing and counter-narratives of belonging. These categories are by no means discrete; like exoticism itself, both are characterized by desire. Moreover, in Jules-Rosette's analysis, both are reflected in the mythology of scientific Africa.[12] In Chapter 1, I discussed France's attempts to contain Beyala within a scientific discourse by positioning her in the exotic category of 'African woman'. In this chapter, I shall be discussing the ways in which Beyala engages with the discourse of 'scientific Africa' in her novels through an analysis of her fictional negotiations of 'authenticity'.

As James Clifford demonstrates, any claims to ethnic purity or 'true tradition' are 'always subverted by the need to stage authenticity *in opposition* to external, often dominating alternatives. [...] If authenticity is relational, there can be no essence except as a political, cultural invention, a local tactic.'[13] Senghor's Negritude was such a tactic, positing as it did the notion of a black essence in response to racist representations of blackness. However, the critics of Negritude have since failed to acknowledge its interventionist role, reducing it instead to yet another dominating set of clichés about black people in the world. While, as Clifford observes, 'Senghor's brand of negritude has yielded to Aimé Césaire's more syncretic, impure, inventive conception of cultural identity', it is the Senghorian version that provides the more common intertext in Beyala's fictional writings.[14]

Beyala's erotic novel *Femme nue, femme noire* (2003) takes its title from one of Senghor's best-known poems, a poem that has been criticized by feminists for its essentializing images of African women. The poem is quoted three times – in the title, the epigraph and the opening lines of the novel – only to be immediately dismissed as the opposite of what will follow. Beyala writes: '"Femme nue, femme noire, vêtue de ta couleur qui est vie, de ta forme qui est beauté..." Ces vers ne font pas partie de mon arsenal linguistique. Vous verrez: mes mots à moi tressautent et cliquettent comme des chaînes' ['Naked woman, black woman, dressed in your colour that is life, in your form that is beauty...' These lines are not part of my linguistic arsenal. You will see: my words rattle and jangle like chains] (*FNFN*, p. 11). From these words the reader infers that Senghor's language is not appropriate for the articulation of this narrator's experience. Immediately after the denunciation of Senghor, the narrator elaborates: 'ici il n'y aura pas de soutiens-gorge en dentelle, de bas résille, de petites culottes en soie [...] et encore moins ces approches rituelles de la femme fatale' [here there won't be any lacy bras, fishnet tights or silk panties [...] never mind any of that femme fatale ritualistic behaviour] (p. 11). By association, then, Senghor's imagery is rejected as the stuff of male heterosexual fantasy, as inappropriate to the narrative as sexy underwear. So the reader immediately assumes that what will follow will somehow write against essentializing gender norms. Paradoxically, though, in this same novel, Beyala appropriates and condemns what she presents as Senghor's essentialist imagery in a text that has itself been criticized for reducing African women to another form of racist stereotype. Through its crude depictions of the narrator-protagonist's extraordinary sexual adventures, the novel appears to promote and perpetuate the colonial myth of the African woman as a primarily sexual being. This will be discussed later in this chapter.

In my view, these Senghorian intertexts signal Beyala's desire to expose the way in which Africa has been represented as a series of 'invented authenticities' by both African and non-African writers. Huggan identifies such a strategy as a common feature of the postcolonial writer's agenda. Drawing on Clifford's work, he writes that:

> Post-colonial writers are generally suspicious of effecting a 'salvage ethnography' of their own in which 'native authenticity' or 'native point of view' – whatever either of these might mean – are somehow rescued from the imprisoning conventions of Western representation. They are more likely to turn their attention instead to the (sometimes disguised or surreptitious) fiction-making processes underlying all forms of cultural representation.[15]

As well as denouncing Senghor and his Negritude, Beyala, like Ouologuem before her, uses fiction to denounce what Huggan calls the 'anthropological fraudulence' exemplified by ethnologists like Leo Frobenius, and exposes the fetishization of authentic African culture by critics and anthropologists alike.[16] As both Beyala and Ouologuem were accused of literary theft, a sympathetic reader might extend the comparison to argue that Beyala's plagiarism, like Ouologuem's, is another way of reversing the exoticist gaze. It might be argued that, by appropriating other people's words, Beyala resists containment within the ethnological category of 'African writer' while at the same time challenging the notion of textual ownership which has its roots in Western culture. A similar tactic was employed by Ouologuem, whose case has subsequently been accorded an overtly political agenda. Writing about Ouologuem, Huggan, among others, reads *Le Devoir de violence* as 'a satire on origins, textual as well as cultural, for Ouologuem also takes every opportunity to violate the protective copyright of artistic originality'.[17] Surprisingly, perhaps, Beyala has never appropriated such an agenda into the complex armoury of her defence that we discussed in the previous chapter. Yet, as we have seen, outside her fiction Beyala turns anthropological fraudulence to her own advantage, reclaiming her place in the sun as an 'authentic African woman' and encouraging the cultural voyeurism of the ethnological gaze.

Part of Beyala's self-positioning as an 'authentic African woman' involves persistently reminding readers of her impoverished background in the New Bell area of Douala, Cameroon. *La petite fille du réverbère* is the only novel in which Beyala makes an explicit autobiographical pact between herself and her narrator, Beyala B'Assanga Djuli, nicknamed Tapoussière because she is always dirty. The publisher's blurb, however, describes the text not as autobiography but, more ambiguously, as 'largement autobiographique', and labels it a novel. Nevertheless, the decision to name her narrator Beyala forces readers to assume that at least some of the details of Tapoussière's impoverished childhood are similar to Beyala's own. She also frequently talks about her childhood in published interviews, on television and on radio, and writes about it in her first essay, *Lettre d'une Africaine à ses soeurs occidentales*. While the printed details of Beyala's childhood vary quite considerably, the most often-quoted biographical information includes the stories that her father abandoned his wife and twelve children, that she lived in a 'bidonville' [shanty town] and was raised by her grandmother 'dans les valeurs de la noblesse traditionnelle dont [sa grand-mère est issue]' [in the values of the traditional nobility that her grandmother came from].[18] Africa as autobiographical home is represented as a place of poverty and squalor where men play a minimal role and where women – in Beyala's case, her grandmother and her late sister, Assèze – make extraordinary sacrifices for their children, and are the keepers and transmitters of tradition. While she acknowledges New Bell's role as a source of inspiration, Beyala emphasizes the material and cultural impoverishment of her birthplace, stressing the devaluation of intellectuals in Cameroon as well as the political and economic corruption there.

An equally negative picture emerges in the novels set in real and imagined African contexts, reflecting for sympathetic critics such as Gallimore the horror of postcolonial Africa.[19] Beyala's first three novels, *C'est le soleil qui m'a brûlée*, *Tu t'appelleras Tanga* and *Seul le diable le savait* (republished as *La Négresse rousse*), are all set in fictitious African locations but, in *Assèze l'Africaine*, Beyala explicitly identifies Cameroon. In *Les Honneurs perdus*, Beyala even presents a brief parody of Cameroonian political history when she describes Bida who, in an ironic reference to Oedipus Rex, is blinded by his political opponent, 'Le Président à vie' [the President for life] (*HP*, p.122). Here, Beyala is treading slightly dangerous ground, for Bida's phonetic proximity to Biya is difficult to deny.[20] This shift from imagined African nations to a locatable Cameroonian context can best be explained by fear of censorship: it is easier for Beyala to openly criticize the country of her birth when she is safely established as a best-selling writer in exile in France. Nonetheless, Beyala's novels paint an extremely damning portrait of contemporary life in Africa, whether they are located in the fictional or the 'real'.

Drawing on the work of Andrew Gurr, Ayo Abiétou Coly suggests that the reconstruction of home in Beyala's early works conforms to a pattern for writers in exile.[21] Africa in these novels is indeed, as Coly suggests, 'a collapsing continent',[22] characterized by stifling heat, decay and filth. By way of example, Beyala's very first description of the imagined city of Awu in *C'est le soleil qui m'a brûlée* illustrates this point: 'Chaleur étouffante. Soleil accablant, un escadron de grosses mouches noires patrouille au-dessus d'une montagne d'ordures. Des rats jouent à cache-cache. Des chiens et des chats pelés se disputent quelques détritus' (*CSB*, p.15) [A stifling heat. The sun is overwhelming, a squadron of fat black flies is on patrol above a mountain of waste. Rats are playing hide-and-seek. A few mangy dogs and cats are fighting over a bit of rubbish (*SHL*, p. 3)]. Portraits of squalor continue throughout Beyala's fiction: in her more recent novel, *Femme nue, femme noire*, she describes people defecating in the street and children taking dead rats home for dinner. The shocking realities of poverty and disease are never ignored, even when Africa is re-viewed from the comfort of exile: 'Lasse et cendreuse, je [Assèze] pensais à cette vie en dégénérescence qui continuait en Afrique. La lutte pour la survie: la faim, la soif, la rougeole, le paludisme, le Sida, qui tuaient sans ordre de grandeur' [Weary and ashen, I [Assèze] thought about this degenerating life which continued in Africa. The struggle for survival: hunger, thirst, measles, malaria, AIDS, which killed you however tall or small you were] (*AA*, p. 287). Crushed by economic deprivation, African people are represented by a string of negative metaphors: men are 'la boue' [mud] and la crasse [filth]; women are 'les fesses' [arses][23] and 'les pondeuses' [good layers], emphasizing their function as exchangeable commodities. African countries are depicted as prisons from which the only escape is death.

Beyala's fiction also alludes to abuses of human rights in Cameroon and elsewhere in Africa, particularly through the descriptions of the appalling treatment of the prisoners Tanga and Anna-Claude.[24] Both women are imprisoned because of what is seen to be their subversive behaviour: Tanga is accused of helping street children to forge money; Anna-Claude is arrested for drawing the public's attention to the sudden disappearances of some of her students by walking around with a billboard. When the latter requests a cigarette from one of the prison guards, he tears off her clothes and forces her to run naked around the cell. One of his colleagues then defecates inside the cell, joking that, in place of a cigarette, he is giving her a cigar (*TTT*, p. 69; *YNT*, p. 43).

All heterosexual relationships are characterized as inherently abusive or motivated by financial gain. What is presented as the essential incompatibility between men and women is reflected in the natural symbolism of *C'est le soleil qui m'a brûlée*: men are represented as the sun which burns or mud that clings; women as the stars that illuminate or water that cleanses and purifies. Sex between women and men is generally presented as either rape or prostitution. Where there is a suggestion of heterosexual love, for example in the case of Assèze and Alexandre (*AA*) or M'am and Etienne Tichit (*MAA*), it is specifically the reserve of Beyala's migrant heroines and fulfils a very particular function (see Chapter 3). In Beyala's Africa, love between men and women simply does not exist, for men are the representatives and perpetuators of patriarchal tradition.

'Tradition' is presented as the justification for the perpetuation of oppressive practices against women, one of the most controversial of which is the genital mutilation of young girls as a right of passage into womanhood. The first written reference to this practice by a francophone African woman writer appeared in Awa Thiam's groundbreaking sociological text, *La Parole aux Négresses*, published in 1978.[25] Apart from Thiam, however, women in francophone Africa have on the whole been reluctant to speak about what is euphemistically referred to as 'female circumcision'. This was particularly the case in the 1980s when Beyala began to publish.[26] Her outspokenness on such issues has continued throughout her career with her novels exposing such 'traditional' practices as virginity testing ('le rite de l'oeuf' [the egg ritual]), in which the tester attempts to insert an egg into a girl's vagina to ascertain whether her hymen is still intact, the dowry system and polygamy. In *Lettre d'une Africaine* Beyala openly criticizes those African men who intellectualize the oppression and mutilation of women by conflating such practices with tradition. These men, she writes, condemn the cultural hegemony of the West and preach salvation through African tradition (*LASO*, p. 88). In Beyala's novels, many of the characters also brandish tradition as a protective shield against what they see as the dangers of modernity.

At the same time, however, the texts condemn so-called traditional practices and social structures as responsible for creating the widespread negativity and inertia, 'le Rien' [Nothingness] and 'le Vide' [Emptiness], of the communities they describe.[27]

Africa is a place of oppression and corruption in Beyala's fiction: the President sends corn to the people of Saïda's village in an attempt to seduce voters (*HP*, p. 121) and eventually polls 118 per cent [*sic*] of the votes (p. 169); Tanga's shack has been razed to the ground ten times to make way for important visitors, highlighting the way in which neocolonial African governments attempt to conceal the poverty of their peoples (*TTT*, p. 38). Women and children are raped and exploited within the domestic space and also outside the home – sometimes by family members, sometime by strangers, sometimes by representatives of the neocolonial government. Tanga, a child-prostitute, is raped by her father and becomes pregnant by him; Ateba is forced to perform fellatio on two men (Jean Zepp and another man with whom she poses as a prostitute (*CSB*)). Like Sony Labou Tansi, Beyala uses sex to illustrate the failure of postcolonial African governments. In *Femme nue, femme noire*, butcher Saturnin's success with local women is explained by the impotence of their husbands, 'parce qu'elle sont mariées aux suppôts des dictateurs dont les couilles, à force de magouiller, de piller le pays, deviennent si molles qu'ils n'ont plus qu'une seule distraction: envoyer des balles dans la nuque des opposants' [because they are married to the dictators' henchmen whose balls become so soft from plotting and pillaging the country that the only way they have left to pass the time is by firing bullets into the backs of their opponents' necks] (*FNFN*, p. 203). Indeed, in Beyala's world, political power seems to be inversely proportional to sexual potency: whereas the political henchmen are impotent, the rest of the population seems to be having sex all the time, creating an atmosphere of sexual and political decadence.

The violence of Beyala's Africa can be read as a form of textual resistance against the corruption of neocolonialism, as critics such as Gallimore suggest. However, this resistance is limited by the fact that the novels offer few alternatives to the horror they describe. Whereas Christiane Ndiaye suggests that Beyala's novels offer fictional solutions to real African problems, I find little evidence to support this view.[28] Through explicit descriptions of oppression and violence, linguistic decadence and the exposure of taboos, Beyala's fiction offers some resistance to the misery it portrays, but this resistance remains at the level of revelation. Individual acts of rebellion have little impact on the surrounding communities. In other words, by revealing violence and corruption, Beyala's novels challenge that same violence and corruption, yet at the same time offer no alternatives other than a utopian 'ailleurs' [elsewhere] that exists only in dreams or the imagination.[29] The relentless female suffering of *C'est le soleil qui m'a brûlée* ends with the death of Ateba's friend, Irène, a prostitute who dies after an illegal abortion. Ateba then goes to a nightclub where she poses as a prostitute and goes home with a man she does not know. When the man forces her to perform oral sex on him, Ateba kills him by hitting him over the head with a heavy copper ashtray. She then bangs his head on the stone floor and stabs him repeatedly. The scene ends with her urinating on his dead body, then kissing him and calling him Irène. This is followed by an ambiguous dénouement in which Ateba is reconciled with 'Moi', the narrator of the novel, and Ateba's 'true self'. By concluding the novel in this way, Beyala could be read as suggesting that the only way out of female oppression is through acts of violence against men; only then will women find their 'true selves'. On the other hand, Ateba appears not to recognize 'Moi' and walks away towards the horizon and what the text describes as 'les eaux complexes des femmes à venir' (*CSB*, p. 174) [the intricate waters of women to come (*SHL*, p. 12)], implying that only in another time and another place will women escape patriarchal oppression.

Beyala's Africa seems then to be frozen in a state of pessimism and inertia: Tanga observes that 'dans mon pays, la montre s'est arrêtée là où commence la culture...' (*TTT*, p. 27) [in my country, the clock has stopped where culture begins... (*YNT*, p. 14)]. The people of Beyala's African nations are depicted either as zombies – the living dead – whose only activity seems to be endlessly waiting, 'attendre à Iningué est une forme de suicide' (*TTT*, p. 89) [waiting in Iningué is a form of suicide (*YNT*, p. 57)], or as abusers like the prison guards who thrive on others' suffering. In particular, Africa in Beyala's novels is depicted as a continent with no future through the representation of the abuse of children. This is particularly marked in *Tu t'appelleras Tanga*, which presents the exploitation and neglect of the children of Iningué. The content of this novel is summed up by Nancy Arenberg as the 'hell of surviving in a modern African city that exploits children, robbing them of their innocence and subjecting them to widespread violence and debauchery'.[30] Childhood here is 'mutilée' [mutilated], with children forced to act as adults from a very early age, hence Tanga's naming of herself as 'femme-fillette' [girlchild-woman]. This point is further emphasized in the disturbing descriptions of Tanga's visits to a local abattoir. When she sees a butcher chopping up a pig she is reminded of 'l'enfance égorgée. La vie éventrée' (*TTT*, p. 100) ['childhood's slashed throat. Life disembowelled' (*YNT*, p. 65)]. She later returns to ask the butcher to cut her own throat in a scene that ends with Tanga playing the role of 'maman improvisée' (*TTT*, p. 103) ['improvised mamma' (*YNT*, p. 66)] while the butcher suckles her breasts. What seem to be almost surreal descriptions of children posing as adults represent the very real situations of child prostitutes and increasing numbers of street children in many contemporary African nations, but also reflect the profound sense of hopelessness for the future of Africa that dominates Beyala's novels.[31] As Harrow observes in his fascinating discussion of this novel, Beyala's early fiction is 'consonant with the age of a new, harsh urban landscape' in which the people of Cameroon live in an increasing state of despair and repression.[32]

Thus Beyala takes a very critical backward look at 'home' in Africa which, for some critics, presents simply another version of an invented authenticity. Odile Cazenave, for example, reads Beyala's images of Africa as 'generic and cliché-like' because they are 'decentred, shaped in part by her own experience as an African woman who has been living in France for more than a decade, and who starts seeing Africa with distant eyes', the eyes of the former colonial power.[33] Extending her argument to consider the impact of a predominantly French readership on Beyala's fiction, Cazenave suggests that Beyala's representations of Africa and its peoples is indicative of a 'gallicizing' of her writing, by which she means that Beyala's point of reference has shifted from Cameroon to France.[34] 'To the French reader', Cazenave argues,

> The insertion of African words and expressions, or literal translations of proverbs, etc. will appear as truly authentic and evocative of African/Cameroonian environment. But they will appear as such because French readers are not in a position to make an informed judgement. As a result they adhere to this representation of Africa and Africans.[35]

Cazenave's aim is not to denounce Beyala as an 'inauthentic' writer, but her conclusions do rightly raise questions about the degree of complicity between Beyala and her French readers. In her analysis of

Beyala's subversion of stereotypes, Cazenave concludes that 'part of [Beyala's] writing seems to be feeding into French readers' fantasies about Africa and their quest for a renewed version of exotic literature. Hence the controversy, where African readers may object to a certain artificiality of her representation of African [sic] and Africans.'[36] The implication here is twofold: first, Cazenave suggests that, now that she is living in France, Beyala has to a certain extent 'sold out' to her predominantly French readership. But secondly – and more importantly – Cazenave seems to be supporting the view that African writers should present realist visions of Africa in their fiction. Tunde Fatunde makes a similar point when he implies that Beyala has a responsibility to act as a literary ambassador for Africa, a belief that leads him to charge her with 'Afro-pessimism'.[37]

I would suggest that what some see as Beyala's pessimistic and/ or clichéd images of Africa are not so much further evidence of the incorporation of Beyala into France, but rather are symptomatic of the migratory experience. While it is certainly true that visions of Africa as a backward continent characterized by misery and political instability are as much Eurocentric clichés as the celebration of noble savages in lands uncontaminated by civilization, Beyala's 'Afro-pessimism' is not as surprising as it might at first seem. Indeed, the negativity of Beyala's fictional relationship with Africa is, as Elleke Boehmer reminds us, a common feature of migrant literatures which 'represent a geographic, cultural and political retreat by writers from the new but ailing nations of the postcolonial world back to the old metropolis. The literatures are a product of that retreat; they are marked by its disillusionment.'[38] The distance that exile brings will almost necessarily generate a more critical evaluation of 'home'. This is not to underestimate the market pressures and cultural hegemony facing a francophone writer in France, but rather to suggest that Beyala is doing something more than simply confirming another Eurocentric version of normative African 'authenticity'. Later in this chapter, I discuss the ways in which Beyala's critical visions of Africa in fact present a challenge to the very notion of African 'authenticity' and confirm the widely held view that, as Kwame Anthony Appiah remarks, 'there is no longer a fully autochthonous *echt*-African culture awaiting salvage by our artists'.[39]

Although she knows unparalleled success in Europe and the United States, Beyala's work is relatively unknown among francophone African readers. Beyala is, of course, read in translation in anglophone African countries thanks to her place in the Heinemann African Writers Series (see Chapter 1). However, in francophone Africa she has failed to make the kind of impact she experiences in the West. According to US-based Cameroonian critic Ambroise Kom, 'Même au Cameroun, son pays de naissance et univers d'élection de nombre de ses créations, tout indique qu'au-delà de ses bruyantes apparitions à la télévision d'Etat lors de ses occasionnelles visites au pays natal, Beyala et son œuvre passent totalement inaperçues' [Even in Cameroon, her birth country and chosen setting for many of her creations, everything points to the fact that, apart from her boisterous appearances on state television during her occasional visits to her home country, Beyala and her work go totally unnoticed].[40] Here Kom is undoubtedly overstating the case concerning Beyala's alleged anonymity in Cameroon since it is hard to believe that someone whose work is totally unknown would be invited to appear on national television. Moreover, a substantial number of reviews and analyses of Beyala's work have been produced by critics based in Africa. Beyala does, however, admit that her books are not easily obtainable in Cameroon. This, in her view, is the fault of Cameroonian booksellers who are not prepared to pay for the books from the publisher in advance. Beyala claims to demand publication in cheap paperback format in order to make her books more easily available to African readers, but she fails to mention that the economic reality of many African countries makes buying books a low priority, even in low-priced editions.[41]

What is also interesting in Kom's analysis is his description of Beyala's novels as 'en nette rupture avec les textes africains précédents' [making a clean break with the African texts that have gone before].[42] Heinemann publishers make a similar point in the blurb for the English translation of *C'est le soleil qui m'a brûlée*, presenting it as a 'shocking novel [which] deconstructs the illusions about African women which négritude literature has produced'.[43] In their attempts to emphasize the originality of Beyala's fiction, both Heinemann and Kom choose to ignore the resonances between her writing and that of other members of the new generation of writers that emerged in francophone Africa in the 1980s.[44] That aside, both descriptions place Beyala firmly outside the established canon of African literature in French represented in the first instance by the Negritude generation and then, some years later, by such pioneers of women writing in francophone Africa as Mariama Bâ. While Bâ implicitly criticizes

Negritude through the essentializing gender politics of many of her male characters, Beyala's intertextual references to Senghor mark a greater distance from Negritude's celebration of woman as the ultimate symbol of African authenticity.⁴⁵ This distance is crystallized in Beyala's choice of *Femme nue, femme noire* as the title for her first erotic novel, as discussed above.

On the other hand, Beyala's relationship with Negritude is more ambivalent than her reference to *Femme nue, femme noire* suggests. In my analysis it is an example of what will emerge as a pattern of alternating rejection and recuperation of 'authenticity' in her writing. As we saw in the previous chapter, Beyala claims that her philosophy of 'Féminitude' derives from a rather different – and more positive – interpretation of Negritude's images of women. This would appear to contradict the angry rejection of a key poem in Negritude's construction of African femininity. Such ambivalence is perhaps what leads Claudia Martinek to levy at Beyala criticisms similar to those made of Senghor's poetry in Beyala's text. Martinek condemns *Femme nue, femme noire* for failing to deconstruct the image of the African woman as Europe's seductive and sensual Other. According to Martinek, '*Femme nue, femme noire*, malgré son dénouement tragique, renforce cette idée en présentant l'Africaine comme détentrice d'un pouvoir sexuel guérissant. A la fin, le roman laisse une impression plutôt décevante et un arrière-goût amer' [*Femme nue, femme noire*, despite its tragic dénouement, reinforces this idea by presenting the African woman as holder of a healing sexual power. At the end, the novel leaves a rather disappointing impression and a bitter aftertaste].⁴⁶ While I agree with Martinek that the ending of the novel is disappointing, I do not share her view that Irène's role of sexual healer reinforces Otherness. Having abandoned her position as healer, Irène decides to return to her home in New Bell where she is beaten by men with iron bars, raped repeatedly and left for dead. The final line of the novel, narrated by Irène, describes her mother crying over her dying body: 'Ses larmes coulent doucement et c'est tout' [Her tears fall gently and that is it] (*FNFN*, p. 224). Irène is killed for accidentally stealing the body of a dead baby at the beginning of novel and not for the sexual amorality that takes up most of the narrative space. What the rather cursory conclusion seems to suggest is the absurdity of Irène's death at the hands of these men: their behaviour is ultimately far more depraved than her own. It also draws attention to the lawlessness and hypocrisy of contemporary Cameroonian society, a point that is repeated in the novel through the references to the barbaric killings of petty thieves.[47] Ultimately, Irène is not able to heal anything, least of all the horror that surrounds her.

Martinek, however, is not alone in her criticism of what she sees as Beyala's reductive stereotyping. Ayo Abiétou Coly is similarly critical, this time of *Les Honneurs perdus*. Although she claims to take issue with criticisms of Beyala pandering to Western audiences, Coly nevertheless accuses Beyala of recreating Conradian images of Africa as a 'heart of darkness' and of presenting African characters as dehumanized, 'strange creatures'.[48] For Coly, like Cazenave and Martinek, such representations of Africa reinforce the exoticist incorporation of Beyala discussed in the previous chapter: 'if the satisfactory response to the urge for Otherness qualified Beyala for membership in the select club of metropolitan writers, her lack of open critical engagement with Western hegemonic discourses [on Africa] constitutes another qualifying factor'.[49] Yet while Coly begins by challenging Beyala's apparent complicity with the imagery of racist colonial discourse, the second part of her article reveals a rather different, more subversive agenda in Beyala's fiction. Here, Coly's interpretation comes closer to my own reading of Beyala as a player who, from her position at the 'centre', (re)views both France and Cameroon with highly critical eyes. Such a privileged position, however, does not amount to Beyala switching sides to that of the former colonial power. As I shall argue in the rest of this chapter, beneath Beyala's criticism of Africa lies a subtle yet powerful criticism of those who colonized and mythologized the continent.

Africa, Beyala emphasizes, cannot be reduced to a single version of itself. The diversity of its cultures and peoples already resists any monolithic definition of African authenticity other than from a Eurocentric point of view. Furthermore, the influences of European colonization as well as the more recent infiltration of American cultural models through the media compound the difficulty – and the undesirability – of attempting to reduce Africa to a single version of itself. As Beyala's novels reveal, the postcolonial continent is in a continuous state of flux, reinvention and hybridity:

> Les nouvelles modes, les changements, nous les vivions de manière naturelle. Que le chrétien s'amène à l'église avec des cauris, que le musulman refuse de manger du porc tout en dévorant des morceaux de jambon calamiteux, cela nous paraissait normal. (*HP*, p. 75)

[The new fashions, the changes, we lived through them naturally. That a Christian should go to church with cowries, that a Muslim should refuse to eat pork while at the same time devouring morsels of wretched ham, that seemed normal to us.]

By drawing attention to the religious syncretism of Africa the text suggests that there is no 'authentic' interpretation of faith. In the same way, Beyala's texts remind us that there is no 'authentic' version of African culture, a point made by David Murphy in his article, 'Will the Real Africa Please Stand Up?' Drawing on Appiah's study, *In My Father's House*, Murphy writes that:

> 'Popular' African cultures are not hermetically sealed, frozen in time at some distant, pre-colonial, pre-European moment. For example popular African music borrows heavily from 'Western' musical styles (which in turn have been hugely influenced by the music of the African-American community), as well as borrowing from other cultures within Africa itself.[50]

On the other hand, whereas Murphy's example of popular African music represents a positive blending of different cultural influences, Beyala also suggests that the combination of European and African social expectations can generate examples of a more negative hybrid, associated with what she calls 'Afrique domino' [domino Africa], and typified by the character of Tanga's lover: 'Hassan. Il était de cette Afrique qui se mariait sans se marier, qui divorçait sans divorcer, cette Afrique domino, le cul entre deux chaises, qui revendiquait la négritude d'un côté et pourchassait les frigos et les gazinières de l'autre' (*TTT*, p. 29) [Hassan. He belonged to that Africa that would marry without getting married, would divorce without divorcing, that domino Africa, its ass between two chairs, which would claim negritude on the one hand and pursue refrigerators and gas stoves on the other (*YNT*, p. 15)]. Aspiring to 'Western' material comforts, yet clinging to 'traditional' practices that privilege the male, Beyala's 'domino' Africans are similar to the migrant 'in-betweens' I shall discuss in Chapter 4. Both groups manage to negotiate competing sets of cultural references without any real difficulty but always on a superficial level. They choose those elements of culture that suit their own agendas but are never presented as achieving a coherent sense of self.

Just as Murphy is right to deplore the history of European colonialism in Africa, so he is also right to remind us that that same history of colonial violence means that the 'African world' and the 'European world' are no longer discrete categories: 'there is no "authentic" Africa nor is there an "authentic" West'.[51] Indeed, Cameroon's continued political, economic and cultural dependence on France after independence is consistently exposed and criticized in Beyala's novels. As she writes, 'il suffisait qu'en France un chef de section au troisième sous-sol d'un bureau oubliât de se moucher pour qu'à Douala tout le monde marchât la morve au nez' (*AA*, p. 103) [a section head on level minus three of an office in France only had to forget to use a handkerchief for everyone in Douala to walk around with snotty noses]. As well as postcolonial dependency, neocolonial political instability is also exposed through references to demonstrations, attempted political coups, torture, curfews, and the cynicism of the people when new government initiatives are announced.

So, Beyala's fiction dismantles the myth of an 'authentic' Africa, uncontaminated by 'civilization' and fixed in the kind of noble yet primitive state that liberal ethnologists would have us believe still exists. In *Tu t'appelleras Tanga*, Anna-Claude's unhappiness in Paris, where she works as a philosophy teacher, leads her to invent an imaginary African lover, Ousmane, 'tissé à la dimension de ses rêves (*TTT*, p. 12) [fashioned to fit her dreams (*YNT*, p. 3)]. Ousmane, she imagines, is tall, handsome and intelligent; he belongs to a people uncorrupted by the knowledge that causes war and represents the quintessential object of colonial desire: the beautiful and noble primitive. So consumed is she with her fantasy lover that Anna-Claude eventually requests a transfer to the fictitious former French colony of Iningué where she spends most of her time looking for her Ousmane and his people. To her intense disappointment she discovers that, as quoted in the epigraph to this chapter:

> Le peuple d'Ousmane N'EXISTE PAS. Celui qu'elle a trouvé sait infliger la mort en dépit d'armes antédiluviennes. Il sait compter les monstres et faire pousser ses cornes à la terreur. Orfèvre en cruauté, il porte sa gangrène détressée dans les mains. (*TTT*, p. 150)
>
> [Ousmane's people DO NOT EXIST. What she found was a people that knows how to inflict death despite their antediluvian weaponry. A people that know how to count monsters and make their horns grow against terror. Goldsmiths of cruelty, they carry their gangrenous affliction in their hands. (*YNT*, pp.101–02)]

The emphasis here is on Anna-Claude's investment in a fictionalized version of Africa. She hoped to find the people who had not invented gunpowder, an allusion to Aimé Césaire's *Cahier d'un retour au pays natal* which celebrates what Beyala's fiction denounces as the nostalgic essentialism that was Negritude.[52] Anna-Claude's Africa is thus another invented authenticity and bears little resemblance to the horror she discovers when she actually arrives. In a sense, her journey is like a touristic vesion of Sartre's 'Orphée noir': in place of 'authenticity' she is confronted with a kind of hell.[53]

As Iain Chambers advocates, 'to return, rather than simply to re-visit or re-view, that is, to apparently turn back and return "fully", to African, Caribbean or Indian roots in pursuit of a displaced and dispersed authenticity today hardly seems feasible'.[54] This view is confirmed in Beyala's fiction through the treatment of manifestations of 'traditional' African cultures by narrators and protagonists in Paris. In *Comment cuisiner son mari à l'africaine*, the narrator attempts to find a traditional African solution to her problem of how to attract a man: Aïssatou visits a marabout in Paris, 'le professeur Gombi'.[55] On the way there she has an encounter with a Rastafarian who attacks her for not responding to his advances, claiming that she is living proof of the alienation of blacks in France. Here the text begins to problematize the notion of authenticity. The Rastafarian claims that he is the true descendant of the Queen of Sheba and therefore authentically 'Black'. Women in Jamaica, he claims, unlike Aïssatou 'n'ont pas perdu leur âme' [have not lost their soul] (*CCMA*, p. 50). This scene is juxtaposed with Aïssatou's meeting with the marabout himself who, it quickly transpires, is a charlatan. When Aïssatou arrives, this so-called symbol of African mysticism is watching football on television and lamenting the fact that he did not place a bet. The only advice Aïssatou receives is delivered by the marabout's wife, Maïmouna, who tells her that the reason she cannot meet a man is that she is too skinny (p. 54).

The cultural roles of the Rastafarian and the marabout are not the same in France as in Jamaica or Cameroon. In France, they are exoticized by the majority ethnic population and treated with a certain level of caution by other resident blacks: for Aïssatou, the Rastafarian is simply someone who smokes cannabis and is best avoided. Uncomfortable in the marabout's waiting room, she feels the need to justify her presence there. Neither figure appears to represent an 'authentic' black culture that Aïssatou might want to recuperate. The tension lies in the way in which this text undermines the authenticity of black culture on the one hand, and simultaneously presents a collection of 'authentically' African recipes on the other. Many of the recipes contain ingredients which most Western readers would find unusual, if not unappetizing. Bush tortoise, antelope, boa constrictor, crocodile and porcupine are the ingredients least likely to find their way onto a French dining room table. Paradoxically, however, such recipes can also serve to reinforce the dismantling of 'authenticity' that emerges in the text since, as Bell and Valentine observe, 'the consumption of foods viewed as traditional by "insiders" and as at best unappetizing by "outsiders" – [such as crocodile and porcupine] – is a powerful statement of identity and difference, but also a nostalgic and "invented" one'.[56] The same can be said of the fact that these foods are presented in the form of recipes since they will also contribute to the invented tradition that is sub-Saharan African cuisine.[57]

Thus, *Comment cuisiner* functions not only as an invented story, but also as an invented representation of African cooking: a regional recipe book. Beyala's recipes are clearly separated from the narrative; each recipe lists ingredients and method, sometimes annotated by the narrator but always clearly presented and easy to follow. Of course, some critics would identify an African recipe book as something of a cultural contradiction. Political scientist Igor Cusack, for example, claims that 'most Africans have not learnt how to cook from written recipes but orally from mothers and grandmothers. African cuisine is, by reputation, largely an oral cuisine. Cookery books assume a literate population, as do recipes published in newspapers.'[58] According to Cusack's analysis, Beyala's text is doubly inaccessible to the uneducated cooks of Cameroon, since it requires both literacy and proficiency in French.[59] However, Cusack is here in danger of essentializing Africa: most Europeans do not learn to cook from recipe books either. By presenting her text as the antithesis of African invented authenticity – i.e. as a printed text and a recipe book – Beyala begins to dismantle the myths that populate the discourse of 'scientific Africa'.

A similar agenda emerges in *Les Arbres en parlent encore*, a novel that Beyala promotes as her 'return to Africa':

> Ce retour en arrière était un retour sur moi-même. Il vaut mieux savoir d'où l'on vient pour savoir où l'on va. Dans ce livre, j'ai utilisé toute la mythologie beti. Le livre est divisé en veillées et j'ai repris les modes de narration où l'on commençait avec une réflexion philosophique pour finir avec une autre. J'ai exploré tous

les domaines, c'est un livre épais: l'enfance, la vieillesse, les relations homme-femme, la sorcellerie. Il était question de retrouver la philosophie africaine parce qu'on nous a toujours dit qu'elle n'existe pas. Moi, j'ai justement voulu montrer qu'elle existe.[60]

[This backwards journey was a turning in on myself. It is better to know where you come from in order to know where you're going. In this book I've used the whole of Beti mythology. The book is divided into 'veillées' [evening gatherings] and I've recaptured the modes of narration where you began with a philosophical reflection and finished with another. I've explored all the areas, it's a dense book: childhood, old age, relations between men and women, magic. It was about reclaiming African philosophy because we were always told that it didn't exist. I precisely wanted to show that it does exist.]

Without reading the novel, it would seem that *Les Arbres en parlent encore* represents Beyala's version of 'salvage ethnography'. While it is true that African philosophy is generally ignored or discredited in the academic world, oral storytelling has long been heralded by tourist-explorer-critics as that which is quintessentially African.

In Beyala's earlier novel, *La petite fille du réverbère*, Beyala appears to affirm the links between storyteller and writer, as Mildred Mortimer has convincingly argued.[61] However, while such an affirmation could be read as reinforcing the mythology of 'Tradition', the novel's narrator, Tapoussière, also gently mocks aspects of that same 'Tradition'. For example, when Jean Ayissi accuses Tapoussière's grandmother of stealing his virility because he owes her money, the narrator makes the following observation:

> Je savais inconsciemment que je n'avais pas fini d'entendre parler de cette histoire. Plus tard, mes mots bâtonmanioqués tenteront d'assembler ces instants pour donner un nom à l'absurde naïveté. Plus tard encore, je comprendrai que combattre l'absurde équivaudrait à tuer l'Afrique, à assassiner ses magies et ses mystères qui dominent notre civilisation aussi fortement qu'un fantasme collectif. (*PFR*, p. 76)

[I knew deep down that I hadn't heard the end of this story. Later, my cassava-stick words would try to put together these moments in an attempt to give a name to absurd naivety. Even later, I would understand that fighting against the absurd would be like killing Africa, assassinating its magic and its mystery, which dominate our civilization as strongly as a collective fantasy.]

Here the association of the magic and mystery of Africa with a collective fantasy begins to invalidate any claim to essential spirituality there. At the same time, though, as Tapoussière's remark suggests, the absurd and the supernatural form part of Africa's imagined authenticity and so are very much part of its invented 'Tradition'. As the chief of the village in *Seul le diable le savait* observes, 'Tout le monde connaît la lourdeur de la tradition, ses impostures, son fanatisme, ses superstitions, ses mensonges' [Everyone knows the weight of tradition, its impostures, its fanaticism, its superstitions, its lies] (*SDS*, p. 93).

It is in *Seul le diable le savait* that the supernatural is most evident, but here too the narrative swings between what might be seen as salvage or preservation of supernatural events and implicit dismissals of these so-called traditions. Following one of the most extraordinary scenes in the novel, in which the villagers of Wuel are entertained by a talking dog and duck, a spirit appears and some of the villagers appear to be possessed, Mégri goes back to the hut of the mysterious stranger who claims to be the Devil. In the hut, Mégri is surprised to find icons of the Devil next to a portrait of General de Gaulle (*SDS*, p. 88). Here the humorous juxtaposition of the two images defuses the reader's suspension of disbelief and points to an anti-colonial agenda. The emphasis throughout the novel is on the effects of what has happened rather than the reasons why things happened, reinforced by the disruption of chronological time in the narrative: the reader is told what will happen but not why or when. What all of this seems to stress is that, in Africa, many things have happened for reasons that cannot be explained, and that colonialism is the most significant 'supernatural' happening of them all. In this respect, Yvan Audouard is right to describe the novel on the back cover as 'le reportage le plus vivant sur une Afrique d'autant plus inconnue qu'elle dissimule ses secrets sous l'aveu de ses fausses évidences' [the most vivid record of an Africa that is all the more unknown because it hides its secrets under the claims of false evidence]. But whereas he points the reader to the supernatural behind the reality, I am inclined to do the opposite. The supernatural chapter culminates in Mégri flying naked to Paris by helicopter with L'Etranger to meet with dead colonial figures and to erase history, but this is ultimately dismissed by L'Etranger as another collective fantasy (*SDS*, p. 103).

Les Arbres en parlent encore continues this careful balancing act by alternately promoting and undermining the oral tradition of storytelling in Africa. In this novel, the principal storyteller is Edène, the now aged daughter of Assanga Djuli, former chief of the Issogo clan. Assanga Djuli, we are told, was the 'héritage de tout ce que nos ancêtres connaissaient' [legacy of everything our ancestors knew] and his story 'n'est autre que celle de l'Afrique' [none other than the story of Africa] (*APE*, p. 7). The fact that Assanga's (and Africa's) stories are here being retold by his daughter, Edène, appears initially to foreground the importance of the woman storyteller in Africa whose memory, as Trinh reminds us in 'Grandma's Story', is often described as the world's earliest archive or library.[62] Indeed, the novel's title, *Les Arbres en parlent encore*, emphasizes story as a continuum and also recalls the archetypal symbol of storytelling in sub-Saharan Africa: the 'arbre à palabres' [tree for stories and discussions] beneath which griots often perform tales before an audience. However, as will emerge in the course of my reading, what initially seems to be a celebration of women storytellers gradually transforms into a playful interrogation of what is loosely termed the 'oral tradition'.[63]

In an interview published in *Amina*, Beyala explains the title of *Les Arbres en parlent encore* by alluding not to the 'arbre à palabres' but to the fact that printed books are made from trees.[64] Indeed, the relationship between written and spoken words is discussed in the opening lines of the very first 'veillée' in which, following the call-and-response, 'On disait que... Que quoi?' [People said... What did they say?] the narrator states:[65]

> Une confession écrite dans une langue étrangère est toujours un mensonge. C'est dans la langue de Baudelaire que nous mentons. On racontera de préférence ce qui est facile à exprimer, on laissera de côté tel fait par paresse de recourir au dictionnaire. On comprendra aisément que cette histoire racontée dans notre dialecte n'aurait plus la même teneur. (*APE*, p. 9)

> [A confession written in a foreign tongue is always a lie. It is in the language of Baudelaire that we tell lies. What is told is that which is easy to express, certain facts are left out because we are too lazy to resort to the dictionary. It will easily be understood that, told in our dialect, this story would no longer be the same.]

Writing, it is suggested, betrays the truth. When the colonial commandant requires the villagers' names to be written down, Assanga Djuli is outraged: 'Qu'est-ce qu'un homme à qui on enlève son identité de cette façon?' [What is a man that his identity can be removed in this way?] (p. 46). What this question begins to expose is the tension between written stories about Africa (often written by colonial explorers) and the reality they purport to describe. In the case of the written narrative that is *Les Arbres en parlent encore*, Assanga's question can be read as an interrogation of the usefulness of the novel itself. As a written tale about Africa, the story begins to tell against itself.

But it is not just the written word that is not to be trusted: as the story unfolds it becomes apparent that a spoken version in the language of the Issogos would not only have a different content (as suggested above), but would be equally unreliable. When Espoir de Vie, for the love of Michel Ange de Montparnasse, unwittingly condemns the village to the forces of evil, no storyteller is able to tell what happened next:

> Qu'est-ce qui se passa par la suite? Je ne saurais le dire précisément. Nos griots, nos chroniqueurs, nos cancaniers, nos batteurs de nouvelles eurent beau taper les bouches, secouer les faits, les retourner, battre le rappel de leur mémoire, ils ne purent fournir un témoignage fiable et concordant. (pp. 218–19)
>
> [What happened next? I could not say exactly. Our griots, our chroniclers, our scandalmongers, our news drummers tried in vain to bang their mouths, shake up the facts, turn them over, summon up their memory, but they could not provide a reliable testimony that tallied.]

On the level of characterization, oral testimonies are constantly devalued in the text. When Edène claims to have seen a ghost, the villagers accuse of her telling lies.[66] This is followed by the men of the village inventing a story about the same 'blancfantôme' [white-phantom] (Michel Ange de Montparnasse) whom they pretend to have captured (p. 12). Indeed the village is characterized as a place of rumour, hearsay and different versions of the truth: 'Certains disent que [...] D'autres jurent' [Some say that [...] Others swear'] (p. 41). The black interpreter mistranslates Assanga's words to the colonial commandant (p. 45). Even the narrative voice is unstable in the novel, switching between three different storytellers: the named first-person narrator (Edène); a supernarrator who suddenly appears to be recounting Edène's words (pp. 27; 113); and a traditional griot playing the nvet (p. 113).[67] These different narrative layers, each telling stories of stories, undermine the authority of the first-person narrative and create an effect of hearsay, reinforced by the constant gossiping among characters in the text. Just as gossips are often selective with the truth, so Beyala's text emphasizes the unreliability of stories and, to a certain extent, begins to challenge the reification of the oral tradition by critics in both Africa and the West.

Gradually, this novel begins to emerge as a self-conscious example of what Alioune Tine calls 'oralité feinte' [feigned orality]: 'L'oralité feinte n'est en quelque sorte qu'une simulation, qu'une "modélisation" possible de l'oralité proprement dite, qu'un artefact, qu'une réécriture de l'oralité' [feigned orality is in a way simply a simulation, a possible 'modelization' of orality proper, simply an artefact, a rewriting of orality].[68] For Tine, the relationship between what he calls the 'ethno-text' and written African fiction is one of feigned, affected or fake orality. Ethno-texts can be myths, legends, tales, praise songs, riddles and proverbs, but also gossip, traditional psychotherapeutic discourses and everyday conversations. Fictional narrators, Tine writes, 'imite[nt] ou simule[nt] une performance narrative proche de celle d'un griot, d'un récitant ou d'un personnage de la tradition orale' [imitate or simulate a narrative performance close to that of a griot or a recitalist or a character from the oral tradition].[69] Of course, as Tine points out, writing in French can do nothing more than simulate the discourse of, for example, a griot. What interests me about Tine's analysis, however, is that it implicitly draws attention to the performative nature of many written African narratives, thereby connecting with the inherently performative oral tradition, but also highlighting the artificial or 'inauthentic' nature of written African stories.

In *Les Arbres en parlent encore*, the narrative takes the notion of 'oralité feinte' one step further in that it is self-consciously artificial, and so implicitly challenges the authenticity of both stories and storytellers. An entertaining example of this is presented in the figure of Awono Awono, a charlatan faith healer whom some people believe to be a new messiah. In particular, the young French doctor, Tristan, is fascinated by Awono Awono, seeing him as a potential ticket to fame and fortune in the scientific world. Tristan imagines them both receiving standing ovations at international conferences (*APE*, p. 372). However, Awono Awono makes a sudden disappearance, having stolen money from one of the villagers, Fondamento de Plaisir. His departure eventually leads the villagers to see him as nothing more than a 'brigand [...] sans une raclure d'ongle de talent de guérisseur' [crook without a toenail scraping of talent as a healer] (p. 380). However, another story is later told about him when a travelling merchant arrives with the tale of a tramp he had buried at the edge of a forest. According to the merchant, the tramp claimed he had been bewitched by Fondamento and had run away to save his soul. All his money, he says, he had distributed among the poor. The villagers deny all knowledge of the tramp, reluctant to admit that they might have been deceived, again rewriting a story that had already had many versions. Of all the tales surrounding Awono Awono, it is Tristan's that has the most serious repercussions. Having created a narrative of the so-called healer as an exciting scientific discovery, Tristan is carried away on a stretcher and shipped back to Europe; the other whites believe him to be mad.

On one level, Tristan's tale illustrates the European obsession with fixing what they believe to be the truth. Tristan's story of Awono Awono challenges Western notions of what is true and so the other whites refuse to listen. On the other hand, it draws attention to the ways in which the discourses of science and ethnology, among others, have simultaneously reified and corrupted that which was seen to be 'authentically African'. Beyala's narrator writes: 'Ceux qui ont peu de mépris pour les gens simples disent qu'ils ont en eux l'authenticité. Ils prétendent que nous avons la mémoire des choses passées. C'est vrai que nous en connaissons parfaitement une partie' [Those who have little contempt for simple folk say that they have authenticity in them. They claim that we have the memory of things past. It is true that we know a part of it perfectly] (p. 145). What the well-meaning ethnological storytellers fail to recognize is that, as Trinh writes, 'each story is at once a fragment and a whole; a whole within a whole. And the same story has always been changing, for things which do not shift and grow cannot continue to circulate.'[70] Once a story becomes fixed in a third party's interpretation of it, then the story is lost, as it only exists in the process of transformation that is its telling.

It is no coincidence that Beyala chooses to name her narrator after the original paradise lost. As James Clifford notes in his discussion of the pastoral, Eden is an ultimate point of reference in the quest for authenticity.[71] It connotes a pre-'civilized' time which in many ways resembles the images of 'Afrique nature' promoted by both Negritudinists and ethnologists alike. The fact that Beyala's Eden constantly draws attention to the unreliability of her own narrative voice further exposes the fallacy of ethnographic salvage: Edène's stories can neither be rescued nor lost since they do not exist in any kind of uncorrupted 'virgin' state. Implicitly, Beyala's text also undermines the authority of the Bible as the master narrative of the Christian church.[72] This challenge is by no means unique to *Les Arbres en parlent encore*. Throughout her fiction, Beyala plays with Biblical stories and references, most notably by turning the myth of original sin on its head and blaming men for dragging women into a life of pain and suffering. The figure of Eve, 'la femme fautive' [the guilty woman], ironically flags the way in which texts such as the Bible and the Koran have been exploited as justification for patriarchy. No story, Beyala suggests, ever exists in a version that is 'authentic' or 'pure'.

This emphasis on the constantly changing nature of story adds another layer to Beyala's challenge to the notion of African authenticity. For many people, the tradition of oral storytelling encapsulates what distinguishes the African continent from the rest of the world. While Beyala's writing is marked by what can loosely be defined as 'oral elements', it also clearly resists reification of the 'oral tradition', implicitly warning that the very concept of the 'oral tradition' risks becoming another 'invented authenticity' in the context of African texts written in European languages. An oral tale is no less and no more 'authentically' African than a written text might be, but the very concept of something called an 'oral tradition' is here called into question. After all, as Ivorian poet Bernard Dadié reminds us, the oral tradition was introduced to Western cultures by European colonists and ethnologists such as Frobenius and Delafosse.[73] Trinh makes a similar point when she writes that, 'the question "What is oral tradition?" is a question-answer that needs no answer at all. Let the one who is civilized, the one who invents "oral tradition", let him define it for himself.'[74] In other words, the oral tradition, like authenticity, is both an overdetermined and an empty signifier, invented by European tourist-explorers to make the unfamiliar familiar.

One of the paradoxes of authenticity is, as Huggan explains, the fact that it depends on 'an illusion of transparency – that it is externally recognisable as authentic, that it is what it appears to be – its authenticity also remains to be discovered, a mysterious essence hidden beneath the veil of surface appearances'.[75] In other words, authenticity is both locatable and elusive, both 'there' and 'not there'. Ultimately, the very concept of authenticity reflects a desire to contain the other in his or her relation to the self as both familiar and different. The search for an authentic other, a 'native' betrays a refusal to accept the fact that, as Clifford remarks, postcolonial identity is never 'authentic':

> Intervening in an interconnected world, one is always, to varying degrees, 'inauthentic': caught between cultures, implicated in others. Because discourse in global power systems is elaborated vis-à-vis, a sense of difference or distinctness can never be located solely in the continuity of a culture or tradition. Identity is conjunctural, not essential.[76]

There is, however, a danger in dismissing authenticity out of hand since to do so would be to ignore the important part played by counter discourses and movements in acts of resistance against colonialism. In 'The Myth of Authenticity', Gareth Griffiths is careful not be read as denying the importance of what he terms recuperative 'alter/natives' to colonialist discourse, and I share his concern here.[77] On the other hand, Griffiths' conclusion, based on reading Australian Aboriginal texts, is also demonstrated in Beyala's fiction:

> such texts reveal through the process of mimicry how the contemporary dominant discourse replicates its own divisions through the construction of myths of purity and authenticity which enable the continuity of the idea of a stable dominant discourse even at the very moment it appears to 'recognize' the other as 'authentic'.[78]

By alternately reclaiming and rejecting myths and stereotypes about Africa, Beyala's novels undermine the 'stable dominant discourse' that Griffiths describes. Such mimicry is central to Beyala's fictional and personal performances of identity since it allows her to both appropriate and dismantle the dominant discourse to suit her own agenda. Just as Beyala's public performances reveal her ambiguous relationship with the myth of the erotic-exotic African woman, so Beyala's fictional images of Africa demonstrate her ability to position herself inside and outside the authenticities invented by (post)-colonial France.

CHAPTER THREE

Migrating Subjectivities

> J'ai immigré. J'ai franchi des frontières. J'ai laissé des empreintes digitales et à chaque fois, un lambeau de chair, un peu de mon âme.[1]
> [I've immigrated. I've crossed frontiers. I've left fingerprints behind and, on every occasion, a shred of flesh, a bit of my soul.][2]

Six of Beyala's novels deal explicitly with the cultural and psychological effects of migration from sub-Saharan Africa to France. Although, as we saw in the previous chapter, Beyala's early novels limit most of the geographical space of the narrative to the African continent, Paris is, in fact, a centripetal force throughout her oeuvre. For a number of the Africa-based protagonists, France is presented as a promised land. For example, in an attempt to escape the horror of their own existence, girlchild-woman Tanga organizes 'trips' to Paris for her friends:

> Autrefois, Paris était mon refuge. J'y allais à pied chaque fois que les aberrations du monde m'attrapaient. J'appelais mes copains. Je leur clamais Paris, la belle vie qu'on aura. Le départ pour Paris est la plus belle chose qui ne soit arrivée dans ma putain de vie. [...] Quelquefois, je tapais dans mes mains, je devenais grande rien que pour croquer la pomme de France et le jambon. (*TTT*, p. 128)

> [Before, Paris was my refuge. I'd go there on foot every time the world's absurdities grabbed hold of me. I'd call my friends. I'd hold forth about Paris – the lovely life we'd have there. Leaving for Paris is the most exquisite thing that could have happened in my goddam life. [...] Sometimes, I'd clap my hands, I'd grow up for no reason other than to bite the apple of France and some ham. (*YNT*, p. 85)

In fact, Tanga's 'trips' to Paris take the form of stealing French foodstuffs from a supermarket and then burying them in a cardboard box. She explains: 'Il y a un moyen d'aller à Paris sans prendre l'avion: c'est d'enfermer ses symboles dans une tombe' (*TTT*, p. 29) [There's a way of going to Paris without taking a plane: you lock up its symbols in a tomb (*YNT*, p. 86)]. Since economic deprivation makes geographical migration impossible, Tanga makes imaginary journeys in her head, sealing the souvenirs in the ground as a record of her trip. Burying the symbols of Paris also points to the reification of the French capital as a kind of promised land. The reality, however, for those able to make the physical journey there, is nothing like 'la belle vie' that Tanga imagines.

In *Seul le diable le savait*, Mégri's first visit to Paris is on her honeymoon: a supernatural naked journey by helicopter with her mysterious new husband, L'Etranger, and a dog and a duck. As 'Princesse Mégri' she is taken to the Elysée palace to meet the French President where she suddenly finds herself speaking with someone else's voice: 'Je ne reconnaissais plus ma voix, elle ne m'appartenait plus. C'était comme si quelqu'un d'autre s'était introduit en moi et prononçait ces paroles' [I no longer recognized my voice. It no longer belonged to me. It was as if someone else had been introduced into me and was speaking those words] (*SDS*, p. 97). What this scene suggests is that migration offers the possibility for African women to perform their identities differently, to speak with another voice. On this night the history of colonization is magically wiped out, but, as the previous chapter revealed, Mégri wakes up the following morning to find that the marriage and the trip were nothing more than 'un rêve collectif' [a collective dream] (p. 103). Viewed from Africa, Paris becomes part of a dreamscape in Beyala's early fiction, a utopian space – an elsewhere – where women can escape the reality of their everyday lives and reinvent themselves, at least in their imagination.

When Beyala's protagonists physically migrate to France, they are confronted with a very different picture. For Beyala's first migrant, Mégri, the reality of Paris bears little resemblance to the images of monuments, cafes, intellectuals and elegance she had imagined from the picture postcards she had seen (*SDS*, p. 63). Instead, she finds a 'ville sans larmes, rien que des blessures secrètes' [a city without tears, only secret wounds] (p. 9), suggesting a dehumanized place where emotions are repressed. However, as most of *Seul le diable le savait* is narrated with hindsight, we learn little more about Mégri's Parisian experience. It is in the following novel, *Le petit prince de Belleville,* that Beyala begins to focus explicitly on the experience of African migrants in France through the first-person child narrator, Mamadou Traoré, nicknamed Loukoum, who lives in Paris. The action of the two 'Loukoum novels' (*Le petit prince de Belleville* and *Maman a un amant*) centres on African immigrant life in the Parisian twentieth 'arrondissement' of Belleville, as does that of Beyala's other migrant novels: *Assèze l'Africaine, Les Honneurs perdus, Amours sauvages* and *Comment cuisiner son mari à l'africaine*.[3] In each of these texts, the female protagonist retraces Beyala's own itinerary from Cameroon to Paris, and in each the experience of migration leads male and, in particular, female characters to renegotiate their identities across what emerges as the constantly shifting borderspace between Africa and Paris. In the previous chapter, I discussed the way in which relationships with Africa are renegotiated and ultimately reconfigured as a result of the migrant experience. The present chapter will begin by considering the representation of Paris as viewed through the eyes of Beyala's migrant characters, and the way that this relates to changing notions of 'home'. Just as the image of the French city is transformed through the process of migration, so migrant subjectivities — and in particular gender identities — are reconfigured and renegotiated. The remainder of this chapter will focus on the personal trajectories of Beyala's migrants as they attempt to reconcile competing sets of cultural expectations in France.

Like their author, Beyala's fictional characters occupy a space of ambivalence in their adopted country of France. Although an 'immigrant' is, by definition, relocated from one home to another, the label, Stuart Hall explains, 'places one so equivocally as *really* belonging *somewhere* else', as belonging to some other home to which the immigrant will eventually return.[4] Whether it is through voluntary expatriation, enforced exile or asylum, migration generates anxieties about national identity, forcing the migrant to re-evaluate his or her relationship with 'home' and often generates feelings of homelessness. 'Home' is no longer an easy place to locate and so becomes, as Ireland and Proulx suggest, a common preoccupation in migrants' literary production.[5] Is home the place where you are born or the place in which you find yourself? As we saw in Chapter 2, geographical home in Africa begins to be (re)viewed differently from a migrant perspective. On the other hand, the unfamiliarity of the host nation also prevents it from being identified as 'home'. This ambivalence is reflected in the ways in which characters' memories of Africa oscillate between positive nostalgia and critical condemnation while, inversely, their relationships with Paris swing between admiration and contempt. Migration challenges the dichotomy of 'home' and 'abroad', or 'here' and 'there', since 'here' becomes collapsed into 'there', and the migrant's place of residency is neither 'home' nor 'abroad'.

Whenever she has free time, Eve-Marie, the protagonist of *Amours sauvages*, wanders up and down the Faubourg Saint-Honoré, gazing into the windows of the exclusive designer shops. An illegal immigrant, Eve-Marie supports herself through prostitution when she first arrives in Paris. Whereas she finds it difficult to imagine buying anything in these shops, other women move in and out of them with ease: 'les autres femmes ne semblaient pas partager [s]on avis. Des vendeuses habillées comme des hôtesses de l'air leur ouvraient les portes. Elles y pénétraient comme chez elles' [the other women did not seem to share [her] view. Shop assistants dressed like air hostesses opened the doors for them. They went inside as if they were entering their own homes] (*AS*, p. 13). Here, freedom of movement is suggested not only by the reference to air travel in the description of the shop assistants' clothing, but also by the way in which women enter the shops as if they were their own homes. On the other hand, the reference to the shoppers as 'les autres femmes' as well as Eve-Marie's position outside the closed shop doors emphasize the way in which migrants lack the economic freedom of their majority-ethnic neighbours, never feeling totally 'at home' in Paris.[6] Watching the women shopping among the luxurious excesses of the Faubourg Saint-Honoré often causes Eve-Marie to have nostalgic thoughts of her village back in Cameroon. However, she is always quick to leave those memories – and that country – behind, remembering the economic motives for her decision to migrate: 'je quittais mon pays, parce que Dieu s'était montré plus généreux en Europe' [I left my country because God proved himself to be more generous in Europe] (p. 14). Here the imperfect tense points to the fact that, like Tanga, Eve-Marie spent a long time migrating in her head before the physical migration to France actually took place.

Most of Beyala's main protagonists leave Africa for economic reasons. The exceptions are Mégri (*SDS*), whose migration is motivated by psychological rather than economic pressures, and Saïda (*HP*), whose mother, on her husband's death, gives her money to find a better life in France. In *Assèze l'Africaine*, the character of Sorraya (Awono's daughter and Assèze's adoptive sister) travels to France with independent means and eventually becomes a successful dancer married to a rich French record producer. Assèze leaves Douala when her adoptive father, Awono, leaves her nothing in his will, hoping to find in France a land of 'soie, dentelles, bijoux, galeries' [silk, lace, jewels and shopping malls] (*AA*, p. 231) and to return 'rutilante de diamants' [sparking with diamonds] (p. 232). Although, in the 'Loukoum' novels, M'am travels to France to be with her husband, Abdou, she nevertheless also presents her migration as a search for increased wealth. She tells her anonymous interlocutor: 'On m'avait dit que là-bas, dans ton pays l'argent tombait des arbres, qu'il avait de l'argent à gagner avec son corps, avec son esprit, avec son âme' [They had told me that over there, in your country, money fell from the trees, that there was money to be earned with your body, with your spirit, with your soul] (*MAA*, p. 49). As well as economic freedom, there is a shared belief that, as in Mégri's dream, women will be able to reinvent themselves in France and 'speak with another voice', no longer constrained by normative gender roles: 'Maintenant', Saïda's mother tells her just before she leaves, 'tu peux dire ce que tu veux, ce que tu penses, y aura personne pour te l'interdire. [...] Je t'offre la liberté' [Now you can say what you want and what you think. There'll be no one to contradict you. [...] I'm giving you freedom] (*HP*, p. 177). Such remarks illustrate and confirm Jane Freedman's conclusion that 'for many women immigration [to France] is a positive life choice as they hope to find a freer society or a more urban lifestyle than that which they experienced in their country of origin'.[7]

The reader also learns that, as independent, single women, the majority of the migrant women in Beyala's fiction are, in fact, illegal immigrants. This reflects the fact that since 1974, immigration into France has generally been granted only for reasons of family reunification or political asylum. In the 'Loukoum' novels, M'am is the only legitimate wife of Abdou as far as the French authorities are concerned, polygamy being illegal in France. Ironically, according to French immigration law, it is the co-wife, Soumana, and not M'am who would be permitted to stay in France with their husband because it is she who is the mother of his children.[8] Although Abdou was granted residency in 1981, Soumana is not recognized as mother because she and Abdou are not legally married; Soumana simply borrowed M'am's identity papers when the children were born. Where family reunification does occur in Beyala's novels, it too is illegal: in *Amours sauvages*, Eve-Marie's aged mother travels overland from Cameroon through Morocco and then Spain, hidden first in a tanker and then under a tarpaulin in the back of a lorry (*AS*, p. 25). As illegal immigrants, Beyala's women live a precarious existence since, without legal residence status, they have no access to social security or healthcare and risk expulsion at any time. As Saïda observes in *Les Honneurs perdus*, 'vivre sans papiers, sans véritable domicile, sans mari, sans enfants équivalait à ne pas avoir d'existence' [living without legal documentation, without a husband, without children was the equivalent of having no existence] (*HP*, p. 283). Many of Beyala's women work as prostitutes in Paris. When they do look for jobs outside the sex industry, the migrants tend to end up in traditional (usually illegal) immigrant occupations such as cleaning or factory work where they are paid cash in hand, and have no security of employment or union representation.

Paris is certainly not, then, a city whose streets are paved with gold as far as immigrant women are concerned. Eve-Marie's window-shopping ends with her return to her life as a prostitute in Belleville 'où les rues étaient sales, étroites et laides' [where the streets were dirty, narrow and ugly] (*AS*, p. 15) in sharp contrast to the elegant stone buildings and flower-covered balconies of Faubourg Saint-Honoré. On the other hand, whereas among the exclusive shops Eve-Marie remained anonymous, the moment she returns to Belleville she is pleased to find people she knows and who recognize her. As long as the migrant's place of living is defined solely by economic circumstance it has the status of a temporary residence. Only when she experiences acknowledgment and recognition from other inhabitants of that space does the migrant identify her place of living as a home. It is, of course, on the back of recognition that, some argue, identification is constructed.[9] Identification, Beyala's texts reveal, is based solely on racial criteria and not on shared cultural or even economic capital. Despite living in France as the wife of a wealthy, white, French record producer, Sorraya tells Assèze that she will never be acknowledged as an equal in France:

> J'ai toujours appartenu à une minorité, reprit-elle [Sorraya]. Vous ne m'acceptiez pas, parce que j'estimais que j'avais certains droits, que tout n'était pas bon dans nos traditions. En France, j'appartiens encore à une minorité. Jamais je ne serai considérée comme une Blanche. Je n'appartiens à rien. Une hybride. Un non-sens! (*AA*, p. 339).

> [I've always belonged to a minority, she [Sorraya] continued. You wouldn't accept me because I believed I had certain rights, that not

everything was good about our traditions. In France I still belong to a minority. I'll never be treated like a white woman. I belong to nothing. A hybrid. A nonsense!]

In Cameroon Sorraya was marginalized because of her feminist ideals; in France she is viewed as an outsider because her skin is black. She is thus unable to identify with anyone, which for her is equivalent to having no identity. What she has not realized is that, as Hall explains, identification is a construction and is always 'in process'.[10] It is not achieved through the fantasy of incorporation that Sorraya describes. As this book will show, only those migrants who recognize the ambivalent and contingent nature of identification will survive the experience of migration.

Sorraya's lament is also interesting in so far as it reveals that even when migrants achieve equality of wealth and status, they still strive to be integrated on other people's terms. The fantasy of incorporation is perhaps particularly endemic among migrants in France given the emphasis on assimilation in French immigration policy. Another important example of this desire for recognition occurs in the second 'Loukoum' novel, *Maman a un amant*. This text is unique among Beyala's novels in that it describes the Traoré family taking a holiday. The financial success of the jewellery business M'am sets up at the end of *Le petit prince de Belleville* means that she can now afford to pay for the whole family to travel to the Southern French village of Pompidou. On one level, this holiday presents a radical new version of a migrant journey: when they leave the boulevard périphérique, Loukoum remarks, 'Nous avons immigré dans la France profonde' [we immigrated into deepest France] (*MAA*, p. 26). More significantly, as Aedín Ní Loingsigh observes, the holiday demonstrates the ways in which immigrant-tourists obey the rules of travel dictated by the host culture. Having pretended to their friends that they were holidaying in Cannes, the family see Pompidou as something of a rural backwater. This, according to Ní Loingsigh, confirms 'that they have bought into tourism's discourse of rusticity, and relate to their surroundings in the manner of sophisticated Parisians'.[11] Ironically, though, as Ní Loingsigh points out, the family 'continue to be perceived according to skin colour and racial stereotypes'.[12] Indeed, I would add to this by stating that the villagers in Pompidou receive the family not just in terms of racial stereotypes but also as a kind of travelling spectacle or freak show:

> Les gens sortaient de leur maison, exprès. Ils nous regardaient, ils fouillaient nos tronches de garnison exotique. Pas comme à Paris où blanc, jaune ou noir, personne ne fait attention à ta gueule et tu peux toujours te la casser au coin d'une rue, tout le monde s'en fout. J'étais très fier. C'est vrai, quoi! C'est pas tous les jours que ceux-là voyaient des Nègres en colonie. (*MAA*, p. 65)
>
> [People came out of their houses, deliberately. They looked at us, they scrutinized our exotic soldier faces. Not like in Paris where white, yellow or black, no one pays any attention to your mug and you can always hide it on a street corner, no one gives a damn. I was proud. It's true, you know! It's not every day that that lot saw a Negro colony.]

Here, Loukoum's misplaced pride at being stared at in the street reinforces what in Beyala's novels can be read as an example of the migrant's desire for recognition on majority ethnic terms: he prefers being identified as an 'outsider' to what he sees as the impersonal anonymity of Paris. Alternatively, Loukoum's affirmation of his otherness can be seen as a retreat into ethnic essentialism in reaction to a feeling of non-belonging. Paradoxically, either interpretation reinforces the suggestion that, even as tourists, the Traorés remain trapped in the majority ethnic gaze.

The insider/outsider dichotomy constantly generates the question, 'Where are you from?' and reflects the way in which 'insiders' refuse to accept the possibility of alterative subjectivities outside the 'us' and 'them' divide. Following Stuart Hall, Claire Dwyer writes:

> The politics of positioning [...] is so often a requirement demanded from those who are ascribed as 'outsiders' within politicized and racialized discourses of national belonging. This positioning is required not because the identities of the [people] themselves are 'in crisis' but instead because of the refusal of others, those at the 'centre', to engage in the re-making or the re-thinking of identity.[13]

What Dwyer observes among young Muslim women in Britain extends to Beyala's fictional immigrant communities in France, which position themselves in the various 'insider' spaces they have established for themselves. When Assèze arrives at her destination in Paris (a grim block of flats somewhere near the Gare du Nord), her African contact and future landlady, Madame Lola, asks her where she is from. Assèze tells her she is from Douala. Madame Lola, apparently ignorant of Cameroonian geography, has no idea where Douala is and so replies, 'Je veux pas d'Antillais chez moi!' [I don't want

Antilleans in my house!] (*AA*, p. 236). This attempted rejection of Assèze because she is believed to be Antillean (and therefore French) amounts to an interesting reversal of the insider/outsider dichotomy. Coming from a French overseas department would, it seems, exclude Assèze from the insider space of the immigrant community in France. Once it is established that Assèze is a 'true' migrant, she is welcomed as an insider in what is nationally an outsiders' space.

Recognition is also important in terms of the individual recognizing home as a familiar, locatable space and feeling that she belongs there. Sometimes, as Dwyer has shown in her discussion of young British Muslim women, the experience of not feeling you belong to one particular 'home' may result in 'a desire to fix and root identities through other essences or "homes"'.[14] The extreme example of this is found in the recent rise in religious fundamentalism among immigrant communities in Britain and in France. Some of Beyala's migrants are portrayed as having lost their 'repères' [points of reference] and so find it difficult – and sometimes impossible – to find a sense of place. In *Le petit prince de Belleville* Abdou repeatedly complains that he feels lost and that his apartment has become defamiliarized and strange: 'Plus rien n'est nommé. Je ne reconnais plus la géographie du pays dessiné dans MA MAISON' (*PPB*, p. 133) [Nothing is called by its name any more. I no longer recognize the geography of the land drawn in MY OWN HOUSE (*LPPB*, p. 91)]. The capitals invoke Abdou's desperation to find a space he can call his own; although this is his own house in so far as he lives there, he does not feel at home there any more. Conversely, when Loukoum sees his father weeping over his mother's adultery, he suggests that all that is needed is a return to Africa: 'Bientôt, on retournera au Mali et tout redeviendra comme avant' [Soon we'll go back to Mali and everything will be like it was before] (*MAA*, p. 206).

The metaphor of migrants losing their way appears repeatedly in the 'Loukoum' novels. Loukoum himself wants to dress like Sylvester Stallone and not like his father 'de crainte de se sentir perdu' (*PPB*, p. 198) [for fear that he'll feel lost (*LPPB*, p. 138)], stressing the way in which migrants and their children create a sense of home out of familiar reference points. The fact that Abdou can no longer find his way whereas Loukoum creates new points of reference in Western culture/Hollywood presents the two generations adopting similar strategies for building homes but drawing on very different sets of cultural references. Whereas Loukoum's model of home is one in which he is recognized by his peers, conservative Abdou hoped to base his new home on values and 'points de repère' from his former home in Africa. What both characters demonstrate is the migrant's search for an identifiable community. In Abdou's case, this search potentially challenges and undermines the French constitution's emphasis on a nation that is 'unie et indivisible' [united and indivisible] since it is based on the promotion of cultural difference.[15] Loukoum, on the other hand, looks for points of identification with the host culture but without ever completely abandoning his roots. Although he wants to dress like Stallone, he also describes his pride in going to the mosque wearing a djellaba and a chechia just like his father (*PPB*, p. 80; *LPPB*, p. 53).

Unlike his son, Abdou feels that he has no access to the imagined community of France. In his musings to his imaginary majority ethnic friend he explains:

> [Loukoum] a repoussé les frontières. Il a installé son monde dans ton monde à toi, l'ami, là où je ne peux pas pénétrer, car sa nation, la tienne, l'ami, s'est formée et se protège jalousement. Sens interdit, je ne passe plus. (*PPB*, p. 223)

> [[Loukoum] has pushed his frontiers away. He has set up his world inside that world of yours, friend, which I cannot penetrate, for his nation, which is yours, friend, has been formed and protects itself jealously. A one-way street, I can no longer pass through. (*LPPB*, p. 156)

Abdou, then, has no place to go: the private space is foreign to him and the public space is closed. As a refuse collector he lacks economic status; as an illiterate, Muslim, first-generation immigrant he lacks the social capital to participate in French cultural life. The privileges accorded to cultural insiders are therefore unavailable to him. Having resigned himself to never learning the cultural language of the host nation, Abdou fears his identity is disappearing under the failure of his assimilation – shedding over space and time, as the prefatory quotation to this chapter suggests.

Abdou's dilemma is one of the possible outcomes of transculturation, as Kevin Robins notes: 'Continuity and historicity of identity are challenged by the immediacy and intensity of global cultural confrontations. The comforts of "Tradition" are fundamentally challenged by the imperative to forge a new self-interpretation based upon the responsibilities of cultural Translation'.[16] Drawing on the work of

Homi Bhabha, Robins demonstrates the impossibility of maintaining a 'coherent and integrated sense of identity' in a globalized world.[17] This impossibility becomes crystallized in the cultural confrontation that a migrant like Abdou experiences: unable to negotiate the very real difficulties of cultural translation, Abdou fails to recognize that, as Stuart Hall reminds us, 'there can be no simple "return" or "recovery" of the ancestral past which is not experienced through the categories of the present'.[18] Abdou is trapped in an 'invented authenticity' that he has created for himself. It is a safe space for a migrant, but one that is ultimately unsustainable.

Those who, unlike Abdou, recognize the need to re-evaluate the past through the present are what Salman Rushdie calls 'translated' peoples. Loukoum is a good example of what Rushdie is describing. 'Translated' individuals embrace the plurality of their cultural heritage and thus locate themselves in at least two – and sometimes several – 'homes' rather than in a single geographical, cultural or physical space.[19] Whereas Abdou fails to reconstruct his identity through translation rather than through the imaginary space of 'Tradition', Beyala's migrant women and children generally operate more effectively as cultural translators. I shall return to the discussion of translation later in this chapter and shall suggest that, for Beyala, men's role is that of mediators through which women translate themselves.

According to Pius Adesanmi, Beyala's Belleville also functions as a site of 'Tradition' rather than translation. Drawing on Arjun Appadurai's concept of the 'ethnoscape', Adesanmi identifies Belleville as 'a complex ethnospatial entity with its own norms and mores'.[20] Despite his assertion that Belleville is an example of the way in which 'migrant groups inevitably deterritorialize their original cultures and attempt to reterritorialize them in their new locations', Adesanmi's analysis is restricted to a brief discussion of gender and space in the Traoré household.[21] The suggestion that Belleville is an 'ethnospace' is, however, an interesting one since it seems to imply that this is a space that requires little translation or negotiation; a veritable 'home from home'. Indeed, in a similar way, Beyala herself has described the setting of her Belleville-based novels as a kind of 'Afro-Paris', explaining, 'Je ne parle pas de Paris en tant que tel. Je parle de l'Afrique transposée à Paris' [I'm not talking about Paris as such. I'm talking about Africa transposed to Paris].[22] Like Adesanmi, Beyala views Belleville as a kind of ethnic ghetto which is both separate from and included in the surrounding space of Paris. Belleville thus begins to collapse the dichotomy of 'here' and 'there' since it is simultaneously both and neither, a hybrid space, an 'in-between' (see Chapter 4). In *Amours sauvages*, Belleville is enigmatically described as 'un quartier parenthèse à l'intérieur de Paris' [a parenthesis-area of Paris] (*AS*, p. 73). The polyvalent metaphor of the parenthesis suggests both marginality and inclusion, containment and rupture, and points to the ambivalent relationship between Belleville and Paris.[23]

When, in *Assèze l'Africaine*, Assèze goes with her lover, Océan, to a Chinese restaurant in Belleville, she is struck by the multicultural spectacle she witnesses in the surrounding streets:

> Le quartier était altéré. Il ressemblait plus à rien, à tout. [...] Tout ici était théâtral. Les êtres dans les rues, Chinois, Nègres, Juifs, faisaient leur entrée comme des *prime donne*, convaincus peut-être que le reste du monde était peuplé d'hommes destinés à saluer leurs performances traditionnelles. C'étaient des djellabas-Salamalékoum, des kippas-shalom, des dragons avec leur langue couleur de sang et d'or qui retenaient toute l'attention. Même les Français étaient bizarres, car leurs différences culturelles et vestimentaires par rapport aux autres se faisaient trop insistantes et fortes. (*AA*, p. 292)

> [The area was altered. It no longer resembled anything or everything. [...] Everything here was theatrical. The people in the streets, Chinese, Blacks, Jews, made their entrances like prima donnas, convinced perhaps that the rest of the world was populated with people destined to acclaim their traditional performances. It was djellaba-Salamalekoums, kippa-shaloms, dragons with their tongues the colour of blood and gold, who held all the attention. Even the French were bizarre, for their differences in culture and dress, compared to the others, became too insistent and too strong.]

Here we have almost a reversal of Loukoum's experience in Pompidou; this time the migrant, Assèze, becomes the observer of a performance of identities, all of which appear exotic and 'other', including those of the majority ethnic French. The suggestion here is that the immigrant cultures of Paris have made strange the majority ethnic culture of France. However, the description of the French as too strongly marked by their difference also hints at a fear that French culture will somehow be eroded by an increasing influx of people from 'outside'. Just as Abdou attempts to take refuge in an essentialized version of his own cultural heritage, so, in Assèze's description, the majority ethnic population are attempting to promote a version of themselves that is 'too insistent, too strong'.

This 'making strange' is echoed in Beyala's controversial writing style which demonstrates the impact of another language and cultural framework on French. Drawing on Spivak's concept of a 'frontier style', Elleke Boehmer describes the distinctive feature of postcolonial women's writing as its 'mosaic or composite quality'.[24] The figure of the mosaic can usefully be applied to Calixthe Beyala's migrant novels, which are characterized by a nexus of different cultural contexts, writing styles and speaking positions. The most obvious examples are found in the 'Loukoum' novels where the lyrical musings of first Abdou then M'am are juxtaposed with the streetwise Parisian vernacular of their son, Loukoum. But the whole of Beyala's oeuvre is marked by shifting narrative voices, as Eloise Brière remarks: 'Beyala accueille et intègre dans ses textes des voix et des perspectives multiples et divergentes qui interdisent de les simplifier' [Beyala introduces and integrates into her texts multiple and divergent voices and perspectives that prevent them from being simplified].[25] This cross-hatched style of writing reflects the way in which migrant subjectivities emerge from a patchwork of different cultural codes. Describing her decision to write the story of her life, narrator-protagonist Saïda Bénérafa explains: 'J'ai assemblé ma vie de travers comme tous les immigrés. Mais peu importe, notre monde à nous est désintégré et on recolle les morceaux comme on peut' [I have assembled my life sideways like all immigrants. But it doesn't matter, our world is disintegrated and we stick the pieces back together in any way we can] (*HP*, p. 403). What Saïda is describing identifies her as what Lionnet calls the 'paradigmatic postcolonial subject' whose world and identity are constructed as 'diffracted, yet recomposed'.[26]

The language of all Beyala's novels is marked by a range of registers and tones, switching as it does between the oneiric and the obscene. Beyala also injects her novels with traditional songs and poems from the oral tradition, Africanized expressions, 'petit-nègre' [pidgin] and words in her mother tongue, Eton.[27] Such techniques, Boehmer suggests, 'work against the unifying viewpoint more typical of European tradition' and are, she argues, a common feature of postcolonial women's writing.[28] The effect of Beyala's mosaic writing style is a hybridized French that polarizes critics (see Chapter 1) and allows Beyala to stage the linguistic interference produced by migration. French is not the mother tongue of any of Beyala's protagonists but they are forced to operate in French if they are to gain access to French culture. Conversely, the majority ethnic host culture and its language are, in turn, transformed. The French language has, of course, always been seen as the route by which colonial assimilation would be achieved. Beyala's language subverts the French of the Académie Française and reworks it to it own ends, thereby implicitly undermining the ideology of France's 'mission civilisatrice' and its contemporary legacy, integration. The violence of the (post)-colonial encounter is both reflected and reversed in the unconventional French of Beyala's novels. Just as the migrant's identity is diffracted and recomposed, to borrow Lionnet's words, so Beyala diffracts and recomposes the French language to mirror the way in which migrants and indigenes have an effect of cultural interference on one other. By writing in French, the language of the former colonizer, and at the same time twisting that same French to reflect the multi-faceted reality of the formerly colonized, Beyala shows that, despite resistance from both sides, cultural interference is a two-way process and thus the responsibility for cultural and linguistic translation is shared.

The impact of migratory translation on individual migrants is most strongly felt, in Beyala's fiction, in the ways in which gender identities become interrogated and remodelled in the cultural contact zone. In *Assèze l'Africaine*, the first stage in the eponymous heroine's migration takes place inside Cameroon when she moves from rural Eton country to Douala to live with Awono and his daughter, Sorraya. On arrival in the city, Assèze is struck by what she describes as 'cultural transsexuals' sitting outside the Ramsec Hotel:

> A droite, en face de Monoprix et de Prisunic, il y a le *Ramsec Hôtel* où des Nègres blanchisés imitent leurs confrères blancs. Ils sont ce qu'ils sont, ni Blancs, ni Nègres, des espèces de transsexuels culturels, vaguement hommes d'affaires, voyous sur les bords, et tout au fond pouilleux. (*AA*, p. 66)
>
> [On the right, opposite Monoprix and Prisunic, is the Ramsec Hotel, where whitified Blacks imitate their white colleagues. They are what they are, neither Whites nor Blacks, sort of cultural transexuals, vaguely businessmen, slightly loutish and basically undesirable.]

Here, the text begins to draw a parallel between acculturation and gender identity, suggesting that, through imitating the behaviour of whites, these African men have become both racially and gender non-specific. As 'ni Blancs, ni Nègres', these 'cultural transsexuals' appear to confuse normative codes of race and gender by associating themselves with another culture. By extension, Beyala's fiction suggests that the migratory process also has a destabilizing effect on normative gender roles. This is not to suggest that migration from Africa to Europe necessitates lactification (cultural 'whitening'), but rather to begin to tease out a thread in Beyala's writing that associates acculturation with gender instability. By the end of her stay in Paris, Assèze feels that she has lost sight of her own gender identity: 'ce qui me perturbait par-dessus tout, c'était mon propre état de femme. Je n'étais plus sûre, en réalité, d'en être une!' [the thing that bothered me more than anything else was my own womanliness. I was no longer sure, in fact, that I was a woman!] (*AA*, p. 343). Having found herself confronted with other people's notions of what and how a woman should be, Assèze's femininity begins to fall into crisis. Although she does not go so far as to see herself as the kind of 'cultural transsexual' she observed in Douala at the Ramsec Hotel, Assèze now finds it difficult to identify herself as a woman.

Thoughout Beyala's migrant novels, France is presented as a space where traditional African notions of both femininity and masculinity are interrogated and destabilized. When Aïssatou, the protagonist of *Comment cuisiner son mari à l'africaine*, bumps into her sweetheart Bolobolo shopping for food in the local grocery store, she tells him, 'Vous vous êtes finalement bien adapté à l'Occident qui voudrait que l'homme soit une femme et l'inverse' [You've ended up well adapted to the West which would like men to be women and vice versa] (*CCMA*, p. 44). These constant references to gender switching form a metaphorical thread in Beyala's fiction. Abdou claims that women generally have 'travesti [leur] pagne en pantalon' (*PPB*, p. 159) [changed [their pagnes] for trousers (*LPPB*, p. 108)], the choice of verb suggesting not just African women wearing Western clothes (trousers) rather than the traditional African 'pagne', but also women choosing to perform their gender role differently – to 'dress up as men' – and, in Abdou's eyes, to misrepresent or 'travesty' this role.[29]

Migration from Africa to Europe often forces individuals to reconsider the traditional gender roles which their countries of origin took for granted. Alec Hargreaves writes:

> Most immigrants of Third World origin come from countries where even formal equality does not exist: power is vested primarily in the father, whose authority extends over most decision-making areas and who generally serves as the breadwinner while the mother attends primarily to domestic tasks.[30]

This is certainly the kind of family model that Abdou Traoré exports from Mali to Paris in the 'Loukoum' novels: M'am and her co-wife, Soumana, perform all the household chores while Abdou works as a refuse collector and is initially the sole breadwinner. Only when M'am begins to undergo her personal transformation is Abdou forced to reconsider the socio-cultural models he unquestioningly imported from sub-Saharan Africa. Significantly, it is the French state's failure to acknowledge traditional African – in this case, polygamous – family structures that ultimately strips Abdou of his patriarchal authority and prompts M'am to re-evaluate her own gender role.[31] When French feminist Madame Saddock reports Abdou to the authorities for making false claims for family allowance, M'am takes his place as head of the household, running her own company and becoming her husband's boss when he is eventually released from prison.

Abdou returns from prison apparently transformed. Whereas, before his incarceration, he encapsulated the racist stereotype of the black African immigrant male – dishonest, sexually voracious, polygamous and physically violent – on his release from prison he is presented as a radically different man. Having lost his job, Abdou claims to now be happy working for his wife. He also helps M'am with the cooking, buys her jewellery, and showers her with flowers and compliments. According to Loukoum 'il n'est plus vraiment le même. [...] Il fait tout' (*PPB*, p. 245) [He truly is not the same any more [...] He does everything (*LPPB*, p. 172)]. It is as if the exile of prison has provided a second experience of migration allowing Abdou to reinvent himself outside the safe place of 'Tradition' he previously tried so desperately to inhabit. Indeed, Abdou appears at first to have travelled the route of the Ramsec hotel guests, returning from prison a feminized version of his formerly stereotypically masculine self: Loukoum describes him caring for a houseplant 'comme si c'était un bébé' (*PPB*, p. 245) [as if it were a baby (*LPPB*, p. 172)]. The fact that Abdou is again presented as performing a stereotypical, polarized version of masculinity (this time an 'effeminate' male) further confirms his inability to negotiate conflicting cultural models. Moreover, Abdou's 'feminization' after his exile in prison is another example of Beyala's 'cultural transsexualism'. In *Maman a un amant*, Loukoum notes that, 'Il [Abdou] s'est transformé en maîtresse de maison pour faire régner la bonne humeur. Il lave la vaisselle, il torche les mômes. Il fait la cuisine et c'est tellement sa nature que la cuisine et vraiment bonne' [He [Abdou] has transformed himself into the mistress of the house in order to keep everyone happy. He does the washing up, he wipes the kids' arses. He does the cooking and it's so much his thing that the cooking is really good] (*MAA*, p. 188). Through the eyes of Loukoum, however, Abdou is presented as emasculated. Whereas in *Le petit prince de Belleville*, Abdou was portrayed as a man to be feared, in the sequel Loukoum describes his father sobbing, spitting and suffering from bulimia. M'am's affair with Tichit further threatens Abdou's masculinity in the eyes of his community such that Monsieur Kaba prays for Abdou's dignity to be restored (*MAA*, p. 154). In Pompidou, the French police inspector implies a lack of respect for Abdou when he discovers M'am's affair (p. 114), suggesting that Abdou's new version of his masculinity is no more accepted by majority ethnic culture than it is by the black community of Belleville.

Like exile, education is also potentially damaging to normative gender roles, according to the so-called 'Traditionalists' in Beyala's world. When Assèze decides to travel to France as an illegal immigrant, the only form of identification she carries is her school identity card. Metaphorically, her education becomes her passport to France. In her village in Cameroon, however, education for women is viewed with suspicion. When Assèze returns to visit her village after moving to Douala to live with Awono and Sorraya, she meets with considerable hostility from the other women there. The aptly named Sotteria claims that women's qualifications are useless, adding that, 'ces femmes des livres, c'est comme des femmes qui deviennent des hommes à force de faire du sport' [these bookish women, they're like women who become men through playing sports] (*AA*, p. 134).[32] Her implication is that both education and migration defeminize women, challenging the normative role they have been allocated by 'Tradition'. Assèze concludes that 'elles [les autres femmes] voulaient que je paie pour avoir osé étendre mes frontières au-delà de notre village' [they [the other women] wanted me to pay for having extended my horizons beyond our village] (p. 135).

Similarly, in *Maman a un amant*, literacy is presented as a means for migrants to overcome barriers and gain entry into majority ethnic culture. However, the suggestion here is that this freedom of movement also comes at a price:

> Pourtant, j'ai dû franchir la barrière. Accepter cette préférence d'apprendre à lire et à écrire. Je sais que c'est un scandale qui efface chacune de mes complicités avec la communauté nègre. Un privilège,

déporté sur l'éloignement culturel – l'enfer, en somme. (*MAA*, p. 208)

[Yet I had to break through the barrier. Accept this preference for learning how to read and write. I know it's a scandal that wipes out all my connections with the black community. A privilege, deported into cultural estrangement – in short, hell.]

By using the language of migration, Beyala stresses the cultural separation between the immigrant ghetto of Belleville and the surrounding majority ethnic space of France. M'am chooses voluntary 'deportation' from her reconstructed home to another form of exile in autonomous subjectivity. Like Saïda in *Les Honneurs perdus*, M'am uses reading as a route into social and cultural mobility. In M'am's case, her newly acquired literacy is also connected to her adultery with the white Frenchman, Etienne Tichit, since her attendance at evening classes is partly a ruse for continuing the affair. Similarly, education gives Saïda the confidence to begin a sexual relationship with Marcel Pignon Marcel. Education for migrant women is linked to both integration and sexual freedom, hence M'am's succinct remark about what she learnt in the arms of her lover: 'J'y ai appris à lire le Blanc' [There I learnt how to read the white man] (*MAA*, p. 241).

For a long time, Loukoum wrestles with his mother's transformation from passive, conventional housewife to educated, independent woman, attempting to contain M'am within the space created for her in the family: 'une bonne ménagère, une bonne cuisinière et une bonne mère pour nous tous' [a good housewife, a good cook and a good mother to us all] (*MAA*, p. 184). However, he is forced to re-evaluate his image of her when he sees her reading the menu in a Chinese restaurant: 'La lecture l'emporte sur le terre à terre digestif. Acte éblouissant. Dépassement de soi. Femme de personne. Mère de personne. Quel orgueil à elle seule! Besoin sourd de creuser la terre pour trouver le sens des choses' [Reading has the edge over the mundane question of food. It was a dazzling act in which she surpassed herself. Nobody's wife. Nobody's mother. What pride she has in herself! A silent need to dig into the earth and find the meaning of things] (*MAA*, p. 226). Having initially attempted to explain his mother's transformation as some kind of diabolical possession, Loukoum learns to translate between the normative gender roles he has inherited from his father and the alternative femininities explored by M'am in France. This point is echoed in the text by Loukoum's translations of his mother's 'memoirs' from Bambara into French and demonstrates the way in which second-generation migrants function more effectively as mediators between different sites of 'home'.³³ Loukoum's role as linguistic translator mirrors the cultural translation of M'am's identity in France. According to Homi Bhabha, 'in order to objectify cultural meaning, there always has to be a process of alienation and of secondariness *in relation to itself*. In that sense there is no "in itself" and "for itself" within cultures because they are always subject to intrinsic forms of translation.'³⁴ Bhabha's notion of cultural translation, which draws on the work of Walter Benjamin, 'denies the essentialism of a given original or originary culture', a point that is repeatedly demonstrated in Beyala's fiction.³⁵ Through acts of translation, both literal and metaphorical, the novels point to the instability of cultural norms including 'Tradition' and 'authenticity'. The absurd suggestion that M'am's memoirs have been translated from Bambara by Loukoum undermines any exoticist notions of 'authenticity': since M'am's only education has been through the medium of French, it is implausible that she should formulate her 'memoirs' in Bambara, particularly as she is addressing them to a majority ethnic friend.

The importance of translation is also reflected in Beyala's decision to present a number of her migrant heroines – M'am, Saïda, Assèze and Eve-Marie – as renegotiating their femininity after a sexual encounter with a majority ethnic male in France. Sexual relationships with white men are a form of metaphorical migration, which empower the women to reassess normative gender roles and to reassert themselves as women on their own terms. After her affair with Etienne Tichit, M'am describes herself as 'plus tout à fait la même ni tout à fait une autre [no longer completely the same nor completely another] (*MAA*, p. 187). Whereas before meeting Tichit she had internalized the traditional premise that 'la femme est née à genoux aux pieds de l'homme' [woman is born kneeling at man's feet] (pp. 21, 240), at the end of the novel she sees Abdou no longer as her master but as her 'soleil déchu' [fallen sun] (p. 240). The sexual encounter with Tichit leads M'am to reassess her role within the family, and to evaluate more critically that of her husband, Abdou. Her love, she claims, 'reinvents' her (p. 208). Similarly, in *Les Honneurs perdus*, when Saïda Bénérafa finally loses her much-prized virginity, it is again with a white Frenchman, Marcel Pignon Marcel.³⁶ This experience is presented as a rebirthing in the text: 'Je me sentais une femme neuve' [I felt like a new woman] (*HP*, p. 396). No longer identified as a fifty-year-old virgin, Saïda is able to redefine herself: 'J'étais forte. Pas d'enfants. Pas encore de mari. Mais indestructible' [I was strong. No children. No husband yet. But indestructible] (p. 397).

For Assèze, the black–white sexual relationship is a little more complicated. She meets Monsieur Alexandre, a rich, white, French record producer in Paris, while she is trying to secure a record deal for her exploitative black lover, Océan. Although she knows that Alexandre is married, Assèze's relationship with him reads as a love affair between equals. The complication lies in the fact that, unbeknown to Assèze, Alexandre's wife is Sorraya, her former friend/adoptive sister and the girl she lived with in Douala. Initially, Alexandre fulfils a similar narrative function to Tichit and Marcel in that, through her relationship with him, Assèze begins to question her future with Océan whom she eventually leaves. Ultimately, though, the majority ethnic lover in *Assèze l'Africaine* has a more complex role in that, when Sorraya commits suicide, unable to live as a hybrid (*AA*, p. 339), Alexandre decides to marry Assèze. The book opens with Assèze living a self-effacing lifestyle, going to church every day, her husband threatening to divorce her for her passivity. Like M'am and Saïda, Assèze uses the knowledge she gains from a migrant sexual relationship to change, albeit to adopt a more conventionally 'feminine' role.

The example of Eve-Marie in *Amours sauvages* is similarly ambiguous in that, initially, the protagonist is delighted to be able to identify herself as 'Mme Eve-Marie Gerbaud' rather than as 'Mlle Bonne Surprise' (the name she used when working as a prostitute); she also begins to eat more because her husband prefers her plump. By African norms, Eve-Marie's marriage to white French poet, Pléthore, is unconventional since her husband stays at home while Eve-Marie works as an office cleaner and subsequently sets up an illegal 'maquis'-style restaurant. Eve-Marie's mother is not impressed by her daughter's domestic arrangements: 'Son regard vide erra vers quelques lointaines sagesses: – J'aurai tout vu! Ce pays des blancs fait voir des miracles!' [Her empty gaze wandered towards some far off words of wisdom: 'I've seen it all now! This white man's country makes you see miracles!'] (*AS*, p. 34). The ambiguity of Eve-Marie and Pléthore's relationship again demonstrates the difficulties of acculturation for migrant women in France. Although she claims to be 'un exemple parfait d'intégration pour toutes les négresses' [a perfect example of integration for all black women] (p. 55), Eve-Marie oscillates between two sets of normative values. When she discovers Pléthore in bed with her neighbour, Flore-Flore, Eve-Marie's reaction is to broadcast the news to the people of Belleville. This leads her neighbours to accuse her of behaving like a white woman (p. 77). Only when Eve-Marie decides to befriend Flore-Flore does she regain the approval and recognition of other migrant women: 'Pour elles, j'étais une femme trompée, qui acceptait sa rivale et vivait cette situation avec hardiesse. [...] Etait-ce perdre son âme d'Africaine que d'aspirer à l'amour total?' [For them, I was a woman who'd been cheated on, who accepted her rival and who bravely put up with this situation. [...] Was it losing your African soul to aspire to total love?] (p. 90). The problem identified here is how to reconcile two sets of competing cultural expectations: does a desire for what is perceived as a Western model of monogamy amount to a negation of one's roots in a culture where polygamy is widely tolerated? Like the mixed relationships in the other novels, Eve-Marie's marriage forces her to reassess and renegotiate her set of cultural values and thus functions as a site of translation between migrancy and 'Tradition'.

As Durand rightly concludes in his engaging analysis of *Le petit prince de Belleville*, it is women and children who negotiate migratory spaces more successfully than men in Beyala's novels.[37] Those who, like Soumana, are unable to translate between European and African cultural models ultimately fail to survive the migratory experience. When she talks of her impossible dreams of leaving her husband and becoming an actress, Soumana ends up weeping with frustration in the kitchen. Indeed, Soumana's failure to adapt to what Durand calls the 'survival materialism of the migratory space'[38] culminates in her physical deterioration and eventually her death.

Whereas characters like Soumana and Abdou lose their way either permanently or temporarily on their migratory journeys, others characters cope much better. These are those individuals in Beyala's fiction who, like the symbolically nicknamed 'Resourceful Women' ('Les Débrouillardes'), do not attempt acculturation into the majority ethnic culture of France, nor seek refuge in the imaginary space of 'Tradition'. The fixity connoted by 'Tradition' is an obstacle to transculturation, and is described through the narrative of Saïda Bénérafa as 'l'énorme danger que suppose un raidissement dans un heureux processus d'adaptation' [the enormous danger posed by intransigence in a happy process of adaptation] (*HP*, p. 235). Rather than following Abdou's experience of migration as a process of shedding 'bits of their souls', these women shake off those 'traditional' myths that contain them within a fixed and so-called 'authentic' gender identity, translating between and across the different cultural spaces they inhabit. As Assèze remarks, 'les Débrouillardes étaient sans scrupules: elles avaient l'habitude de tout mélanger' [The Resourceful Woman had no scruples: they tended to mix everything up] (*AA*, p. 242), suggesting a more fluid approach to exile, and one that is based on an eclectic mixing of cultural norms rather than the polarized clash of 'Africa' versus 'France'. Like M'am, the 'Débrouillardes' have learnt to travel without an agenda fixed in a particular geographical or cultural space. They follow 'un chemin dont on ignore l'itinéraire' [a journey with an unknown itinerary] (*MAA*, p. 5). Such journeys imply strategic appropriation rather than acculturation or assimilation, and so represent the migrant woman's role as one of activity rather than passivity in the migratory experience.

Moreover, rather than take refuge in the past, Beyala's successful migrants focus on the present and the future. This point is emphasized in *Assèze l'Africaine* by the discovery of the narrator-protagonist's gift of clairvoyance: 'Dès lors, rêver au passé devenait totalement absurde. Dès lors, l'engouement pour mes prédictions trouvait un terrain propice' [From then on, dreaming of the past became totally absurd. From then on, the interest in my predictions found fertile ground] (*AA*, pp. 274–75). This looking to the future connects with what Hall describes as 'the process of becoming':

> Though they seem to invoke an origin in a historical past with which they continue to correspond, actually identities are about questions of using the resources of history, language and culture in the process of becoming rather than being: not 'who we are' or 'where we came from', so much as what we might become, how we have been represented and how that bears on how we represent ourselves.[39]

Throughout Beyala's fiction there is an emphasis on becoming through the repetition of the verb 'devenir' [to become]. Indeed, *Seul le diable le savait*, which begins with Mégri in Paris and ends with her decision to leave Africa, is framed by the sentence, 'Dans la famille nous aimons les grands projets. D'ailleurs, j'en ai un: DEVENIR' [In our family we like big projects. Besides, I've got one: TO BECOME] (*SDS*, pp. 9, 281).[40] Migration thus becomes a space of possibility rather than fixity. Paul White writes:

In migration, above all topics, the levels of ambivalence, of plurality, of shifting identities and interpretations are perhaps greater than in many other aspects of life. The relationships between people and their contextual societies and places are intimate ones which are transformed by movement. Adjustment processes may never be fully completed: indeed, since we all continually refine our self-identities throughout our life-course it may be more truthful to say that migration intervenes in that process of renegotiation as a lasting force, rather than as a single event.[41]

White's point is an important one: identity is not fixed in any individual – migrant or indigene – and we all respond continuously to external events. The difference, White argues, is that migration is not a single event but a 'lasting force'. The next chapter discusses whether, once settled in France, Beyala's migrants are ever able to resist and adapt to this lasting force or whether it positions them forever 'out of sync'.

CHAPTER FOUR

'Afro-française': In-Between or Out of Sync?

> Moi je suis plus un vrai Nègre vu que je vis en France.[1]
>
> [Since I've been living in France, I'm not a real Black anymore.]

In 2000 Beyala produced her second essay, *Lettre d'une Afro-française à ses compatriotes*, in which, according to the publisher's blurb, 'l'écrivain Calixthe Beyala réagit et pousse un coup de gueule contre le racisme, elle qui aime la France et les Français, ses frères' [the writer Calixthe Beyala, she who loves France and the French people, her brothers, reacts and rants against racism].[2] The title of this essay marks a significant shift in Beyala's self-positioning, particularly when compared to that of her earlier essay, *Lettre d'une Africaine à ses soeurs occidentales* (published in 1995).[3] From the geographically located 'Africaine', Beyala's chosen identity tag has now moved to the more ambiguous, hyphenated neologism, 'Afro-française'. Moreover, Afro-French appears to foreground French rather than African identity; the ethnic descriptor 'Afro' functioning as a sub-category or 'type' of Frenchness. This new label is echoed in *Lettre d'une Afro-française* when Beyala criticizes French journalists for always labelling black people 'Franco-something':

> Les journalistes parlant des personnalités noires, n'omettent jamais de préciser: Le Franco-sénégalais, Franco-camerounais, Franco-malien, toujours ce Franco et quelque chose, qui situe l'autre dans des sphères de différences, l'éloigne de la communauté nationale et crée en son sein des sous-communautés nationales. (*LAFC*, p. 40)[4]
>
> [When talking about black personalities, journalists never fail to specify 'Franco-Senegalese, Franco-Cameroonian, Franco-Malian', always this 'Franco-something', which positions the other in realms of difference, away from the national community, at the heart of which it creates national sub-communities.]

Such a pro-Republican statement is rather surprising from an author who, as president of Collectif Egalité, condemns French universalism for not respecting its 'minorités visibles' [visible minorities] (*LAFC*, p. 33) and who actively campaigns for positive racial discrimination in the form of quotas. At the same time, it implicitly points to the tensions around locating immigrant identity in a Republic which, although ostensibly multicultural, is determined to remain 'unie et indivisible'. Perhaps inevitably, it appears that Beyala is beginning to identify herself – and immigrants more generally – in terms of nationality rather than ethnicity. This is reinforced by the shifting identification of Beyala's intended readership for each essay: whereas *Lettre d'une Africaine* was addressed to her 'soeurs occidentales', *Lettre d'une Afro-française* is addressed to Beyala's male and female 'compatriotes'.

2000 was also a year in which Beyala publicly confirmed her Frenchness on national television, telling France 2 presenter, Philippe Bouvard:

> Je suis plus française que vous. Je connais une plus grande partie de la culture française que 90% de mes compatriotes. Donc suis-je immigrée? Je ne pense pas. Je pense dire de moi que je suis immigrée, c'est presque une injure. Je ne suis pas immigrée en France. Je suis chez moi. C'est ma terre. Je l'aime.[5]

> [I'm more French than you are. I know more about French culture than 90% of my compatriots. Am I an immigrant, then? I don't think so. I think that to say I'm an immigrant is almost an insult. I am not an immigrant in France. I am at home here. This is my land. I love it.]

Similarly, in *LAFC* she writes: 'Française je suis; française je reste; française je suis fière d'être, n'en déplaise à certains' [I am French; I'm staying French; I'm proud to be French, whether people like it or not] (p. 30). This apparent lack of ambiguity does not, however, completely map onto Beyala's newly coined label, 'Afro-française'. Although, as outlined above, the term appears to privilege French over African, the hyphen also points to an identity that might be located somewhere in between. Having discussed the strategic positioning of Beyala's public self in Chapter 1, this chapter will turn to the representation of the 'Afro-française' in her fictional writings. It will ask whether Beyala's characters reflect the incorporation into Frenchness that she herself appears here to embrace, or whether they in fact reflect an African immigrant identity that is permanently 'out of sync' with the host culture of France. Beyond these questions I shall consider whether, in Beyala's fiction, any of her 'in-between' characters represent an alternative, more complex formation of identity that might be positioned beyond the insider/outsider divide in a space of postcolonial ambivalence.

In a discussion of performance artist Guillermo Gomez-Peña, Homi Bhabha describes the way in which what he calls 'hybrid hyphenations' emphasize the incommensurability of the two cultural spaces linked by the hyphen while at the same time promoting identification on the basis of this same incommensurability. To put it another way, the hyphen is both a link and a barrier: in Beyala's appellation, 'Afro' is both linked to 'française' and the same time separate – and excluded – from it. 'What is at issue', Bhabha writes, 'is the performative nature of differential identities: the regulation and negotiation of those spaces that are continually, *contingently* "opening out", remaking the boundaries, exposing the limits of any claim to a singular or autonomous sign of difference'.[6] So, according to Bhabha, the hybrid hyphenation is both restrictive and enabling as an identity tag, suggesting an identification that is 'neither One nor the Other but *something else besides, in-between*'.[7]

The previous chapter discussed the ways in which white male lovers in Beyala's fiction act as mediators for migrant women to translate their own gender identities. In other words, men such as Etienne Tichit (*MAA*), Monsieur Alexandre (*AA*) and Marcel Pignon Marcel (*HP*) function as what Bhabha calls 'objects of otherness', with and through which the female subjects identify.[8] As such, cross-cultural sexual intercourse crystallizes the process of hybridity, which, as Bhabha explains, generates new cultural meanings and new subjectivities:

> If [...] the act of cultural translation (both as representation and as reproduction) denies the essentialism of a prior given original or originary culture, then we see that all forms of culture are continually in a process of hybridity. But for me the importance of hybridity is not to be able to trace two original moments from which the third emerges, rather hybridity to me is the 'third space' which enables other positions to emerge.[9]

While postmodern discourses on hybridity tend to follow Bhabha in celebrating the potentiality of cultural synthesis, the original meaning was, as Jayne Ifekwunigwe reminds us, one of racial contamination.[10] In the nineteenth and early twentieth centuries, it was widely believed that interracial breeding led to diminished fertility, and that this was evidence that black and white were not different races but rather different species that should not be combined. This view was based on evidence from biological science in which hybrids are a cross between two different species, and are incapable of reproduction. The most common example of the hybrid is the mule, which is the sterile offspring of a horse and a donkey.[11] The application of such a model to the question of interracial breeding among humans generated a number of possible positions, as summarized by Robert Young in *Colonial Desire*. In all but one of the five theories Young describes, sexual unions between different races are either infertile or lead to offspring that are in some way degenerated from their parents. The one exception is what Young calls the 'amalganation' thesis, which is 'the claim that all humans can interbreed prolifically and in an unlimited way; sometimes accompanied by the "melting-pot" notion that the mixing of people produces a new mixed race, with merged but distinct new physical and moral characteristics'.[12] This model is the one that comes closest to contemporary definitions of hybridity in the cultural sphere. Interestingly, this model can also be read as a biological precursor of Senghor's polemical notion of 'métissage culturel' [cultural mixing].[13]

Although both Young and Ifekwunigwe trace the link between biological theories of hybridity and its contemporary reformulation as a diasporic space, sometimes cultural hybridity becomes disconnected from its biological antecedent. In Beyala's novels, however, the concept of hybridity as a genetic deviation returns, first in the figure of the 'cultural transsexual', which fuses the cultural with the biological (see Chapter 3). Secondly, and more commonly, Beyala produces fictional echoes of nineteenth-century genetics through the deaths of migrant women who become impossible hybrids. Echoing the view that miscegenation would create hybrids of 'weaker constitution', Beyala presents some characters that are unable to cope with the negotiation of more than one cultural space. Here she is not suggesting that hybridity is in itself impossible or undesirable, but rather that conceiving of ethnic and cultural differences in essentialist terms prevents any kind of workable hybridity.

The deaths of women such as Soumana (*MAA*) and Sorraya (*AA*) demonstrate the problematic nature of the kind of polarized hybridity that Bhabha rejects in his discussion of the 'third space'. These characters' failure to negotiate what they perceive to be the incompatible cultural spaces they inhabit is based on an adherence to essentialist views of racial difference. Sorraya describes her own frustrated attempts to acculturate in terms of an opposition between 'le Blanc' and 'le noir':

> Toute ma vie, j'ai vécu le cul entre deux chaises. J'ai essayé de singer le Blanc. C'est pas de ma faute! En Afrique, on nous faisait croire que nous étions des arriérés et moi, j'y ai cru. Je voulais me franciser, désincruster toute trace de noir en moi. Parce que le noir c'est la saleté. Le noir c'est la misère. Le noir c'est la malédiction. Je m'en voulais d'être africaine. Je voulais ressembler à Dupond, à Durand. C'était ridicule. (*AA*, p. 331)

> [All my life I've lived with my arse between two stools. I've tried to ape the Whites. It's not my fault! In Africa they made us believe we were backward, and I believed it. I wanted to Frenchify myself, dig out every trace of black in me. Because black is dirt. Black is destitution. Black is a curse. I hated myself for being African. I wanted to be like Dupond, Durand. It was ridiculous.]

Such negative hybridity results from an attempt to bridge a gap between two apparently discrete cultures, and is the given explanation for Sorraya's suicide. Metaphorically, Sorraya's death is inevitable since she attempts to fix her identity through acculturation. Only much later, after her sister's death, will Assèze recognize the positive hybridity that Sorraya might have represented. Recalling a dance Sorraya performed in her bedroom to music by Mozart, Assèze comments that: 'Aujourd'hui, avec du recul, je dirais qu'il régna dans cette chambre une ambiance très french cancan, revue et corrigée par les pom-poms girls, et relevée par une touche culturelle bien africaine' [Today, with hindsight, I would say that the prevailing atmosphere in that room was very French cancan, revised and corrected by the pom-pom girls, and spiced up with a cultural touch that was certainly African] (*AA*, p. 112). In Assèze's memory, Sorraya's dance confirms the impossibility of shedding one's ethnic origins: the dance is still identifiably African in the same way as it is identifiably French. A similar image is conveyed by the description of Sorraya's bedroom where posters of French chanteuse Dalida are side by side with books by French canonical authors such as Baudelaire, Du Bellay, Hugo and Sartre, as well as handbooks on traditional African medicine (p. 111). For Sorraya, however, there is no value in African culture. She wants to become a dancer in Europe, she says, because in Africa people do not even know how to blow their noses properly. Such contempt for her own people demonstrates the extent to which Sorraya has been indoctrinated by racist ideology. Ironically, of course, she appears to be oblivious to her own internalization of colonial mythology, telling Assèze immediately after their conversation about dancing that, 'Blanche ou noire, cela n'a d'importance que pour les imbéciles' [Whether you're white or black only matters to imbeciles] (p. 113), failing to see the contradictions in her own discourse.

In *Le petit prince de Belleville*, M'am's co-wife, Soumana, also dies once she is brainwashed by the ideology of the white feminist, Madame Saddock. Soumana wants to acculturate but, unlike Sorraya, lacks the economic means to gain entry to the cultural space of France. Despite the significant differences in their economic circumstances, what both Soumana and Sorraya have in common is the mistranslation of both their own gender identities and those of French women as essential and given. Similarly, as we saw in the previous chapter, Soumana's husband, Abdou, refuses to recognize the fictional nature of normative gender roles in both Mali and France. Although Abdou does not die in the novel, his essentialized approach to hybridity, leads him to experience his exile as a 'poison' that eats away at his flesh (*PPB*, p. 7; *LPPB*, p. 1). What these characters represent is not Bhabha's 'third space' but the alienation that ensues when a migrant individual attempts to privilege one set of cultural meanings over another.

Not all Beyala's hybrid characters are doomed. There is, however, a refrain running through the migrant novels that living in the West makes you mad: 'L'Occident nous rend dingues!' [The West makes us crazy] thinks Eve-Marie, remembering that there are more blacks in psychiatric hospitals than in prison in France (*AS*, p. 117). Africans in France, various characters suggest, are 'complexés' [full of hang-ups] (*AS*, p. 145), particularly when they choose to have relationships with majority ethnic whites. Following a line that can be traced back to Fanon's *Peau noire, masques blancs*, black characters with white lovers are condemned as alienated by and from the exiled black community who thereby perpetuate the racist biological myth of what Saïda calls 'l'accouplement ignoblement contre nature d'une Négresse avec un blanc' [the basely unnatural coupling of a Negress with a white man] (*HP*, p. 218) or vice versa. In *Amours sauvages*, the text goes so far as to equate a black man's desire for a white woman as a challenge to his masculinity when Océan's relationship with Eve-Marie's white neighbour, Flora-Flore, is juxtaposed with the revelation that he is a transvestite (*AS*, pp. 145–47).¹⁴ Océan leaves because, as he explains, 'les nègres de Belleville n'accepteraient pas de me voir déguisé en femme' [the blacks of Belleville would not accept seeing me dressed up as a woman] (*AS*, p. 147).

The alienation that is perceived to be a result of lactification is also interrogated in Beyala's hybrid text, *Comment cuisiner son mari à l'africaine*, which functions as both a novel and a cookery book. Published in 2000, *Comment cuisiner* intersperses the fictional account of the narrator Aïssatou's attempts to seduce her handsome neighbour, Souleymane Bolobolo, with twenty-four of the recipes she prepares as her means of seduction. Many of the recipes are those identified as 'authentically' African in cookery books published in print and in electronic form (generally found in Europe and North America).¹⁵ Dishes such as crocodile in tchobi sauce and porcupine with wild mango kernels immediately load the text with markers of the exotic. However, in terms of marketing and readership, this novel is very much a French, and more specifically Parisian, cultural product. Furthermore, the narrator/protagonist is immediately identified as a Parisian in the publisher's blurb, which promotes *Comment cuisiner* as the story of 'mademoiselle Aïssatou, *Parisienne pure black* en proie aux tourments de l'amour' [Mademoiselle Aïssatou, a *pure black Parisian woman* prey to the torments of love].¹⁶ Although the reader later learns that Aïssatou has, in fact, migrated from Cameroon to France, the implication is that her positioning has shifted from outside to inside. Her primary identification is with the city in which she now finds herself rather than with her origins or her ethnicity. This point is rather overstated in the text itself with Aïssatou's repeated refrain of 'j'ignore quand je suis devenue blanche' [I don't know when I became white] suggesting a total assimilation into majority ethnicity in France.

In this novel-cum-recipe book, Beyala illustrates the way in which migrant women are influenced by the conventions of physical beauty established in their host nation. In *Consuming Geographies: We are Where we Eat*, cultural geographers Bell and Valentine explain that the effect of majority ethnic beauty norms on women from ethnic minorities tends to be underestimated:

> some writers [...] claim that eating disorders like bulimia are less common among black and Asian women, suggesting that they are less prone to be influenced by Western ideals of the slender body, others have argued that it is naive to believe that because black

women have largely been excluded from these representations, they are free from the pressures on white women. [Others] point out, for example, that this very obliteration of black women's experiences of their own bodies actually serves to construct 'beautiful' black women as those with light skin and straightened hair.[17]

In *Comment cuisiner*, the influence of European representations of the feminine body translates into the suggestion that Aïssatou, like an increasingly large number of majority ethnic women and girls, is suffering from an eating disorder. She informs the reader that, 'bien manger est une dégradation parce que cela engendre une surabondance de chair, impure aux regards' [eating well is damaging because it it generates an overabundance of flesh which looks impure] (p. 13).[18] Back in Africa, a 'surabondance de chair' is viewed as desirable since not only is it an indicator of wealth and elevated social status but also, as butcher-gigolo Saturnin explains, 'La diète en matière de sexualité atrophie le plaisir' [As far as sex is concerned, dieting shrivels desire] (*FNFN*, p. 203). This explains Saïda's distress in *Les Honneurs perdus* when her lover, Ibrahim, suggests that she needs to lose some weight: she sees him as having internalized European beauty myths.

The suggestion here is that the slender body is synonymous with the lactified body. To achieve integration into the predominantly white community that surrounds her, Aïssatou strives to look 'white'. She has straightened hair, bleached skin, and diets obsessively, eating only three grated carrots or a packet-soup for her evening meal. On one level, then, she appears to represent the 'Négresse blanche' she claims to be, seduced by the cultural norms of France. Indeed, the description of the three-carrot meal provides a stark contrast with a conversation she has immediately beforehand with an overweight woman in a bar. When the woman asks her if she diets to stay thin, Aïssatou responds with a detailed list of the food she eats:

> Et je lui cite, exaltée, les mets succulents dont mes entrailles se régalent depuis ma naissance: le coq au vin, arrosé d'un bon beaujolais nouveau; les épaules d'agneau aux champignons noirs, le ris de veau à la crème fraîche et le couscous mouton à la tunisienne. Je continue mon énumération jusqu'à ce que je voie deux larmes poindre au bord des ses paupières. (*CCMA*, pp. 21–22)

> [Full of excitement, I list for her the succulent dishes that my guts have relished since the time I was born: coq au vin, washed down with a good beaujolais nouveau; shoulder of lamb with mushrooms,

calf sweetbreads à la crème, and lamb couscous à la tunisienne. I carry on with my list until I see two tears appear in the corners of her eyes.]

What is interesting here is not only the high calorific value of the dishes she mentions, but also the fact that all are identifiable staples of French national cuisine.[19] Even couscous, the closest French equivalent to chicken tikka masala in Britain, is here incorporated into the national cuisine of France.[20] The label 'à la tunisienne' establishes a certain geographical distance between what is presented by Aïssatou as the exotic home of couscous (Tunisia) and the local site of its preparation and consumption (France). The mention of couscous also points to one of the few ways in which Maghrebian immigrant culture has affected the majority ethnic culture of France. According to Bell and Valentine,

> migrant groups, often bearers of ethnic or religious identities, commonly take their food habits with them, altering the culinary culture of host nations along the way. Indeed, the 'national dishes' of countries commonly bear the mark of successive waves of migration.[21]

Although this is far less the case in France than in Britain, some migrant foodstuffs from North Africa and Vietnam are readily available in French restaurants and supermarkets. The same cannot be said, however, of dishes from sub-Saharan Africa. Apart from a relatively small number of specialist restaurants in those areas with substantial immigrant populations, West and Central African cooking has made few inroads into the food habits of France.[22] By stating that she eats and enjoys quintessentially French cuisine, Aïssatou stakes her claim on majority ethnic culture, at least in terms of her public performance. Paradoxically, her dieting serves an identical purpose: by starving herself she hopes to achieve the breastless, bottomless body of the waif celebrated by French fashion houses and glossy magazines.

Significantly, her decision to try to seduce her neighbour, Bolobolo, leads to Aïssatou's rejection of French foodways and her return to African cooking. What this reveals is the way in which the migrant woman is prey to conflicting cultural norms. As a 'Négresse blanche' Aïssatou is presented as constantly oscillating between the traditional African gender role she has inherited from her mother who would tell her that a woman's role is to satisfy her husband sexually, keep the house clean and be a good cook, and the post-feminist interrogation of this role she is presented with in France. When, as a ruse to win Bolobolo's affections, she offers to look after his mother while he is at work, Aïssatou remarks, 'J'ai l'impression que mon discours est en décalage, espace et temps. Je sais que j'ai eu une réaction africaine où chacun se mêle des casseroles étrangères' [I feel like my words are out of sync in space and time. I know I had an African reaction where everyone has their finger in everyone else's pies] (*CCMA*, p. 35). The metaphor of speaking from a position of 'décalage' in relation to that of her interlocutor provides an interesting version of 'in-betweenness'. Whereas geographical theorists of migration tend to present the migratory process as the compression of time and space, Beyala presents the migrant woman as spatially and temporally 'out of sync': faced with an African man in a non-African context, Aïssatou becomes culturally illiterate because she feels unable to communicate with him in shared space and time.[23] Similarly, in *Les Honneurs perdus*, Saïda experiences feelings of being incorrectly aligned with her environment: without the 'repères' [points of reference] she left behind in Africa, her universe is 'désaxé' [off beam] (*HP*, p. 357). To be 'out of sync' suggests a level of normative synchronicity that might ideally be achieved and also emphasizes the way in which migrants are often not 'tuned in' to what Hargreaves and McKinney identify as the circuits of communication on which cultures are constructed.[24] To continue the signal processing metaphor, Aïssatou and Saïda are not on the same wavelength as the majority population, nor are they able to communicate easily with other Africans in France. The implication is that the experience of exile has produced a level of interference that impedes all communication, reducing some characters, as we have seen, to silence.

These various negative interpretations of what Salman Rushdie calls 'mongrelization' suggest that many migrants remain fixed in and by the essentializing discourses of colonial times. As Robert Young puts it, 'the nightmare of the ideologies and categories of racism continue to repeat upon the living'.[25] Death, madness and alienation are the fates of those who have lost a locatable identity. This loss, as we have seen, is a common thread in Beyala's migrant fiction. It is also symptomatic of what Gloria Anzaldúa defines as living in a 'borderland'.[26] In her groundbreaking study of what she calls 'the new mestiza', Anzaldúa writes:

> Chicanos and other people of colour suffer economically for not acculturating. This voluntary (yet forced) alienation makes for psychological conflict, a kind of dual identity – we don't identify with the Anglo-American cultural values and we don't totally identify with the Mexican cultural values. We are a synergy of two cultures with various degrees of Mexicanness or Angloness. I have so internalized the borderland conflict that sometimes I feel like one cancels out the other and we are zero, nothing, no one.[27]

In fact, Beyala's novels sharpen Anzaldúa's analysis in that it is specifically the gender identities of African people that become dislocated through individuals' experiences of the border zone. As we saw in the previous chapter, normative notions of femininity and masculinity become destabilized and threatened by the expectations of the majority ethnic culture of France such that many of the characters end up feeling that they are 'zero, nothing, no one'.

In response to the 'borderland conflict' that is symptomatic of exile, many migrants find themselves in a position of ambivalence, as Paul White observes:

> A common feature of many migrants and migrant cultures is ambivalence. Ambivalence towards the past and the present: as to whether things were better 'then' or 'now'. Ambivalence towards the future: whether to retain a 'myth of return' or to design a new project without further expected movement built in. Ambivalence towards the 'host' society: feelings of respect, dislike or uncertainty. Ambivalence towards standards of behaviour: whether to cling to the old or to discard it, whether to compromise via symbolic events whilst adhering to the new on an everyday basis. The choices (or the paths taken, since in many cases 'choice' is not actually perceived to exist) depend not just on the individuals involved but also on the constraints of the situation in which migrants find themselves.[28]

Ambivalence, it could be argued, is a version of 'in-betweenness', and is characterized by uncertainty and/or contradiction. For women such as Aïssatou in *Comment cuisiner*, ambivalence is a disabling state. Her inability to reconcile conflicting cultural expectations causes her to feel permanently out of sync. White's point about the constraints of the individual migrant's situation is pertinent since, as Beyala's fiction reveals all too clearly, the situation of African women in France is radically different from that of African men. That is not to say that none of Beyala's male migrants experience exile as being 'out of sync', but rather that far more men than women are successfully able to negotiate exile through different forms of ambivalence.

In *Les Honneurs perdus* Beyala depicts the ambivalent figure of a Moroccan immigrant, Ibrahim, who, while apparently happy to sleep with Blandine in exchange for a plane ticket to Paris, refuses to have sex with his fiancée, Saïda, leading Ngaremba to accuse him of impotence:

> Ce type est impuissant, dit-elle [Ngaremba]. C'est normal. Quelle vie ont les immigrés? Certains restent si longtemps sans toucher à une femme qu'ils en perdent les moyens dès qu'il s'en présente une. (*HP*, p. 350)

> ['That bloke is impotent', she [Ngaremba] said. 'It's perfectly normal. What sort of life do immigrant men have? Some of them spend so long without touching a woman that, as soon as one appears, they forget how to do it'.]

In fact, the narrative implies that Ibrahim cannot cope with the fact that, at fifty, Saïda is still a virgin. While Ngaremba is right to suggest that his 'impotence' is a result of his migration to France, it is more specifically the transformation of his moral and sexual codes which are at the root of his rejection of Saïda. For this Moroccan immigrant male, Saïda embodies the gender clash between the cultural spaces of Islam and France, since she is a Muslim woman who is both a virgin and prepared to have sex with him outside marriage.[29]

Indeed, Ibrahim represents the cultural contradictions that can emerge through attempted assimilation. In a conversation in a cafe, he tells Saïda that he spends his free time teaching Arabic to second-generation immigrants in France, telling her 'Ce qui est surprenant, c'est que les enfants d'immigrés pensent qu'ils n'ont pas d'identité parce qu'ils sont nés en France. Ils sont convaincus que cette société s'est dressée entre eux et leur culture. Après ils se retrouvent' [What's surprising is that the children of immigrants think they've got no identity because they were born in France. They're convinced that this society stands between them and their culture. Afterwards, they find themselves again] (*HP*, p. 318). Here Ibrahim presents French society as an obstacle between Beur children and their origins. This obstacle, he claims, can only be overcome through Arabization. Conversely, when he criticizes Saïda for putting on weight, she responds by saying, 'tu es plus français que je ne le pensais [...] les Africains aiment les grosses' [you're more French than I thought you were [...] African men like fat women] (*HP*, p. 323). It appears that Ibrahim selects those elements of French and Moroccan culture that suit his personal agenda. As such, it could be argued that he functions successfully as an 'in-between'. Sitting with Saïda in a nightclub he declares enigmatically that 'on n'est jamais aussi bien que chez soi' [you never feel better than when you're at home] (*HP*, p. 340). Home, for Ibrahim, seems to be wherever he chooses it to be.

Similarly, after his departure from Belleville, Océan in *Amours sauvages* appears to find a sense of personal freedom in ambivalence – this time of gender. When Eve-Marie tracks him down in a Paris gay bar, she finds him wearing a woman's evening dress:

> Rien qu'à le voir on savait que malgré tout ce que la pensée exclusive pouvait dégoiser sur la question, il avait rassemblé tous les morceaux de lui qui étaient bons, précieux et beaux, les avait traînés dans ce bar, poussés dans ce dancing-bar, loin de l'Afrique et de ces interdictions, loin des frontières où se chuchotaient des 'T'as vu machin?' et des 'Qu'est-ce qu'on dira?' (*AS*, pp. 210–11)
>
> [Only to look at him you knew that, despite everything that the snobs could gossip about, he had put together all the bits of him that were good, precious and beautiful, had dragged them into this bar, pushed them into this disco-bar, far from Africa and its prohibitions, far from the borders where people whispered, 'Have you seen so-and-so?' or 'What will people say?']

Belleville, it seems, can be a difficult space in which to perform alternative gender identities, since to a large extent it functions as a refuge for 'Tradition'. In the rue Sainte-Croix-de-la-Bretonnerie, on the other hand, Eve-Marie finds another 'territoire protégé' [protected territory], that of homosexual men in Paris. The compartmentalization of the city into different socio-cultural zones makes it difficult for in-between identities to emerge. Freedom of movement thus becomes essential, along with adequate financial and personal independence. It is not surprising that most of Beyala's successful in-betweens are men: the majority of migrant women in France are either unemployed or working in poorly paid temporary or part-time positions and so lack the independence necessary to negotiate the city as they choose. Moreover, as Freedman argues, women migrants are caught in a double bind since, on the one hand, they are expected to facilitate the integration of their children into majority ethnic culture, while on the other they are confined to a particular place within that culture's imagination.[30] Whereas men like Océan are able move freely across geographical, sexual and ethnic boundaries, migrant women are often held responsible for the maintenance of those boundaries by both the majority ethnic population and the migrant community they inhabit. As such, they are doubly contained within both dominant and minority ideologies.

The complexity of migrant women's situations is often oversimplified or simply not recognized by feminists in France. In Beyala's 'Loukoum' novels, the blindness of French feminism to the reality of migrant women's lives is represented by the character of Madame Saddock who, having attempted to indoctrinate M'am and Soumana, reports Abdou to the authorities for defrauding the social security system. Although eventually banished from the Traoré family home, Madame Saddock symbolizes the infiltration of Western ideologies into the once-closed communities of African immigrants in France. As such, her role is ambiguous. Madame Saddock's decision to denounce Abdou for illegally claiming child benefits leads to the imprisonment of the sole source of income for the family. However, while Abdou is detained in prison, M'am decides to expand the business of making leather jewellery that Loukoum had started to impress his friends at school. Thus, on the one hand, the Madame Saddock encounter demonstrates the apparent incompatibility of Western feminism and postcolonial migrant women, in this case because the feminist is blind to the notion of cultural difference and to the economic hardships and legal difficulties faced by African working-class women in France. Despite her claim to be acting in the two women's best interests, Madame Saddock fails to consider the financial repercussions for both of the wives. On the other hand, M'am is presented as empowered by this experience: she ejects Madame Saddock from the family home and challenges her own husband's authority, which she had never before questioned. Soumana, however, remains confined within a subordinate position because, as an illegal resident in France, she lacks the means to achieve financial independence.

Although Madame Saddock functions indirectly as a catalyst for M'am's economic success, it is only when the latter is no longer dependent on her husband that she begins to renegotiate her role within the family and beyond. It is no surprise that M'am's affair with Etienne Tichit begins on a family holiday that she has paid for. Beyala establishes a clear link between economic and personal freedom for migrant women in her fiction. For some of the characters, this becomes translated into an association of wealth with happiness. As Yvette and Fathia (two of the 'Débrouillardes') wander with Assèze down the boulevard Saint-Germain, they dream of untold wealth in the form of:

> [une] réussite monumentale avec compte-chèques à la Banque de France, et des directeurs poussiéreux à [leur] disposition. Et dans le pire des cas, on pourrait toujours se contenter d'une rente de cent cinquante mille francs par mois, léguée par quelque mari riche mais un peu radin. (*AA*, pp. 262–63)
>
> [[a] monumental success with a Bank of France current account, and fusty bank managers at their service. In the worst possible case they could always settle for an allowance of one hundred and fifty thousand francs a month bequeathed to them by some rich but rather tight-fisted husband.]

The fantasy of being a woman kept by her husband reminds the reader that, despite the recent increase in the number of African women migrating independently to France, the majority of women migrants are financially dependent on their husbands.

One of the ways in which migrant women can achieve some degree of economic independence is through working illegally in the sex industry. Beyala's figure of the migrant prostitute is an interesting one. Like Beyala's prostitutes living in Africa, the France-based version appears to exercise a certain degree of control over her own destiny. Prostitutes such as Eve-Marie (*AS*) and Aminata (*PPB* and *MAA*) seem to demonstrate independence and resilience. Indeed, Gallimore goes so far as to read Beyala's prostitute as 'une figure positive grâce à sa fonction subversive. Elle peut exploiter sa situation marginale à son profit, refuser l'asservissement et se libérer de l'emprise sexuelle' [a positive figure thanks to her subversive function. She can exploit her marginal situation to her own ends, refuse subjugation and liberate herself from the grip of sex].[31] If this is indeed the case, then Beyala's fictional portrayals of migrant sex workers in France appear to challenge the received view of prostitutes as victims, and to confirm the view of organizations such as Cabiria who claim that, in French political discourse, the emphasis on the victimization of migrant women prostitutes presents a misleading picture and deflects the public's attention from the real issues they face. In response to this discourse of victimization, as Gill Allwood explains, Cabiria emphasizes 'the autonomy and rational decision making of third world women migrating to Western industrialised nations to such an extent that the possibility of any form of manipulation, oppression or abuse appears to be excluded'.[32] While, as Allwood implies, it is difficult to obtain a clear and undistorted picture of migrant prostitution in France, Beyala's novels offer a less biased – albeit fictional – account and one which, I would argue, is more complex than that suggested by Gallimore. For example, although Aminata in the 'Loukoum' novels is initially presented as self-confident, independent and living in a large apartment, the reader soon discovers that her life is managed by a pistol-wielding pimp named Monsieur Mohammed. The prostitute's position is an ambiguous one that lies between autonomy and dependence. To a certain extent, then, she epitomizes the ambiguous positioning of the migrant woman: on the hinge between integration and marginality in France.

Social positioning for second-generation migrants is very different from that of their mothers. In Beyala's fiction, the character who most successfully negotiates different sets of cultural meanings is the ten-year-old boy narrator, Mamadou Traoré, nicknamed 'Loukoum'. As the son of Malian Muslim parents, growing up in France in the late 1980s–1990s, Loukoum is constantly subjected to a wealth of cultural influences from all over the globe: particularly from sub-Saharan Africa and France, but also, of course, though the media, from North America. Indeed, the influence of North American culture is seen to affect other members of the Traoré family, with Soumana dreaming of becoming a film star like Grace Kelly (*PPB*, p. 92) and Loukoum's biological mother, Aminata, listing Frank Sinatra as one of 'nos grands hommes' [our great men], along with Mitterrand, De Gaulle, Senghor, Alain Delon and Martin Luther King (*PPB*, p. 210; *LPPB*, p. 146).[33] Although born in Mali, Loukoum was brought to France at a young age and, as such, his own gender identity is, to a certain extent, constructed around media images of Western masculinity. As mentioned in the previous chapter, Abdou claims that '[Loukoum] répugne à mettre la djellaba. Il veut des costumes comme ceux de Stallone, exactement les mêmes' (*PPB*, p. 198) [[Loukoum] is reluctant to put on his *djellaba*. He wants clothes like those of Stallone, exactly the same (*LPPB*, pp. 137–38)]. The reference to Stallone is an apposite one, highlighting not only the influence of Hollywood cinema on second-generation immigrant youth culture, but also emphasizing the way in which males of immigrant origin – like Loukoum and Stallone – are forced to consciously construct images of socially acceptable masculinity.[34] On the other hand, Loukoum has also inherited cultural codes from his parents and, as a Muslim eldest son, from his father in particular. Although Abdou claims that Loukoum is reluctant to put on a djellaba, when they go to the mosque Loukoum seems proud to be wearing it and even emphasizes the fact that it is the same as his father's (*PPB*, p. 80; *LPPB*, p. 53). For Loukoum, the opposing masculinities represented by the Stallone-style suit and the traditional djellaba do not appear to generate conflict for his own gender identity.

What is unique about Loukoum is the way in which he manipulates his presumed knowledge of both majority ethnic and African cultural systems to his own advantage. For example, his rejection of Madame Saddock is ostensibly based on her lack of knowledge about marriage in Africa: 'Les mariages en Afrique, elle sait pas c'que c'est. Elle comprend rien à notre système de vie' (*PPB*, p. 117) [African marriages – she doesn't have a clue what they're all about. She doesn't know the first thing about the way we live (*LPPB*, p. 80)]; whereas, when Pierre Pelletier asks him what Mali is like, he answers that he does not know because he left when he was too young to remember (*PPB*, p. 51; *LPPB*, p. 31). To a degree, though, Loukoum does feel trapped in his ethnicity, imagining marriage to his majority ethnic girlfriend, Lolita, as an escape road from his blackness (*MAA*, p. 81). He describes his father sweating using a majority ethnic joke ('comme une dinde à la veille de Noël' [like a turkey on Christmas eve] (*MAA*, p. 28)) yet comments on the exotic delight of eating a meal of sausages, green beans and potatoes at the house of his holiday hosts in Pompidou ('c'est tellement bon et tellement différent du maffé et du nfoufou que je me régale' [it's so good and so different from maffé and nfoufou that I stuff my face] (*MAA*, p. 45)), suggesting that the traditional French turkey is cultural capital of an exclusively metaphorical kind.[35]

Loukoum's metaphorical competence is evidence of what Mireille Rosello describes as his fluency in 'code switching (in and out of stereotypes) [which] becomes the language of a constant oscillation between inclusion and exclusion, playing with echoes of political clichés'.[36] In her reading of *Le petit prince de Belleville*, Rosello writes that Beyala's representation of immigrant identity is 'quite remarkable; it is never a principle of inclusion or exclusion by itself'.[37] Indeed, Loukoum's simultaneously inside and outside position is demonstrated in the opening lines of his narration:

> Je m'appelle Mamadou Traoré pour la gynécologie, Loukoum pour la civilisation. J'ai sept ans pour l'officiel, et dix saisons pour l'Afrique.

> C'était juste pour ne pas prendre de retard à l'école. D'ailleurs, je suis le plus grand de la classe, le plus fort aussi. Normal, puisque les Noirs sont plus forts que n'importe qui. C'est comme ça. (*PPB*, p. 6)
>
> [My name is Mamadou Traoré according to my birth certificate; in everyday use it is Loukoum. On official documents I am seven years old, but in Africa I would be ten seasons old. That was just so I wouldn't be put back in school. Besides, I am the tallest in my class, the strongest as well. Quite normal, since black people are stronger than anyone. That's the way it is.] (*LPPB*, pp. 1–2)

What this passage demonstrates is Loukoum's ability to manipulate racist stereotypes, an ability that requires a reasonable level of competence in the culture that generates the myth. Loukoum is the tallest and the strongest in the class because he is three years older than his classmates but the repetition of the racist cliché that blacks are physically stronger (and therefore closer to animals) than whites reveals his familiarity with racist mythology and also his ability to make a joke of it. Furthermore, his insistence that, 'C'est comme ça' undermines this supposed truth. If that really is the way it is, then there is no need for Loukoum to say so.[38] The prefatory quotation to the present chapter makes a similar point. Here, Loukoum suggests that living in France has made him no longer a 'vrai Nègre', suggesting that his blackness has become contaminated, diluted or in some way modified by the experience of exile. 'Un vrai Nègre' is, of course, a meaningless term that harks back to the racist theories of the dangers of miscegenation discussed above. It represents what Said dismisses as 'the silliness of affirming the "purity" of an essential essence'.[39] It also temporarily positions Loukoum outside his ethnic origin since it suggests some kind of objective definition of what 'un vrai Nègre' is. The mention of 'un vrai Nègre' also recalls Senghor's concept of Negritude, which is critiqued throughout Beyala's fiction as an essentializing discourse.

Beyala plays with the concept of 'métissage culturel' that was so central to Senghor's philosophy of Negritude. Just as she criticizes ethnic essentialism, she is also careful to maintain an ironic distance from Senghor's view of cultural hybridity. In an interview with Rangira Gallimore, Beyala explains:

> La négritude a été pour les Nègres, un lieu de retrouvaille; elle nous a permis de prendre conscience de nos valeurs [...] Cette époque est

aujourd'hui révolue. Cependant elle m'est utile dans mon écriture. Si on trouve que j'ai déstructuré la société africaine, c'est d'abord parce que la négritude l'avait structurée sur des bases certes idéologiques et fantastiques.⁴⁰

[For blacks, Negritude was a place to find ourselves; it allowed us to become aware of our values [...] That time has now passed. But it's useful in my writing. If people find that I have deconstructed African society, it's first and foremost because Negritude had constructed it on bases which were certainly ideological and fantastical.]

Negritude was very much an offshoot of the French colonial policy of assimilation. Having been educated in the French educational system, thinkers such as Senghor and Césaire proposed a form of cultural identification that promoted the blending of African diasporic and French cultural influences. In *Assèze l'Africaine*, Sorraya has a mixed-race boyfriend named Océan who is a musician: 'Sa musique? Mettez dans une boîte de sardines James Brown, Johnny Halliday, Cloclo [Claude François], un zeste de balafon, mélangez, et soukouss' [What's his music like? Put into a box of sardines James Brown, Johnny Halliday, Claude François, a zest of balafon, mix, and soukouss] (*AA*, p. 114).⁴¹ Drawing on musical styles from black America, Africa and France, Océan's music represents the kind of cultural blending advocated by Senghor. Indeed, Océan's function as a parody of Negritudinist rhetoric is confirmed when, talking about his music, he tells Assèze that 'Senghor l'a prédit, le métissage c'est l'avenir!' [Senghor predicted it: mixing is the future!] (p. 115). The fact that Océan's dreams of becoming a famous musician are never realized confirms Beyala's view of Negritude as a fantastical basis for African society.

It appears, then, that if Beyala is promoting hybridity, it is distinct from 'métissage'. This may explain why all Beyala's mixed-race figures are presented in a negative light. When Assèze comes across Océan in the Paris metro having last seen him in Africa, he brings her the bad news that her mother and brother have both died of malaria. He then persuades her to move in with him in exchange for 3,000 French francs, after which she spends her time busking for him by telling stories, and sweet-talking record producers in an attempt to secure him a recording contract. In short, their relationship is little different from that of a prostitute and her pimp. This point is emphasized when Assèze challenges her lover for doing nothing all day. Océan's reply is that 'L'Afrique doit se prostituer si elle veut s'en sortir' [Africa has to prostitute herself if she's going to survive] (*AA*, p. 308).

What Océan's response also demonstrates is a level of contempt for the African continent, a view echoed by Beyala's 'métis' characters. In *Comment cuisiner*, Aïssatou's love-rival is a mixed-race woman named Bijou, about whom the narrator comments, 'Bijou me regarde comme si j'étais un macaque. D'entrée de jeu, elle rétablit la moitié de l'océan Atlantique qui sépare les Métis des Nègres, autant dire des sauvages va-nu-pieds des Sept Merveilles du monde' [Bijou looked at me as if I was a monkey. From the start she reestablished the half of the Atlantic ocean that separates the mixed-race from the blacks, in other words the barefooted savages from the Seven Wonders of the world] (*CCMA*, p. 106). From this the reader infers that Bijou is a 'domienne' [from one of the French overseas departments] and therefore a bona fide French citizen, unlike Aïssatou. As an Antillean, Bijou does not identify herself as black and distances herself from Africa: 'Paraît qu'ils mangent des singes, ces Nègres!'[Seems they eat monkeys, those blacks!] (*CCMA*, p. 108).

In the light of the above, Loukoum's remark that he is not 'un vrai Nègre' becomes more ambiguous. Is he lamenting the loss of his blackness or is he proudly asserting his hybridity? It is worth noting that Loukoum makes this remark in response to a white man's (Monsieur Michel) fear that France will be invaded by blacks. Hiding behind essentialism can be read as a means of self-defence, as was demonstrated by Beyala herself in the 'Beyala Affair'. Like Beyala, Loukoum is positioned inside and outside both his own and majority ethnic French culture. His relationships to both Africa and France are characterized by ambivalence. Moreover, the reader's uncertainty about whether the narrator is joking or not relies precisely on Loukoum's 'in-betweenness' and his ability to negotiate different sets of cultural stereotypes and norms. As his father, Abdou comments, 'Il [Loukoum] passe sans s'inquiéter d'un univers à l'autre' (*PPB*, p. 206) [He passes with no worries from one universe to the other (*LPPB*, p. 144)].

Code switching, as we have seen, is a strategy also used by Beyala herself, notably in her public performances when she manipulates racist mythology to her own ends. In *Lettre d'une Afro-française*, she appropriates the racial cliché, 'Je suis noire et le rire est mon moteur' [I am black and laughter is what drives me] only to defuse it with sarcasm: 'Ah, ah, ah, rions donc! Moquons-nous des [sic] ces noirs américains qui réussissent à cause de la couleur de leur peau!' [Ha, ha, ha, let's laugh about it! Let's mock those black Americans who succeed because of the colour of their skin!] (*LAFC*, p. 29). What we see here is a subtle manipulation of racial stereotypes: one moment blacks are essentialized as the kind of laughing caricature seen in the Banania advertising campaign, thereby apparently confirming racial difference; the next, Beyala seems to be expressing her contempt for positive discrimination, a policy that is grounded in recognition of that same racial difference. The effect of the juxtaposition is to undermine ethnic essentialism. What Rosello identifies in the case of Loukoum is then, I would argue, also a feature of Beyala's personal discourse: she plays with racial stereotypes and, conversely, with the concept of authenticity.[42] It can also be read as the fluctuating relationship between mimicry and mockery that characterizes ambivalence in a (post-)colonial situation. As Ashcroft et al. explain, 'mimicry is never very far from mockery, since it can appear to parody whatever it mimics'.[43] According to Bhabha, 'the discourse of mimicry is constructed around an *ambivalence*; in order to be effective, mimicry must continually produce its slippage, its excess, its difference'.[44] This, I would suggest, is the only version of 'in-betweenness' that is not intrinsically flawed in Beyala's fiction. Whereas ambivalent individuals such as Ibrahim in *Les Honneurs perdus* function on a superficial level, his negotiation of the French cultural space is based on contradictory values and a retreat into a traditionalist version of Islam. His dream is to 'voyager sans frontières' [travel without borders] (*HP*, p. 313) but he is still largely contained by his ethnicity. Apart from Beyala herself, then, Loukoum is the only competent code-switcher. His ambivalence is a constant strategy for survival rather than an unconscious coping mechanism; only he is a successful 'in-between'.

Indeed, Loukoum's code switching dramatizes the 'contrapuntal' awareness that Said describes in 'Reflections on Exile':

> Seeing 'the entire world as a foreign land' makes possible originality of vision. Most people are principally aware of one culture, one setting, one home; exiles are aware of at least two, and this plurality of vision gives rise to an awareness of simultaneous dimensions, an awareness that – to borrow a phrase from music – is *contrapuntal*.
>
> For an exile, habits of life, expression, or activity in the new environment inevitably occur against the memory of these things in another environment.[45]

Although all Beyala's characters experience exile as the clash of two cultures, two settings, two homes, only Loukoum manages to perform in both cultural spaces at the same time. As Alain-Philippe Durand suggests, a character such as Abdou remains fixed in the imaginary (and imagined) space of his origins.[46] Others such as Soumana, Sorraya and Aïssatou fail to overcome what they perceive to be the insurmountable gap between the imagined spaces of 'here' and 'there'. Each of their responses is grounded in a monolithic approach to differences between cultures. Loukoum, on the other hand, exercises the plurality of vision that is celebrated by Said as a positive condition of exile and one that relies on an ability to negotiate and therefore to understand the mythification of cultural difference.

I began this chapter with a discussion of Beyala's personal struggle with locational labelling and her recent decision to opt for the ambivalent 'Afro-française'. Odile Cazenave takes Beyala's 'Afro-Frenchness' one step further by choosing to include her among what she terms 'Afro-Parisian writers', i.e. combining 'the cultural influence of both a continent and a metropolitan space, Africa and Paris, in the writing of new identities'.[47] Dominic Thomas, on the other hand, questions the usefulness of these kinds of categories, suggesting instead a transnational approach to migrant literatures.[48] Thomas is right to ask, 'at what point, then, does Beyala stop being a Cameroonian novelist and become an Afro-Parisian one?' As he points out, Beyala's fiction establishes 'on-going associations between the two spaces [of Cameroon and Paris]'.[49] Despite their differences, Cazenave and Thomas both highlight the importance of another space beyond the geographical binary that surrounds the hyphen. For Beyala, I would suggest, this space is characterized by what Bhabha terms the 'ambivalence of mimicry', through which myths of cultural difference are simultaneously articulated, challenged and reformulated.[50]

While the French Republic struggles with what have traditionally been seen as the competing notions of multiculturalism and hospitality, migrant individuals equally struggle to locate themselves in France.[51] Despite Beyala's public declarations of her Frenchness and her allegiance to the Republic, as a migrant woman she is forced to resist constant attempts to deny her access to the 'centre' and relocate her to the margins. Of course, as a francophone writer, Beyala will never be totally incorporated into the canon of French literature, despite her high media profile and her prize-winning success, since, as she reminds us in the epigraph to *Les Honneurs perdus*,

'Le Français est francophone mais la francophonie n'est française' [The French are francophone but Francophonie is not French].[52] This explains the many contradictions in the way Beyala articulates her own identity: like Loukoum she constantly shifts her ideology and her speaking position in response to different situations. For Said, this kind of performance can be read a positive outcome of the exile's contrapuntal awareness: 'there is [...] a particular sense of achievement in *acting* as if one were at home wherever one happens to be'.[53] But it can also, as we have seen with some of Beyala's characters, represent a rather superficial response to the difficulties of exile. The next chapter will consider further the ways in which Beyala and her characters express their identities through performance and improvisation, whether it be conforming to cultural norms, disrupting those same norms, making it up or 'faking it'.

CHAPTER FIVE

Performing Identities

> Je cours me métamorphoser parce que j'en ai assez d'être celle que je suis.[1]
>
> [I rush to transform myself because I've had enough of being who I am.]

Quoting Chinese-Canadian writer Fred Wah, Roger Bromley writes: '"When you're not 'pure' you just make it up" [...] "Making it up", faking it even, is precisely what so much cultural hybridity is about; the inventions and innovations of those "living in the borderlands".'[2] As we have seen in previous chapters, much of Beyala's fiction debunks the myth of authenticity by playing a strategic game of rejection and recuperation. If, as we have concluded, 'authenticity' is an empty signifier, than the concept of 'faking it' might also be problematic in the context of migration, since it implies some kind of authentic identity that is either aspired to by the faker, or is hidden behind the disguise: a fake is always defined in relation to the version presumed 'authentic' or 'real'. However, if we interpret faking it as posing as a socially acceptable version of oneself, then faking it and making it up are useful metaphors for migrant subjectivities. Indeed, they both describe a reaction to two different sets of cultural anxieties. First, the experience of being 'out of sync' generates a need to constantly reinvent oneself in response to the majority ethnic population's attempts to prescribe migrant identity. This leads to an improvisation or performance of identity, often according to an unknown set of rules or expectations. One way of responding to rules that are unfamiliar is precisely to 'make it up'. This chapter will argue that the concept of improvisation or 'making it up' is central to an understanding of both Beyala's fictional staging of the migrant condition and the way in which she performs her own identity.

The second source of anxiety for the migrant individual is the pressure to reassure friends and family back 'home' that migration has indeed led to the anticipated social improvement and economic gain. Attempts to provide evidence to friends and relatives of an individual's successful migration can often quite legitimately be described as 'faking it', as Beyala's fiction reveals. In *Amours sauvages* Eve-Marie left Africa, she tells the reader, because God appeared to be more generous in Europe, but she soon discovers that this generosity does not extend to immigrants. The harsh reality of Eve-Marie's life as a prostitute living in Belleville is, however, temporarily erased in the wedding photograph she sends back to her family in Cameroon. In the photograph, 'des tentures rouges et candélabres donnent à l'ensemble une luxe d'opérette' [red drapes and candelabras give the whole thing the sumptuousness of a light opera] and the French President, presenting her with a huge bunch of roses, is shaking her by the hand. As if the reference to the French President was not enough to put into question the authenticity of the photograph, the narrator's commentary draws attention to the fact it is a fake: 'Je l'ai envoyée au pays parce que je ne voulais pas qu'on sache dans quelle misère je vivais. D'ailleurs personne ne soupçonna jamais que la photo avait été faite chez M. Sallam, spécialiste en trucage' [I sent it back home because I didn't want them to know what poverty I was living in. In any case, nobody ever suspected that the photo had been made up by Mr Sallam, a specialist in fakery] (*AS*, p. 24). So, in what might be read as an ironic reference to the fake passports bought for enormous sums by Africans desperate to migrate to what they see as the promised land of Europe, Eve-Marie creates another form of fake identity card to justify and legitimize her presence in France. In this instance her feigned inclusion is represented by none other than the President himself. Similarly, Tanga's father used to have photographs taken of himself in front of papier-mâché monuments of Paris, which he would send back to his village as symbols of his success (*TTT*, p. 144; *YNT*, p. 97). The difference lies in the fact that he never left Africa; his migration, like his daughter's, took place only in his head.

Photographs appear in a number of Beyala's novels. Tapoussière is portrayed escaping reality in a photo-novel (*PFR*, p. 140) but her book has missing pages, torn out for use as toilet paper during a bout of diarrhoea. In *C'est le soleil qui m'a brûlée* Ateba reads romantic photo-stories, imagining herself as the heroine, in direct contrast to the abusive relationship she experiences with Jean Zepp. Ateba also looks at photographs in an attempt to make a connection with her dead mother, Betty. In one picture, Betty is one of a group of children, all dressed for their first holy communion: 'Immortalisés sur papier glacé, ils [les enfants] deviennent des anges, à l'instar de ces enfants qui meurent avant de perdre leur innocence. Et, derrière leurs regards candides, la grimace douloureuse de l'enfance trop tôt disparue' (*CSB*, p. 88) [Immortalised on glossy paper, they become angels much like children who die before they've lost their innocence. And behind their guileless looks, the painful grimaces of a childhood that's gone too soon (*SHL*, p. 57)]. These photographs, like those of Eve-Marie's wedding and Tanga's father's travels, represent false or incomplete records, preferred versions of subjectivity, and point to Beyala's emphasis on the constructed (i.e. 'fake') nature of identity and life stories, including her own.[3] As she writes in the epigraph to *Assèze l'Africaine*, 'une biographie est une paire de lunettes noires. Face à la vérité, tout le monde est aveugle' [a biography is a pair of dark glasses. Faced with the truth, everyone is blind].

Dark glasses conceal the face of the wearer and also, Beyala suggests, blind them to the truth. They therefore act as a two-way mask, distorting both the subject and the object of the gaze in both directions. One of the most prevalent metaphors in Beyala's novels is that of the mask, which, like masks themselves, cannot be reduced to a single interpretation. In *Les Arbres en parlent encore*, the narrator recalls her father's much-admired ability to hide his thoughts: Assanga Djuli (Edène's father) 'était un vieillard dans le sens éton du terme, c'est-à-dire qu'une lumière magnétique lui conférait le pouvoir de masquer ses vraies pensées' [was an elder in the Eton sense of the term, that is, a magnetic light bestowed on him the power to mask his true thoughts] (*APE*, p. 7). For the Eton people, a metaphorical mask of this kind confers distinction on its wearer. Yet masking the truth does not always signify an individual worthy of respect. Beyala's fictional masks have different functions, reflecting the fact that, in a sub-Saharan African context, masks are rich in meaning. Masquerades are complex performances by men wearing masks made from a variety of materials, the significance of which varies greatly according to context. While the masks themselves are extremely important, once outside the context of the performance they lose their meaning, often being reduced to exhibits in tourist-explorers' collections in museums or private homes. Art historian John Picton explains that sometimes the mask serves to disguise the wearer, sometimes to protect him. In any event, Picton stresses that, 'in masquerade it is the event, the performance that is paramount'.[4] This chapter traces the performances of identity in Beyala's novels (fakery, improvisation, masquerade and mimicry) from Africa to France, and will compare these fictional performances with those of Beyala herself.

Beyala's third novel, *Seul le diable le savait*, frequently draws attention to the way in which identification is based on the ways in which the body presents – or performs – itself.[5] The novel opens with a description of the narrator, Mégri's, life as consisting of two things: the ability to forget and her wardrobe of dresses, 'qui camouflent mon corps et établissent le lien nécessaire entre moi et les autres' [which camouflage my body and establish the necessary link between me and the others] (*SDS*, p. 9). Here, clothes maketh woman, acting as both protective mask and identificatory marker, linking her to her social and gender group. Although her red hair often has the opposite function, leading to her persecution at school and a degree of social alienation, Mégri has learnt how to perform within what society deems to be a framework of normativity. When she decides she wants to seduce L'Etranger, she stuffs her bra with cotton wool and, with the help of some make-up, creates 'le masque idéal de séduction' [the ideal mask of seduction] (p. 67). Similarly, as a child, Ateba hopes her mother will teach her 'l'art de [se] déguiser' (*CSB*, p. 115) [the art of disguising [her]self (*SHL*, p. 77)]. Of course, 'se déguiser' also means to 'get dressed up' in French, pointing to the performance of femininity that a girl learns from watching her mother: Ateba will learn to dress up in the disguise of her prescribed gender. Likewise, Tanga dreams of wearing a white dress with flowers in her hair. This, she believes will make her a woman (*TTT*, p. 74; *YNT*, p. 46).

Throughout Beyala's African novels there are frequent references to the ways in which African women are expected to perform their prescribed gender role. Saïda's father, horrified that his wife has given birth to a daughter, invents the story of his baby having been magically transformed from a boy into a girl (*HP*, p. 25). However, as soon as her biological sex is established, Saïda is obliged to assume the woman's role of cooking, cleaning and holding on to her virginity. Unsurprisingly, biology and gender identity are inseparable for the residents of Couscous (New Bell), just as they are in Beyala's other African locations. Indeed, Beyala's relentless critique of the patriarchal structures of African societies leads Ambroise Kom to accuse her of pandering to stereotypes (of men as holding power and women as oppressed). Ironically, Kom's accusation leads him to into another stereotype when he claims that, contrary to Beyala's portrayal, 'en

Afrique, le prétendu pouvoir mâle n'est souvent qu'une mise en scène, l'homme n'étant, la plupart du temps, que le porte-parole d'un montage dont la femme est le cerveau' [in Africa, the so-called male power is often nothing more than an illusion, the man being, most of the time, only the spokesman for a whole picture in which the woman is the brains].[6] I would suggest that Kom's conclusion is based on a hostile misreading of Beyala's fiction. While he is right to highlight the gender polarization of her early novels, his accusation of false Manicheanism oversimplifies her agenda. For example, in *C'est le soleil qui m'a brûlée* Beyala reverses traditional binaries of masculine and feminine by associating women with change and men with inertia. Here her fictional world is indeed Manichean, but deliberately so.[7]

Beyala's examination of gender roles is not always presented seriously. She sometimes satirizes gender normativity, invoking supernatural women characters who are treated differently because of their failure to conform to human corporeal norms. For example, La Prêtresse-goitrée [the goitred Priestess] is considered an honorary man and allowed to attend men's meetings because, the narrator informs us, she has four eyes and sold her fertility to the forces of evil (*SDS*, p. 81). On the other hand, Akouma, the gorilla woman, claims she wishes she had a tail, in a humorous nod to Freud's concept of penis envy (*APE*, p. 312). Beyala's novels also play with the concepts of masquerade and performance, describing some of the supernatural happenings in *Seul le diable le savait* taking place on a theatre stage while an onlooker asks, 'Que signifie cette mascarade?' [What is the meaning of this masquerade?]. In response to this question, L'Etranger, who appears to be directing the proceedings, offers a rather empty reply: 'Qu'est-ce que la vie sinon une mascarade?' [What is life if not a masquerade?] (*SDS*, p. 84). The playful way in which these concepts are invoked in the African novels prepares the ground for the parodic performativity that is developed in the more recent fiction set in France.

In Beyala's Africa, masquerade pervades all levels of society, as L'Etranger's empty response suggests. Masks are not exclusively reserved for women in Beyala's novels; they signify the imitative nature of both femininity and masculinity. A village chief describes his life as a series of different masks, each marking a different stage of normative masculinity: from obedient child to seductive adolescent to husband and father to chief. The suggestion is that each mask is a copy of one that has already been worn by another boy, another man, another chief. The mimetic nature of this masquerade exposes what Beyala presents as the loss of self through conformity to social and gender norms. The chief describes this as 'ce malentendu avec moi-même' [this misunderstanding with myself] (*SDS*, p. 162). Being in a state of misunderstanding with oneself is characteristic of Beyala's masquerade. Masks only fall when protagonists stop performing society's script. For example, when she is reunited with her long-lost sister, Magdalena, Mégri repeats her dead friend Laetitia's feminist ideals, telling Magda 'tu as arraché mon masque, tu es devenue ma soeur' [you have torn off my mask. You have become my sister] (*SDS*, p. 254).

So, Beyala's Africa-based novels abound in metaphors of masking, simulation, fakery and disguise. As we have seen, Beyala deploys these metaphors not to refer to traditional performances of masking, but rather to critique the socially constructed nature of identity, particularly gender identity, following a line of thought that began with Simone de Beauvoir and can be traced through to the recent work of Judith Butler. Beauvoir is an important intertext in Beyala's fiction: a rewriting of her famous maxim occurs in the lines, 'on ne naît pas noir, on le devient' (*TTT*, p. 53) [You aren't born black, you become black (*YNT*, p. 32)], building on Beauvoir's analysis of the social construction of femininity to include racial identity. Beauvoir is also cited as one of the influences on Mégri's feminist friend, Laetitia, in *Seul le diable le savait* (*SDS*, p. 197). Although the more recent work of Judith Butler is not a direct influence on Beyala's work, the latter's emphasis on performance in masquerade, combined with a feminist agenda, makes an interesting link between the two. As I mentioned in the Introduction, Butler's ideas have made few inroads into postcolonial studies, despite her importance in the fields of feminist theory, cultural studies and queer theory, all of which have contributed to the development of postcolonial theory. There are, however, two brief examples of how Butler might be used in the postcolonial field in the groundbreaking studies of Carole Boyce Davies and Graham Huggan, both of whom have been important influences on my own work.[8]

For Butler, 'gender is in no way a stable identity or locus of agency from which various acts proceed; rather, it is an identity tenuously constituted in time – an identity instituted through a *stylized repetition of acts*'.[9] Drawing on J. L. Austin's analysis of speech acts, Butler uses 'performative' to refer to acts that perform that which they articulate. It is through performative acts that assertions of authority and normativity are made. Thus normative gender roles are asserted through the reiteration – or citation – of what have become representational conventions. Performativity requires repetition since it is only in the recognition of a previously coded act that the performative action succeeds. This is because, as Butler writes:

> [it] echoes prior actions, and *accumulates the force of authority through the repetition and citation of a prior, authoritative set of practices*. What this means, then, is that a performative 'works' to the extent that *it draws on and covers over* the constitutive convention by which it is mobilised.[10]

Austin's theory of the performativity of language has had important implications not just for feminist theory but also for the development of the more recent field of performance studies. As Susan Leigh Foster explains, performance studies takes from Austin the view that 'the enactment of a generalised cultural script will implicate the individual in juridical and political networks of meaning that exercise a determining effect on identity'.[11] By extension, then, the postcolonial subject's identity will be affected by the extent to which she engages with the cultural script of colonialist discourse. In other words, migrant identity is determined by the way in which the migrant performs the role that the host society expects of her.

According to Butler, 'what is called gender identity is a performative accomplishment compelled by social sanction and taboo. In its very character as performative resides the possibility of contesting its reified status.'[12] This means that the performative is potentially – but by no means always – subversive. In her recent essay, 'Critically Queer', Butler returns to the question of drag, which has been adopted by many readers of her earlier work, *Gender Trouble*, as the exemplar of contestatory performativity. Here she asserts that while the hyperbolic nature of drag does highlight the 'taken-for-granted quality' of gender normativity, it does not necessarily subvert these norms in the process.[13] Butler's emphasis on the hyperbolic nature of masquerade echoes that of another key theorist of gender performance, Mary Anne Doane, who, following Joan Riviere, identifies masquerade as a 'hyperbolisation of the accoutrements of femininity', epitomized in cinema by the figure of the *femme fatale*. For Doane, the *femme fatale* always functions as a subversive figure of masquerade because she performs her femininity in order to subvert the law.[14] While her appearance, like that of the drag queen, hyperbolizes gender norms, the *femme fatale*'s actions do exactly the opposite: she looks 'like a woman' but behaves 'like a man'. Of course, the same could be said of male drag artists who rarely convince their audience that they are women. The difference turns around what Butler identifies as the complicated relationship between the 'original' and the 'imitation'.[15] According to societal norms, the *femme fatale* is not 'faking it', although her performance implicitly exposes the fabrication that is femininity. The drag queen, on the other hand, is obviously not a woman according to established gender norms.

There are a number of individuals in Beyala's fiction whose external appearance challenges gender norms. The transsexual prostitute Tatiana is described by Loukoum as a kind of artificial woman: 'Ce n'est pas une vraie fille, bien sûr, vu qu'elle a des seins en postiche et qu'elle peut pas faire des mômes' (*PPB*, p. 13) [Of course she's not really a girl, considering she has falsies and she can't have kids (*LPPB*, p. 6)]. Loukoum's rejection of Tatiana as a woman is, of course, overly simplistic: many women cannot have children and/or have false breasts, but his seemingly naive words signal the arbitrary association society makes between biological sex and gender performance. Despite living and working as a woman, Tatiana remains a man – in Loukoum's eyes – simply because she has a penis. On the other hand, Loukoum makes a similar condemnation of majority ethnic feminist Madame Saddock: 'Je crois que cette femme-là, c'est pas une vraie nana. A parler comme ça à un mec, avec sa cigarette dans sa bouche et qui ne lui fait même pas honte!' (*PPB*, p. 104) [I think that woman isn't a real bird. To talk that way to a guy, with a cigarette in her mouth and it doesn't even embarrass her! (*LPPB*, p. 71; translation modified)].[16] For different reasons both Tatiana and Madame Saddock are rejected by Loukoum as women who do not perform their gender as they should.

The novels also emphasize the way in which colonialism established a set of racial 'norms', according to which black skin marked its wearer as an inferior human being. The legacy of scientific racism has been an internalization of racial hierarchies among some black individuals. Beyala exposes the absurdity of this situation through her unsympathetic portraits of blacks who want to be white. The prostitute Mademoiselle Etoundi's attempts to lactify herself by wearing a blonde wig and bleaching her skin are mocked in the descriptions of the posters she has in her room, among them an advertisement for Omo washing powder with the slogan 'Devenez plus blanc que blanc avec Omo' [Become whiter than white with Omo] (*PFR*, p. 60). Like Butler's use of drag, Beyala's portrait of Mlle Etoundi parodies the performative accomplishment of colonialist discourse: what colonization proclaimed to be the inferiority of blacks has become reified, so much so that some black individuals perform whiteness in a attempt to be identified differently. Because blacks and whites are not essentially different, the various acts of racial difference create the idea of racial difference. Lactification, then, highlights the artificial basis on which racism was based but, rather than challenging it, it allows it to be perpetuated, as Fanon so persuasively demonstrates in *Peau noire, masques blancs*.[17]

As a form of colonial imitation, lactification epitomizes the ambivalent nature of masquerade. Writing about gender masking, Harrow observes that, 'the difficulty lies in knowing when the masquerade [of femininity] is self-consciously adopted by the woman as a means of manipulating men, or when it is unconsciously assumed, and thus is "false" to the woman's desire; when the mask cannot be seen as separate from what lies underneath it'.[18] For Doane, however, there is no difference between 'genuine womanliness' and masquerade. In her influential essay on female spectatorship, Doane argues that masquerade always 'involves a realignment of femininity, the recovery, or more accurately, simulation of the missing gap or distance'.[19] In other words, masquerade risks relocating the performer – from the spectator's point of view – within the very discourse she is attempting to subvert. Thus, in a postcolonial context, what began as an act of resistance may be read as a performance of assimilation. This is Harrow's conclusion in his reading of Beyala. Criticizing her for having plagiarized (badly) and for producing 'Hillbilly' images of Africa in her more recent work, he reduces Beyala's fictional masquerades to the level of assimilative pantomime.[20] By flaunting the exoticism of herself and her characters, Beyala could indeed be read as a kind of postcolonial caricature, and Harrow is not the only one to suggest this. However, if we keep Butler's and Doane's performative figures in mind, it might be more useful to think about Beyala's masquerades in relation to the figures of the drag artist or the *femme fatale*, since both imply the imitative structure of identification. The difference, as we have already discussed, is that the *femme fatale*, like Bhabha's colonial mimic, represents both parody and subversion.

Colonial mimicry, according to Bhabha's definition, 'conceals no identity behind its mask' because it repeats only partial presence, partial representations of both colonizer and colonized.[21] As we saw in Chapter 4, it is not until the publication of *Le petit prince de Belleville* that explicitly mimetic voices begin to emerge in Beyala's fiction, particularly in the characterization of Loukoum. To a certain extent, this shift to parodic mimicry reflects Beyala's growing confidence as a migrant writer. But, as I have already suggested, the shift does not represent a sudden change of direction for Beyala, since the emphasis on masquerade in the early African novels prepares the ground for the colonial mimicry that emerges in the migrant novels later on. In other words, the seeds of Beyala's mimicry are sown as early as in her first novel, *C'est le soleil qui m'a brûlée*, in the unmasking of contemporary society as a performance of socially constructed hypocrisy. During the party organized for the circumcision of the neighbour, Etoundi's son, the guests are presented as voyeuristic gossips interested only in the possibility of free food and wine rather than in this supposedly sacred ceremony of initiation into manhood. At this stage in the novel, Ateba the protagonist is unable to see the crowd for what it is: '[Ses yeux] ne verront que lorsque la mascarade s'étiolera sous la voûte sombre des tonnelles' (*CSB*, p. 38) [Her eyes will only see when the masquerade begins to slacken off underneath the dark vault of the bowers (*SHL*, p. 19)].

Beyala's Africa-based narrators also draw attention to the artificially constructed nature of identity through the use of the vocabulary of filmmaking and the theatre. While a man flirts with her at Ekassi's funeral party, Ateba remembers a quotation from Molière's *Le bourgeois gentilhomme*.[22] The memory prompts her to reflect on the theatricality of existence:

> Chacun au QG joue son rôle, et tout le monde joue à la perfection [...] Sauf elle. Ateba Léocadie doit faire son devoir, elle doit toujours faire son devoir, elle doit être fidèle à son devoir. Mais c'est quoi encore, son rôle? Elle l'avait presque oublié en pensant au rôle des autres. Ça y est, Ateba Léocadie se souvient, elle est la femme, la maîtresse, la femme de l'homme. Elle a trouvé son rôle, elle se sent presque mieux, elle devient tout à coup deux Ateba. La femme et l'actrice. L'ordinaire et l'extraordinaire. (*CSB*, pp. 145–46)

> [Everyone in the QG plays his role, and everyone plays it to perfection [...] Except her. Ateba Léocadie must do her duty; she must always do her duty, she must be faithful to her duty. But what is it then, this role of hers? She had almost forgotten it thinking about the roles of others. That's it. Ateba Léocadie remembers – she is woman,

mistress, man's woman. She has found her role, she almost feels better; suddenly she becomes two Atebas. The woman and the actress. The ordinary and the extraordinary. (*SHL*, pp. 98–99)]

Here the text implies that Ateba's decision to play the role of woman is a matter of choice. Having said that, the text later warns of the danger of such a performance when, having gone home with this man, she looks at herself in the mirror and no longer recognizes what she sees: 'Elle s'est perdue de vue à trop jouer la farce' (*CSB*, p. 149). [She's lost sight of herself through having played the farce too long (*SHL*, p. 101)]. While such comments seem to confirm the existence of some kind of true individual identity (represented in this novel by the figure of 'Moi' [Me]), at the same time the emphasis on role-playing undermines the notion of a natural gender identity. In other words, self and gender are not one and the same. Like the chief I mentioned earlier, Ateba can wear the appropriate gender mask when she needs to, but at the risk of losing sight of herself. Controlled, strategic performance, on the other hand, is generally successful. When Ateba chooses to pose as a prostitute and avenge her friend Irène's death by killing a 'client', she uses her excessive femininity to commit a subversive act, thereby mimicking the performance of the *femme fatale*.

Elsewhere, cinematic terms and stage directions are used to increase the distance between reader and narrator and to reinforce the emphasis on performativity. In Beyala's erotic novel, Irène's hostess, Fatou, describes her role in her marriage to Ousmane as like that of an actress in a porn film. Their relationship, she says, is defined by 'le théâtre, le grotesque, la dépravation, la lasciveté sans âme, ces jeux pervers, excitants mais dangereux' [theatre, the grotesque, depravity, soulless lustfulness, exciting but dangerous games of perversion] (*FNFN*, p. 86). What this rather excessive example demonstrates is Beyala's interpretation of relationships as artificial performances. When Tapoussière is reunited with a man who claims to be her father, Onana Victoria-de-Logbaba, the narrative suddenly switches to dramatic dialogue, with Onana blaming Tapoussière's mother for his absence: '– Tout est de la faute d'Andela. (Grand Silence). Elle aurait pu attendre que je m'assagisse. (Très grand silence et voix montant crescendo.) Je l'aimais tendrement comme une rose du désert. Tu comprends? (Fin!)' [Everything is Andela's fault. (Long Silence). She could have waited for me to settle down. (Very long silence and rising crescendo voice.) I loved her tenderly like a desert rose. Do you understand? (The End!)] (*PFR*, p. 204). As well as highlighting

Onana's hypocrisy, this narrative switch signals the performativity of heterosexual relationships. Onana recites the lines that he thinks are expected of him in a fruitless attempt to reinvent himself as a better 'father'. The final irony emerges when the text reveals that he, like many others, is a fake, pretending to be Tapoussière's father in the hope that she will one day make him rich.[23]

References to filmmaking also emphasize the way in which Africa and its peoples have been constructed through the eyes of the colonizer. The distorting picture created through the lens of colonialism generates the myths and stereotypes of 'Africanness' discussed in Chapter 2. On one level, Beyala appears to reconfirm these stereotypes: her novels are filled with examples of Africans who are stupid, oversexed, lazy, etc. When she returns to her village from Douala, Assèze is struck by the smell of rotting avocados. The villagers tell her that they were advised to get hold of an 'avocat' [avocado/lawyer] to protect them from a cocoa company wanting to take over their land. The rather limp linguistic joke here is made initially at the expense of the villagers and could be read as reinforcing stereotypical notions of African stupidity (*AA*, pp. 129–30). Yet the avocado offensive is, in fact, successful since the cocoa company's vehicles are unable to cross the rotting fruit. Thus the stereotype is implied and then subverted, forcing the reader to reassess any received ideas she might have.

Stereotypes are cited by Beyala's narrators and characters. This is particularly evident in the 'Loukoum' novels where the eponymous narrator repeats one racist cliché after another. As we saw in the previous chapter, Loukoum opens his narration with the claim that 'les Noirs sont plus forts que n'importe quoi' (*PPB*, p. 6) [black people are stronger than anyone (*LPPB*, p. 2)]. Among his later generalizations are the statements that blacks are not intelligent (*PPB*, p. 52) ['Niggers aren't smart' (*LPPB*, p. 32)] and that immigrants are obsessed with sex (*PPB*, p. 198).[24] The frequent repetition of racist clichés about Africans by Africans causes the texts to undermine themselves, to 'decline the stereotype', to borrow Mireille Rosello's phrase. Rosello writes that 'declining a stereotype is a way of depriving it of its harmful potential by highlighting its very nature'.[25] When Sorraya tells Assèze that blacks are 'cons et paresseux' [stupid and lazy] (*AA*, p. 93), Assèze initially protests, reminding Sorraya that she too is black. The latter replies, 'Il y a Nègre et Nègre! Les vrais Nègres sont cons' [There are blacks and blacks! Real blacks are stupid] (*AA*, p. 93). The absurdity of Sorraya's division of blacks into 'blacks' and 'real blacks', underlined by the excessive repetition of 'Nègre', exposes the fallacy of racial hierarchy. After this second remark, however, Assèze chooses to remain silent, commenting that Sorraya probably knows best as she attends the French school (p. 94). Ultimately, this exchange positions Assèze (the narrator) in the role of what Rosello calls the 'reluctant witness', forced by the constraints of circumstance into what could be read as silent acquiescence.[26] At the same time, the reader also becomes a reluctant witness. Unable to intervene, the reader is forced to receive the onslaught of racist clichés, a position that again forces her to re-evaluate the stereotypes articulated by the characters against the more complex identities of the characters themselves.

Stereotypes, like gender, are performative. They rely on their own repeatability and repetition and are therefore self-perpetuating, as Rosello observes. For this reason, Beyala's decision to portray what some read as one-dimensional African characters does indeed risk repeating stereotypes and confirming them at the same time. The initial representation of Loukoum's father, Abdou, as an illiterate drunk who beats his wives and children could certainly be read in this way. However, I propose that what critics such as Kom and others dismiss as reductive, stereotypical representations of Africa and its peoples can more productively be read as demonstrations of the performative nature of stereotypes. Just as, according to Butler, drag 'implicitly reveals the imitative structure of gender itself – as well as its contingency', so Beyala's 'Hillbilly' Africans, as Harrow calls them, draw attention to the contingent and imitative nature of so-called 'African' identity.[27] In other words, stereotypes are exposed and challenged through the apparent complicity of those 'reluctant witnesses' who are Beyala's narrators and protagonists.

Drawing on Dean MacCannell's notion of 'staged authenticity', Huggan analyses the trope of what he calls 'staged marginality', that is 'the process by which marginalised individuals or social groups are moved to dramatise their "subordinate" status for the benefit of a majority or mainstream audience'.[28] 'Staged marginality' can, Huggan acknowledges, have a subversive function, and is related to Bhabha's concept of colonial mimicry:

> by simulating the conditions in which the dominant [...] culture perceives them, marginalised people or groups may reveal the underlying structures of their oppression; they may also demonstrate the dominant culture's need for subaltern others, who function as foils or counterweights to its own fragile self-identity.[29]

If we follow Huggan's argument, then Beyala's decisions to scatter her novels with stereotyped characters and to present other more complex characters repeating stereotypes can be read as a staging of the marginality of African migrants in France. Interestingly, even characters who appear to conform to racial stereotypes, such as Loukoum's father, demonstrate awareness of those same stereotypes. He tells his imaginary French friend: 'Ta légende dit que je suis incapable d'aimer, que mon sexe de cheval me grimpe au cerveau, étouffe mon intelligence et y plante la bêtise' (*PPB*, p. 98) [Your legend tells you that I'm incapable of loving, that my horse-sized genitals creep into my brain, suffocate my intelligence, and implant stupidity there (*LPPB*, p. 66)]. What this remark does is draw attention to Abdou's function as a performer of stereotypes. He adds that he will not be able to remove ten thousand years of prejudice from his friend's brain. On the contrary, however, Abdou's complete transformation into the perfect housewife presents a powerful challenge to racist gender stereotyping.

In the case of the racial stereotype that is Abdou, when he eventually returns to the family home from prison, he is presented as the epitome of the 'new man'. As we saw in Chapter 3, the hyperbolic nature of this shift suggests Abdou's failure to reconcile the different cultural expectations he experiences in France where, he as he sees it, women 'wear the trousers'. His is a polarized world of gender roles that are distinct and culturally variable. Unable to find a middle road of negotiation, Abdou completely transforms his own performance into a parody of its opposite. This demonstrates that, while cultural reconciliation is impossible for Abdou, he is nevertheless able to perform what he assumes to be an acceptable gender role in order to facilitate his reintegration into his altered domestic environment. It also suggests that playing to the ethnic majority's expectations may sometimes be the easier option but that, for migrants, even a performance in bad faith incorporates a degree of agency: Abdou selects a performance that initially conforms to the majority ethnic myth but, as we have seen, he can also choose to perform himself differently. Although he still tries to cling to the traditions that he believes his wife has forgotten, he is able to adapt to a new set of circumstances (*MAA*, p. 205). In other words, migrant identity shifts in relation to other people's expectations which are, to a large extent, determined by historical conditions. Stuart Hall explains:

Cultural identities come from somewhere, have histories. But, like everything which is historical, they undergo constant transformation [...] Identities are the names we give to the different ways we are positioned by, and position ourselves within, the narratives of the past.[30]

Beyala's migrants constantly transform themselves, but their performances, like those of the *femmes fatales*, are opportunistic. Whereas the Africa-based characters, like Butler's drag queens, hyperbolize the construction of their own racial identity, performing the ways in which they have been positioned by colonial history, the migrants perform versions of themselves to suit their own agendas. These agendas are not necessarily subversive but they are almost always self-serving. Here, Beyala's migrant performances attempt to resist performativity since, as Butler notes, the latter is clearly dissociated from any notion of choice or intention:

Performance as bounded 'act' is distinguished from performativity insofar as the latter consists in a reiteration of norms which precede, constrain, and exceed the performer and in that sense cannot be taken as the fabrication of the performer's 'will' or 'choice'; further, what is 'performed' works to conceal, if not to disavow, what remains opaque, unconscious, unperformable.[31]

In other words, performance attempts to mask the performative. This is what Beyala's migrants hope to achieve. They attempt to conceal the identification that their racialized bodies perform and to act out alternative versions of themselves in a strategic attempt to negotiate their exile.

Unfortunately, such opportunistic performances sometimes leave the migrant in a state of cultural limbo. As we saw in Chapter 4, Aïssatou in *Comment cuisiner* actively chooses to perform different versions of herself. Unhappy with her role, she chooses different performances in response to different circumstances. She opts to 'se métamorphoser' [transform herself], swinging between the different public and private interpretations of herself, so much so that she ends up 'out of sync', unable to reconcile the versions of herself that different cultural groups expect. Since, as Butler has shown, gender identity is essentially mimetic, the difficulty for Aïssatou and others like her is which cultural set of gender rules to perform. Abdou's confusion in the 'Loukoum' novels makes a similar point. Having identified himself against a long line of African 'father figures', in France he now finds that everything is out of place and out of sync

(*PPB*, p. 223; *LPPB*, p. 156). His attempts to position himself in relation to his past are no longer sustainable so, like Aïssatou, he flounders around between different (and sometimes conflicting) models of who and how he can be.

The performance of successful integration has also, of course, to be played out before the majority ethnic audience. France's continuing emphasis on the assimilation of difference means that for a migrant's performance of identity to be successful, it will almost necessarily be fake. Faced with racist discrimination in every sphere, migrants have three choices in Beyala's world: to conform to majority ethnic expectations by holding onto their difference and thereby remain forever marginalized; to attempt to assimilate themselves totally in the culture of France; or to become sufficiently adept at negotiating so as to keep one step ahead of the game. This last option is what I refer to as strategic performance, as demonstrated in the description of Assèze busking in Paris:

> Je dansais devant une foule en mal d'exotisme, avec des masques gentils ou inquiétants. J'épuisais les contes de Grand-mère et d'Ahmidou [sic] Koumba. Je décorais de précipices rouge tropical des contes de Grimm et de Perrault. Je faisais le singe, le poirier, la diseuse de bonne aventure. Les Blancs se marraient parce qu'ils croyaient goûter au gâteau sucré des mystères africains. Je les embobinais dans un flot de snobisme et de références cambroussardes. (*AA*, p. 301).

> [I would dance before a crowd hungry for exoticism, with masks to reassure or to frighten them. I exhausted Grandmother's stories and those of Ahmidou [sic] Koumba. I decorated Grimm's and Perrault's tales with tropical red precipices. I monkeyed about, did headstands, was the teller of good stories. The whites had a wonderful time because they thought they were sipping the nectar of African secrets. I would dupe them with a flood of snobbishness and country-bumpkin references.]

Assèze presents her own performance as that of a kind of fake African griot playing to the exoticist desire of her majority ethnic audience. Her performance is self-consciously fake and strategically so: she knows that this type of spectacle will generate the highest financial revenue from the crowd. Of course, giving the public exactly what they want is a difficult game because desires shift all the time. A performance that is too familiar will lack exotic appeal; on the other hand, one that is too exotic risks being rejected as too far removed from the audience's own experience. Assèze responds to this dilemma by combining the familiar with the exotic: the stories of Grimm and Perrault blend with those of Ahmadou Koumba. In order to maintain a balance between familiar and exotic, the migrant's performance is necessarily constantly changing in what becomes a complex improvisation of identity.

Interestingly, Harrow reads the above description of Assèze busking as Beyala's defence of her own plagiarism, 'transforming it from theft into miming, from illicit expropriation to playful imitation'.[32] This is certainly a valid interpretation, particularly as Beyala makes constant reference to her plagiarism in her public performances and her fictional narratives. However, I would suggest that Assèze's busking could also be read as a description of migrants' opportunism in both the public and the fictional spheres. Plagiarism, I have argued elsewhere, is itself a performative act, and one that contributes to the complex performance of public Beyala.[33] Indeed, Beyala's self-representation is constantly transforming through a series of contradictions and repositionings, keeping any sense of a 'true' Beyala forever beyond our reach. In her reading of *Les Arbres en parlent encore*, Brière notes that 'masks and lies are part of the telling'.[34] I would propose extending this idea to Beyala's representation of her self: masks and lies are part of the story that is Calixthe Beyala. This is not to suggest that Beyala is a dishonest woman, according to a particular set of social or cultural norms, but rather that her self-performance is deliberately misleading as she forever resists containment in someone else's image of who or what Calixthe Beyala should be. Just as Assèze panders to her audience with her version of the African storyteller, so Beyala presents many different versions of her self to both appeal to the demands of her tourist-explorer audience and to guarantee her continued success.

In his discussion of Beyala's plagiarism, Harrow makes the brief but controversial suggestion that 'although one ought to be cautious about the employment of African folk figures as symbolic references, one can't help seeing in Beyala's posture the ever-recurring figure of the trickster in this affair'.[35] The African trickster figure is a free spirit whose behaviour is complex and contradictory. Typically represented in animal form, the trickster uses cunning to outwit opponents more powerful than himself and to manipulate situations to his own advantage. In a postcolonial context, Harrow's mention of the trickster recalls Henry Louis Gates's work on the 'Signifying

Monkey' (although Harrow does not himself make this connection). The 'Signifying Monkey' is, Gates writes, 'of the order of the trickster figure' who, common to black cultures in Africa and the diaspora, originates in Yoruba and Fon mythology. Whereas the original trickster functions as a divine messenger, his profane equivalent is, Gates argues, the Signifying Monkey whose role is no longer that of a character in a mythological narrative but rather a vehicle for narration.[36] There are countless songs and tales about the Signifying Monkey in black American culture. These can be traced back to slave narratives as can the black vernacular tradition of 'signifying'.[37]

'Signifying' has specific connotations in black discourse, as Gates explains. In particular, it connotes parody:

> Signifying depends upon the signifier *repeating* what someone else has said about a third person in order to *reverse* the status of a relationship heretofore harmonious; signifying can also be employed to reverse or undermine pretense or even one's own opinion about one's own status. The use of repetition and reversal (chiasmus) constitutes an implicit parody of a subject's own complicity in illusion.[38]

In literature, Gates argues, signifying takes the form of the revision of antecedent texts. One might argue, then, that Harrow's criticism of Beyala for sometimes reproducing texts in 'semi-digested' form could be read in this way.[39] Such, according to Gates, is the nature of 'signifying', which can include 'a fairly exact repetition of a given narrative or rhetorical structure, filled incongruously with a ludicrous or incongruent content'.[40] However, I am not suggesting that Beyala's plagiarism should be read as 'signifying' since to do so would be to ignore important questions of textual ownership and artistic integrity. Indeed, it would be controversial in the extreme to suggest that Beyala signifies on – rather than plagiarizes – texts by Buten, Constant, Okri, Dangaremba et al. Less controversially, though, this book has already demonstrated that Beyala's novels signify upon discourses of so-called authenticity such as the oral tradition and Negritude. She also explicitly signifies on other canonical francophone texts. For example, Samba Diallo, the hero of Cheikh Hamidou Kane's classic novel *L'Aventure ambiguë*, appears as one of Ngaremba's letter-writing clients in *Les Honneurs perdus* (HP, p. 215).[41]

Sunday Anozie explains that the trickster manages to flout or transcend codes of morality or immorality, to defeat enemies, cheat friends and overcome obstacles.[42] The trickster is then an ambiguous character who challenges social orders using cunning and opportunism, shaping his behaviour to the circumstances of the moment. For people who are deprived of power, opportunism is sometimes the only means by which some degree of power can be achieved. Writing about the Hong Kong Chinese, Rey Chow focuses on what she calls,

> the tactics of those who do not have claims to territorial propriety or cultural centrality. Perhaps more than anyone else, those who live in Hong Kong realize the opportunistic role they need to play in order, not to 'preserve', but to negotiate their 'cultural identity'; for them opportunity is molded in danger and danger is a form of opportunity.[43]

Chow's description of the way in which the Chinese community in Hong Kong (before the 1997 handover) deal with living in a space that denies them 'territorial propriety or cultural centrality' applies equally, I would argue, to the migrants in Beyala's France. Diaspora, Chow suggests, requires rethinking identity in terms of opportunistic negotiation, rather than cultural preservation for its own sake.

Opportunism is also, I suggest, the main reason why Beyala has often received a bad press. Her unique position as an extraordinarily successful African woman writer in France gives her the material basis from which she can represent herself in any way she chooses. It is her ability to play with identity that demonstrates the agency that Beyala enjoys as a migrant writer in Paris. This idea that identity can be played like a game is a thread that runs through Beyala's fictional works. It also informs Beyala's relationship with writing, as she explains in her article 'Jouons au cochon pendu' [Let's Play the Hanging Pig], published in 1997 in *Etudes Francophones*.[44] The 'hanging pig' is a playground game where a child hangs upside down by her knees, usually from a metal bar. Beyala's analogy here is a telling one since the game involves a considerable degree of risk: like Beyala the writer, the child hangs in a precarious position and could fall at any time. Arguably, Beyala is now so well established as a postcolonial writer in France that she can afford to take risks. However, as Aijaz Ahmad notes, a privileged experience of cultural hybridity such as Beyala's is by no means representative of the way in which the majority experience migration.[45] Most migrants lack the material means – and the confidence that material capital brings – to manipulate the expectations of the host culture in this way. As we have seen, Beyala's fiction confirms Ahmad's point by presenting a number of migrants who are economically trapped and thus unable to vary the way they perform themselves. Even then, though, like Soumana, they dream of being able to represent themselves differently. When Beyala presents Soumana dreaming of becoming a movie star (*PPB*, p. 92; *LPPB*, p. 61), she emphasizes the possibilities of performance. But unfortunately, even in fiction, personal transformation remains tied to socio-economic reality. M'am only begins to reinvent herself when she becomes a successful businesswoman; Saïda when she begins literacy classes, which gives her the confidence to have sex with Marcel and thus no longer identify herself as a fifty-year-old virgin.

This promotion of identity as something to be played has important implications for postcolonial identities. Is Beyala ultimately advocating nothing more than a postmodern individualistic game? Or does playing with identity in fact resist the containment of postcolonial identities within a colonial paradigm? In other words, to return to the ambivalence of masquerade: do Beyala's performances subvert, parody or reinscribe colonialist ideology?[46] Indeed, the ambivalence of Beyala's reception demonstrates that each of these readings represents a potentially valid response. What my analysis of Beyala's performing identities suggests, however, is that a migrant's desire to play identities, to wear different masks in response to different situations is, in fact, symptomatic of the migrant experience. Migration is, by definition, a transformative experience, an experience of movement, a point that Beyala emphasizes through frequent references to metamorphosis in her novels. Her fiction suggests that transformation is essential for migrant survival. Hall echoes this view when he writes about the diaspora experience:

> The diaspora experience as [he intends] it here is defined, not by essence or purity, but by the recognition of 'identity' which lives with and through, not despite, difference; by *hybridity*. Diaspora identities are those which are constantly producing and reproducing themselves anew, through transformation and difference.[47]

I would also argue that the emphasis on varying performances is more than a postmodern game of slippery subjectivities. One of the few postcolonial critics to engage with performativity is Helen Gilbert. In her analysis of Australian Aboriginal theatre, Gilbert writes that 'continually shifting subjectivities are important here because they forestall attempts to fix the actor/character as the reified object of the viewer's gaze'.[48] While Gilbert is focusing specifically on oral performance texts, her conclusion could certainly be applied more generally to the formation of resisting postcolonial identities and connects with Butler's vision of 'a loss of gender norms [that] would have the effect of proliferating gender configurations, destabilizing substantive identity, and depriving the naturalizing narratives of compulsory heterosexuality of their central protagonists: "man" and "woman"'.[49] The reverse is, of course, also true: proliferating gender configurations can lead to a breakdown of gender norms in the same way as migrants' shifting performances can effect a reconfiguration of the 'insider' versus 'outsider' divide.

In Beyala's fictional world, those migrants who survive the transformative experience of exile are those who are able to 'make it up'. Improvisation is the key to Beyala's representations of the migrant condition. For James Clifford, such is the nature of contemporary identities: 'Twentieth-century identities no longer presuppose continuous cultures or traditions. Everywhere individuals and groups improvize local performances, drawing on foreign media, symbols, and languages.'[50] Clifford applauds what he sees as the 'inventive and tactical "negritude"' of Aimé Césaire, which focuses on transformation rather than extinction. While, as we have seen, Beyala presents a far more ambivalent picture of Negritude in her writings than Clifford, she nevertheless promotes the transformation of black identities in exile rather than a nostalgic state of grieving for an essentialized past. She also emphasizes the need for change not only for the migrants but also for the Africa-based characters. Before Saïda decides to leave Couscousville, her mother advises her that 'la modernité s'amène à grands pas. Il faut changer les choses si on veut survivre' [modernity comes along in leaps and bounds. Things have to change if we are going to survive] (*HP*, p. 118). The difficulty of reconciling 'modernity' with 'tradition' is, of course, a major issue in postcolonial nations of the developing world. Ngaremba's weekly meetings of African intellectuals devote much time to the question of how to embrace progress without losing what they believe to be Africa's identity (*HP*, p. 245).

Ultimately, what Beyala and her migrant characters stage is the conflicting view of identity that, according to Bill Ashcroft, is 'possibly the most deep-seated divide in post-colonial thinking'.[51] On the one hand, characters such as Soumana, Abdou and Sorraya exemplify a view of identity as based on a fixed, essential version of itself; on the other, individuals such as Loukoum, Saïda and Assèze present identity as, in Ashcroft's terms, 'inextricable from the transformative conditions of material life'.⁵² In these novels, the characters who survive the migratory experience are those who embrace transformation. Beyala's rejection of what she presents as such essentializing discourses as Negitude, rastafarianism and the oral tradition demonstrates her lack of sympathy with those who advocate a return to roots as a means of (re)constructing identity in an increasingly globalized world. Indeed, her personal itinerary consists of a series of transformations of identity: from model to writer to plagiarist to prize-winner to TV celebrity to political activist, and so on. Similarly, the content of her novels is constantly shifting: from the angry feminism of the early novels (*CSB* and *TTT*) to the fantastic (*SDS*) to the novels of migration in the 'Loukoum' period (*PPB*, *MAA*, *AA*, *HP*, *AS*, *CCMA*) to traditional storytelling (*APE* and *PFR*) to erotic fiction (*FNFN*) and, most recently, to writing about white Zimbabwean landowners (*LP*). Beyala is keen to promote herself as an innovator or pioneer. She explains this in her interview with Stéphane Tchakam:

> Quand j'ai écrit 'C'est le soleil qui m'a brûlée', est-ce qu'une Africaine avait déjà abordé le sujet? Non. Quand j'ai écrit 'Le petit prince de Belleville' sur l'immigration, personne ne l'avait fait. A chaque fois, j'ai été la personne qui a ouvert au monde littéraire noir des thématiques et des zones d'exploration nouvelles. Même si on ne me salue pas toujours. Effectivement, le pionnier est celui qui travaille [le] plus et récolte le moins en général. 'Femme nue femme noire' est le premier livre érotique africain comme 'C'est le soleil qui m'a brûlée' avait été le premier livre féministe africain, dans le sens propre du terme. Comme 'Le petit prince de Belleville' a été le premier sur l'immigration. Comme 'Les Arbres en parlent encore' est l'un des livres les plus traditionalistes sur la pensée et la philosophie africaines. Ils n'avaient pas pensé à le faire, les autres.⁵³

> [When I wrote *C'est le soleil qui m'a brûlée*, had an African woman already dealt with this subject? No. When I wrote *Le petit prince de Belleville* about immigration, nobody had done it. Each time I've been the person who has opened up the black literary world to new themes and new areas for exploration. Even if I'm still not acknowledged for it. Actually, the pioneer is generally the one who works the most and gets the least reward. *Femme nue, femme noire* is the first African erotic book just as *C'est le soleil qui m'a brûlée* was the first African feminist book, in the proper sense of the word. Just as *Le petit prince de Belleville* was the first on immigration. Just as *Les Arbres en parlent encore* is one of most traditionalist books on African thought and philosophy. No one else had thought of it.]

In the same way, Albin Michel's marketing department has begun to promote Beyala's recent novels as 'firsts' of their kind. *Femme nue, femme noire* is marketed as the first African erotic novel. *La Plantation* is described as a pioneering text in which, 'pour la première fois, un grand écrivain noir se met dans la peau des Blancs, des colonisateurs' [for the first time a great black writer steps into the shoes of the whites, the colonizers]. The blurb even goes so far as to describe this novel as 'un véritable *Autant en emporte le vent* africain' [a veritable African *Gone with the Wind*]. Beyala's and her publisher's immodest (and inaccurate) claims with regard to her pioneering role in several different genres demonstrate their determined efforts to keep her at the centre of African literature in France, and Beyala's strategic approach to her own career.

As this book has shown, what seems to bother so many readers about Beyala is that she performs her identity 'wrongly': she is seen as inauthentic, a 'fake'. For Mongo Beti, Beyala has forgotten that she is African.[54] For Pierre Assouline, she is a plagiarist. Others revel in Beyala's exoticism, happy to see confirmed their received ideas about 'la belle négresse'. Of course, such views reveal the very same essentialist ideology that Beyala and her writings seek to undermine. As a black woman writer in France, Beyala is expected to represent her identity in a way that satisfies her audience, be they African or French. She is therefore subject to the same kind of regulation and control that Judith Butler describes in respect to gender norms:

> In effect, gender is made to comply with a model of truth and falsity which not only contradicts its own performative fluidity, but serves a social policy of gender regulation and control. Performing one's gender wrong initiates a set of punishments both obvious and indirect, and performing it well provides the reassurance that there is an essentialism of gender identity after all.[55]

This conclusion could equally be applied to migrant identity, which is also forced to comply with a model imposed from the outside. In Beyala's case, the polarized nature of reactions to her both as a writer and a public figure reflect a similar model of true and false, 'authentic' and 'fake'. Authenticity in art is, of course, determined by the marketplace, as James Clifford demonstrates in his analysis of what he calls the 'art-culture system', subtitled 'a machine for making authenticity'.[56] The way in which Beyala is able to slide up and down the axis of authenticity, between Clifford's poles of masterpiece and fraud – as prize-winner or plagiarist – reflects the anxieties of critics

Performing Identities 135

and commentators in France about where and how to locate her. But, as I suggested in Chapter 1, it is precisely her slipperiness that compels readers to attempt to fix her identity. In other words, just as the 'Beyala Affair' expressed the literary community's disappointment with the apparent 'inauthenticity' of a prize-winning African novel, so it also manifested that same community's horror at the 'inauthenticity' of Beyala herself. Beyala's own struggle to locate herself in relation to the majority ethnic model in France generates a protean performance, one that is shifting all the time.

Beyala's identity is performative, existing only in the moment of its articulation. As one of the epigraphs to *La petite fille du réverbère*, Beyala quotes Beyala: 'Il en va de l'identité d'un être comme de n'importe quelle matière: elle se recycle' [A person's identity is just like any other matter: it recycles itself]. She revels in her own controversy, willingly donning the mask of a writer who shocks: 'une petite fille bâtarde [...] dont les impropriétés rhétoriques dresseraient les cheveux des Papes de la littérature française' [a little bastard girl [...] whose rhetorical improprieties would make the hairs stand up on the heads of the leading lights of French literature] (*PFR*, p. 146). Like Loukoum, she parodies the way in which she is received by the majority ethnic culture in France. Recalling using the petit-nègre expression 'pardon Missié!' [sorry Mister] when, as a child, she was thrown out of a Douala hotel, Beyala writes:

> Ce tic de langage me reviendra encore: *pardon Missié-oui Missié*! Lorsque, vingt ans plus tard, ceux qui s'attablent avec Missié Riene Poussalire [Assouline] dans la maison de Verlaine me prendront pour cible en dégustant leurs salades de chèvre: 'Salope! Plagiaire!' *Pardon Missié-oui Missié*, lorsque'ils considéreront que j'ai la cervelle à peine plus longue qu'une jupe courte... *Pardon Missié-oui Missié*! A se tordre de rire. (*PFR*, p. 192)

> [This linguistic tic would come back to me again: *sorry Mister–yes Mister*! When, twenty years later, those dining with Mr Nothing Makeshimread [Assouline] target me while they are eating their goat's cheese salad in Verlaine's house: 'Bitch! Plagiarist! *Sorry Mister–yes Mister*, while they are deciding that my brain is scarcely longer than a short skirt... *Sorry Mister–yes Mister*. What a laugh.]

Here she makes indirect reference to Pierre Assouline's suggestion that the prize she was awarded by the guardians of French literature, the Académie Française, was tainted by some kind of inappropriate favouritism and, through mimicry, reverses the exoticist gaze in which Assouline tried to contain her.[57]

In Homi Bhabha's terms, Calixthe Beyala is a mimic. For Bhabha, mimicry is 'at once resemblance and menace' since its very mockery exposes the fragility and ambivalence of colonialist discourse.[58] As Ashcroft et al. explain, 'Mimicry [...] locates a crack in the certainty of colonial dominance, an uncertainty in its control of the behaviour of the colonised'.[59] Beyala resists any form of control; even a criminal record for literary theft failed to stop her meteoric rise to fame. In her fiction, parodies of racist and ethnological discourse pave the way for the subversive mimicry of Loukoum. In public, her protean performances protect her from containment within the other's image. Likewise, her 'inappropriate' behaviour (her outspokenness, her political activism, her plagiarism) undermines the dominant discourse's version of normativity in postcolonial France.

CONCLUSION
Survival in a Post-Exotic Age

From February to April 2005, the Hayward Gallery in London hosted *Africa Remix*, a major exhibition of contemporary African art. One of the works, by Angolan artist Fernando Alvim, consisted of a large, plain canvas consisting only of a mirror and the words 'WE ARE ALL POST EXOTICS' written in pencil.[1] The words are positioned to the left of the mirror so that, when you look into the mirror, the words disappear from sight. The word 'post' is also shaded, unlike the other words. This forces the observer to read the sentence twice: first, we are all exotics; but then the word 'post' seems to shout out from the canvas that exoticism is no more. On one level, Alvim's canvas recalls the on-going debate about the term 'postcolonial', except that here 'post' is very much separate from 'exotics'; there is no hyphenated link to encourage us to question whether exoticism is over. On the contrary, the painting reminds us that, beyond our own gaze, we are all exotic. When we look away from the mirror, we are always identified by the other, and the other's gaze is always a (post) exoticist one. This painting, then, connects with what Huggan describes as 'strategic exoticism', that is, 'the means by which postcolonial writers/thinkers, working from within exoticist codes of representation, either manage to subvert those codes [...], or succeed in redeploying them for the purposes of uncovering differential relations of power'.[2] Alvim simultaneously undermines and reinvents exoticism, albeit a reinvention on rather different terms. Similarly, Beyala both undermines and reinvents the exotic on her own terms. This book has considered the ways in which Beyala positions herself and her fiction within exoticist aesthetics and the different responses that these positionings have provoked.

Beyala's reception, as we have seen, is characterized by ambivalence. If there is one central question that lies behind Beyala's ambivalent reception it is whether she uses exoticism to subvert differential power relations or whether she in fact relies on the perpetuation of exoticist discourses to sustain her own success. In other words, is her relationship with exoticism one of compliance, subversion or manipulation? Having presented 'strategic exoticism' as a potentially subversive positioning, Huggan wonders whether it is in fact simply another symptom of the postcolonial exotic rather than a response to it.³ Certainly, some critics read Beyala as a kind of postcolonial puppet who effectively perpetuates colonialist mythology rather than challenging it. Quoting Judith Butler's point that 'the female body that is freed from the shackles of the paternal law may well prove to be yet another incarnation of that law, posing as subversive but operating in the service of that law's amplification and proliferation',⁴ Harrow concludes that 'as an example of such a figure, we can take the "Beyala" of the Grand Prix of the Académie Française – in contrast to the Beyala of *C'est le soleil qui m'a brûlée* (1987) and *Tu t'appelleras Tanga* (1988)'.⁵ Here Harrow implies that Beyala has somehow become the monster of the colonialist Frankenstein that created her and prevents us from reading Beyala's representations of subjectivity in the later novels as subversive acts of liberation.

If, however, we accept Butler's view that the subversion of cultural norms always takes place within rather than against those same norms, then a different reading becomes possible. According to Butler,

> If subversion is possible, it will be a subversion from within the terms of the law, through the possibilities that emerge when the law turns against itself and spawns unexpected permutations of itself. The culturally constructed body will then be liberated, neither to its 'natural' past, nor to its original pleasures, but to an open future of cultural possibilities.⁶

This leads us to question the extent to which Beyala's performances are indicative of 'an open future of cultural possibilities' for postcolonial identities. Are she and her texts examples of subversive liberation or do they simply repeat and reinforce the law of the colonial father? What if, as we discussed in the previous chapter, Beyala is simply a contemporary version of an African trickster? How, in the final analysis, do Beyala and her fiction contribute to the question of postcolonial identities? In this concluding chapter, I shall suggest that Beyala's strategic exoticism is in fact a cynical response to her positioning in France. I shall also consider whether it is meaningful to talk about a politics of performance in the case of Beyala's opportunistic strategy for migrant identity, or whether what she and her fiction are promoting is nothing more than a self-serving individualistic agenda.

As we have seen in this book, a common charge laid against Beyala is that she is writing for a French audience rather than an African one. Winifred Woodhull develops this by now familiar suggestion when she draws attention to what she sees as the palatable exoticism of the 'Loukoum' novels:

> The publisher of *Maman* seems to have banked on the entertainment value of the novel, which places the European French in the position of natives visited by African tourists from Paris, tourists whose own manners are displayed with gentle irony. The text invites readers to engage in cultural tourism and to be edified by virtue of coming to understand M'ammaryam, her family, and her community better than they did before.[7]

Although it is not totally clear whether Woodhull's charge of exoticism is levied at author or publisher here, her description of *Maman a un amant* presents the text as a complex set of relationships between tourist and native. The majority ethnic French tourist-reader visits the culture of Loukoum's family who, in turn, visit the culture of the French tourist-reader. While Woodhull is suggesting that the reader is placed in the position of super-tourist, the fact that his or her own culture is refracted through the eyes of the African tourists from Paris turns the touristic experience back on itself so that ultimately the positions of tourist and native dissolve into meaninglessness. The reader is left wondering just who is the tourist and who the native.

A similar blurring of boundaries emerges in the phenomenon of Calixthe Beyala as postcolonial icon. The unprecedented nature of her success is countered by an often negative critical reception and a media image that has become something of a parody of itself. Readers are left struggling to locate Beyala just as they have difficulty locating the 'natives' in *Maman a un amant*. Beyala herself is all too aware of what Huggan, referring to Rushdie's Saladin Chamcha, terms 'the provisionality of self-construction'; she clearly understands that 'identities can be staged at different times for different audiences – and different goals'.[8] But critics remain undecided over whether her proficiency as a player is simply evidence of her incorporation into an exoticist image that others have created for her, or whether her performances and her writings suggest a more subversive agenda.

The ambivalence of the figure of Calixthe Beyala is brilliantly encapsulated in Fouad Laroui's novel, *La fin tragique de Philomène Tralala*, published in 2003.⁹ In this satirical text, the eponymous Moroccan-Guinean author is writing her story from prison, having been wrongly charged with the murder of formidable literary critic and magazine editor, Gontran de Ville. Although Laroui does make some attempt to blur the similarities between Beyala and Philomène, he includes a number of fairly transparent references to Beyala's writing and to the 'Beyala Affair'.¹⁰ These include unacknowledged direct quotations from *La petite fille du réverbère*, most notably Beyala's epigraphs to this novel.¹¹ These epigraphs are used by Beyala to cock a snook at those who accused her of plagiarism in 1996 and who imagined that her career would be ruined by the affair. In Laroui's novel, however, the two quotations are taken as evidence that she is indeed a plagiarist. Beyala's chief accuser, Assouline, is also thinly disguised in the character of Gontran de Ville. However, in this fictional parody of the 'Beyala Affair', Laroui turns Gontran into a stalker who, sexually obsessed with Philomène, does accuse her of plagiarism and of having a ghostwriter but also pursues her in both France and Morocco, relentlessly declaring his undying love. Consistently rebuffed, Gontran eventually rapes Philomène who then decides to confront his wife and family with the details of Gontran's campaign of sexual harassment. When his wife leaves him, Gontran returns to Philomène's house where, upon trying to break in, he impales himself on his own knife and dies. This leads to the heroine-narrator's false arrest and subsequent imprisonment for Gontran's murder. The court's decision hangs largely on the so-called evidence of her editor, Plumme, who arrived at the scene of the alleged crime with 'son Albin, son miché', a humorous allusion to Beyala's long-time publisher, Albin Michel.¹²

There is considerable emphasis throughout Laroui's novel on Philomène's exoticism. Alluding to the Hottentot Venus, Philomène claims men stalk her because she is 'à la limite de l'humain, l'exotisme absolu, le presque au-delà' [on the edge of human, absolute exoticism, the almost beyond].¹³ As a refrain in the novel, Philomène repeats 'Je ne suis pas exotique' [I am not exotic] over and over again, the repetition ultimately undermining the protest and suggesting that, like her real-life equivalent, Philomène is keen to keep her exoticism at the forefront of the French public's minds. Rumour has it that she even attempted to seduce editors with photographs of herself naked included along with her first manuscript. This detail reminds readers of Assouline's allegation that the French Academicians awarded Beyala the Grand Prix du Roman on the basis of an exchange of personal – or indeed, sexual – favours rather than literary merit.

Even the cover of Laroui's novel reinforces the representation of Beyala/Philomène as the kind of erotic-exotic object that we discussed earlier in this book. Against a black background all that can be seen is a pair of fleshy pink lips, echoing a point made in the novel by Philomène the narrator when she notes that men only see her as a set of body parts: 'Ils ne voient qu'une paire de jambes, des seins, un ventre, mes grosses lèvres...' [they see only a pair of legs, some breasts, a belly, my thick lips...].[14] Thick lips are of course often cited as a marker of racial difference. To further promote Philomène's eroticism, Laroui uses artistic licence to characterize her as a lesbian who seems to want to seduce every woman she meets. Descriptions of the protagonist with her Russian immigrant lover, Irina, parody the controversial scenes of tenderness between Ateba and Irène in Beyala's first novel and also draw attention to the eroticism that the French public identify in both Beyala and her fiction. Moreover, Plumme encourages Philomène to incorporate lesbian scenes in her novels because 'c'est très *in*' [it's very 'in'], implying that, in the same way, Beyala's choice of subject matter is determined by market trends rather than by creative drive.[15] Certainly, Beyala's recent decisions to write the first African erotic novel (*FNFN*) and then a novel about white farmers in Zimbabwe (*LP*) do suggest a desire to jump on the latest fictional bandwagon in order to guarantee book sales.

However, while it implicitly criticizes Beyala for her careerism, her outspokenness and her lack of solidarity with her fellow Moroccans, Laroui's novel also presents Philomène as an object of editorial manipulation. Philomène/Beyala is presented as the victim not only of an unhinged, rebuffed suitor who happens to be a respected literary critic but also of her over-controlling editor for whom she fulfils the function of 'Blackette de service' [token black woman]. It is Plumme who decides when and where Philomène will appear in public; his aim, he claims, is to promote her to the status of 'vedette absolue' [absolute star].[16] What Plumme cannot control, however, are Philomène's performances in public: in the course of the novel, she manages to publicly insult Benazir Bhutto, Hinduism, a TV journalist, Moroccan traditions and Algeria. Here again Laroui satirizes Beyala's controversial media image and her negative reception in both Africa and France. Following an appearance at the Moroccan Institut Français during which Philomène is attacked as a plagiarist and a traitor, Moroccan newspapers abound in vitriolic condemnations of the author, accusing her of being a traitor to her country, a pornographer, a thief and of having slept her way to the top. In Laroui's version of her story, Philomène/Beyala is, to an extent, a willing pawn in her publisher's game.

What all of this creates is a fictional representation of Beyala as an ambivalent postcolonial cartoon. Despite her editor's attempts to control her, Laroui's parodic figure seems to be spinning out of control: at a debate on Algeria held at the Centre Pompidou, Philomène ends up killing a member of the audience with an ashtray in a hyperbolic moment that recalls the ending of *C'est le soleil qui m'a brûlée*. Such intertextual references blur the distinction between fiction and the 'reality' on which Laroui's novel is based, emphasizing what I have identified as the difficulty readers have in separating Beyala from her texts. They also imply that, like Philomène, the figure of Calixthe Beyala is, to a certain extent, a fictional construct, created by her publishers and reinforced by the media. In what might be read as the ultimate moment of editorial control, Plumme and his companions falsely testify that they saw Philomène stab Gontran. The reader infers that now that she has become something of an embarrassment, it is more convenient for Philomène's publishers that she spend some time in prison, away from the public eye. Philomène, however, remains undeterred by her incarceration. The final lines of the novel describe her fantasizing about enjoying the body of a woman friend and demanding paper, a pen and some books.

Laroui's novel crystallizes the question of Beyala's complicity and leads us to question to what extent she is a victim of our post-exotic age. Brière reads Beyala as controlled by the publishing industry. She explains that, 'Francophone writers who move from the margin to the center of *la francophonie*, as Beyala has done, can easily fall prey to the conflict not only between their writing and the context within which it is read, but also to the power of publishers over writers' careers'.[17] While I agree that, in Brière's terms, 'Beyala is France's "generic" African writer' or what Laroui calls a 'Blackette de service', Brière ignores the possibility that Beyala may be playing the system at its own game.[18] This possibility is implied but not developed in Laroui's story of Philomène Tralala. Although Laroui portrays Philomène as a victim of market forces, he also describes a woman who constantly rises to the challenge. In my view, Beyala is 'strategically generic', meaning that she is happy to play the role of token African woman writer as long as it suits her to do so. In this respect, the relationship is not as imbalanced in terms of the distribution of power as Brière's analysis suggests. Yet to say this also begs the question of whether Beyala's self-serving strategy amounts to the assimilation of the masked performer discussed in the previous chapter. What are the consequences of this kind of post-exotic masquerade? Do Beyala's strategic performances jeopardize the reception of African literature in French?

At a point in time when France has chosen to revise its national curriculum to ensure that secondary school history teachers promote the positive effects of colonialism, is it perhaps better to choose a strategically exotic position that allows access to the 'centre' than to remain in a position of marginality, albeit a more explicitly subversive one.[19] Beyala's privileged position has allowed her to speak within spaces from which African women are normally excluded. For example, it is arguably Beyala's profile as a writer that facilitated the Collectif Egalité's meeting with the CSA discussed in the Introduction to this book. Since the Collectif's intervention, French broadcasting has made an effort to change the terrestrial channel remits to reflect the multiculturalism of the nation and to employ more 'visible minorities' in television programmes.[20] Beyala has also spoken out on AIDS in Africa and stood for a number of key political positions including, in September 2001, the post of Secretary General of the Organisation Internationale de la Francophonie (hoping to succeed Boutros Boutros-Ghali in October 2002).[21] In her own terms, Beyala saw herself as 'une candidate aimée du monde francophone [...] croyant en l'avenir du continent noir et en la Francophonie' [a popular candidate in the francophone world [...] who believes in the future of the dark continent and in 'la Francophonie'].[22] Unlike many other African writers, Beyala apparently sees no political incompatibility between the development of what she refers to as 'le continent noir' and what some see as the neocolonial institution of 'la Francophonie'.[23]

As we saw in Chapter 2, Beyala's public manifestations have led to her rejection by readers back 'home' in Africa. In particular, Mongo Beti condemns her success as irrelevant in an African context:

> Pour séduire le public camerounais, il ne suffit pas de décrocher un grand prix à Paris, ni même d'étaler un génie créateur de Shakespeare,

ni de déployer un style éblouissant. Il faut encore prendre part, sans équivoque, d'une façon ou d'une autre, au combat patriotique de libération nationale.[24]

[To seduce the Cameroonian public, it is not a case of landing a big prize in Paris, nor of flaunting a Shakespeare-style genius, nor of writing brilliantly. One way or another, you have to unequivocally take part in the patriotic struggle for national liberation.]

For Mongo Beti, a Cameroonian writer has a political responsibility to her birth country and, in this respect, he believes that Beyala has failed. As Beti's impassioned criticisms reveal, the case of Beyala leads us to question the role of the African writer in the twenty-first century. Does such a writer have a responsibility to use her position in the service of nationalist politics, as Beti suggests? Are we right to criticize her for advocating a strategy for individual survival when African countries are facing difficulties that affect whole communities?[25] Certainly, it is true to say that Beyala's novels do not promote a nationalist agenda. However, Beti chooses to ignore the fact that Beyala's novels do engage with issues that are relevant to the Cameroonian public, perhaps because these issues affect the everyday lives of women and children rather than the male-centred domain of nationalist politics. Beyala has adopted dozens of orphans in Yaoundé and Douala, demonstrating her continued involvement with her country of origin. She also openly criticizes Biya's government for its lack of women ministers (*LASO*, p. 117). As such, Beyala remains interested in national politics but from the specific point of view of a Cameroonian woman.

What also shocks Mongo Beti is Beyala's 'arrivisme'. Although he wrongly suggests in his article that Beyala has been hoist by her own petard in terms of the effects of plagiarism on her career, Beti is right to observe that she 'a toujours manoeuvré de façon à mettre tous les atouts dans son jeu' [has always manoeuvred in such a way as to play all her trumps to her own advantage].[26] For Beti, Beyala is too individualistic. This is another reason for Beyala's negative reception among African readers: she has made it clear on more than one occasion that she is interested in individuals rather than the wider community. In 1993 she explained to Françoise Cévaër that:

Jusqu'ici l'écriture des écrivains africains était centrée sur le groupe. Car en Afrique le groupe a souvent pris le pas sur l'individu. L'individu n'existe pas; il manque la conscience individuelle. [...] Et moi, j'ai choisi de travailler sur l'individu, non pas sur la masse; la masse, ça ne m'intéresse pas. Et ça c'est très nouveau en Afrique.²⁷

[Until now, African writers focused their writing on the group because, in Africa, the group has often taken precedence over the individual. The individual does not exist; there is no individual consciousness. [...] I've chosen to work on the individual, not on the masses. I'm not interested in the masses and that's very new in Africa.]

As Beyala explains, individualism is not part of African 'Tradition' but, as we have seen elsewhere in this book, 'Tradition' is the focus of strong criticism in her work, emerging as an 'invented authenticity' and an agent of oppression. In Beyala's view, 'un Noir, c'est avant tout et universellement un homme avant d'être un Noir' [before he is a black, a black is first, foremost and universally a man] (*LASO*, p. 99).

Individual opportunism is the key to survival in Beyala's fictional world. This is particularly marked in the migrant novels in which the successful migrants are those who, like their author, adapt their performances to fit their changing environment. Writing about *Le petit prince de Belleville*, Durand sets up an opposition between the two migrant mother figures of Aminata and Soumana. He reads the way in which the two mothers dress as representing polarized images of African women: the outmoded African queen (Soumana in her decorated boubou and sandals) and the Westernized migrant (Aminata in a skimpy, sparkly dress) who exploits her sexuality by working as a prostitute. According to Durand, Aminata epitomizes 'l'espace migratoire et son matérialisme de survie' [the migratory space and its survival materialism].²⁸ He rightly argues that Aminata's clothing signals her successful adaptation to the new space in which she finds herself whereas Soumana's traditional dress connotes a refusal to negotiate. This model of a pair of migrant women in which one is fixed in an essentialized version of her self while the other is a successful negotiator emerges as a pattern in Beyala's Paris-based novels. The pairs of Assèze and Sorraya (*AA*), and Saïda and Ngaremba (*HP*) fulfil a similar function. In each case, one of the pair dies because of her inability to adapt. Unlike Aminata, Assèze, Saïda or even Laroui's Philomène Tralala, Soumana, Sorraya and Ngaremba are unable to constantly reinvent themselves in what Beyala presents as necessary performances of migrant negotiation. As I discussed in Chapter 4, before their death these women view the experience of migration in an overly polarized way. For example, Ngaremba believes that 'pour vivre en France, un immigré doit être très fort, comme elle [Ngaremba], ou simple d'esprit de manière à organiser sa vie sans se poser des questions' [to live in France, an immigrant must be very strong like her [Ngaremba], or simple-minded so as to be able to organize her life without asking questions] (*HP*, p. 357). Such an either/or approach to the migrant condition betrays a lack of flexibility and a failure to recognize that, as Paul White observes, migration is synonymous with change.[29]

The importance of negotiation in the migratory space is central to an understanding of Beyala and her fiction. As Durand explains, 'L'immigré doit [...] subir une remise en question de son identité par l'intermédiaire d'une véritable négociation de l'espace' [the immigrant has to undergo a calling into question of his identity which is mediated through a veritable negotiation of space].[30] As Chapters 3 and 4 have demonstrated, this negotiation can be expressed in terms of a search for an identifiable home or an attempt to position oneself in relation to ethnic and/or national identifications. Alternatively, it can take the form of a constant reinvention of the self in a space that resists location but from and within which alternative subjectivities can emerge. The best example of this approach is Beyala herself who understands, tests, appropriates and manipulates the limits of the space in which she finds herself, forever shifting her position in a complex game of strategic negotiation. What distinguishes Beyala from her migrant women characters is the way in which she remains always in control. As Beyala remarked in a presentation made at the University of Missouri in Columbia in 1995, 'Je est donc étendu et flexible, mais refuse la destruction' [This 'I' is wide-reaching and flexible, but refuses to be destroyed].[31]

According to Carole Boyce Davies, the flexible subjectivity that Beyala describes is synonymous with black femininity. Boyce Davies presents black femininity as a migrating subjectivity that cannot be fixed in a single space and is in a constant state of flux.[32] Beyala's fiction confirms this view, but also suggests that the geographical space of migration facilitates resistance to the monolithic identities imposed on African women and makes it easier for women to position themselves outside the terms of dominant discourses. Migration, Beyala suggests, moves African women into a space that resembles Paul Gilroy's concept of 'the black Atlantic': 'a webbed network, between the local and the global, [challenging] the coherence of all narrow nationalist perspectives'.³³ Whereas the Africa-based women remain trapped within the patriarchal structures that they try to resist and so struggle to retrieve their subjectivity, in the Paris-based novels the implication is that subjectivity, although still uncertain, nonetheless exists in the moment of its performance. Exposure to alternative models of cultural and gender norms gives women the space in which to try out different versions of themselves. This is not to say that migration is necessarily empowering for Beyala's women but rather that it forces them to look at themselves differently. As Smith and Brinker-Gabler rightly note, 'in the practice of everyday life, immigrant women confront and grapple with their status as an "other" within the imagined community as well as their multicultural identifications'.³⁴ What Beyala and her fiction suggest is that migrant women and children can play their multicultural identifications to their own advantage, potentially undermining post-exotic discourse on its own terms.

As I discussed in the previous chapter, Beyala's successful migrants are those who can improvise or 'fake it'. Interestingly, though, Beyala is keen to emphasize that she herself will never dance to someone else's tune. In an interview for the *Cameroon Tribune* published in January 2004, Beyala expressed her contempt for those writers who are driven by a desire to please: 'Je sais qu'il y a des intellectuels qui essayent à tout prix de plaire, et pour cela ils deviennent des saltimbanques. Je ne deviendrai jamais une saltimbanque' [I know there are intellectuals who will try anything to please and for that they become saltimbancos. I will never become a saltimbanco].³⁵ The figure of a saltimbanco is an intriguing choice of metaphor since it not only connotes an Italian street performer, but also a quack who harangues his audience and plays the fool. Thus despite Beyala's dismissal of the possibility that she might be a saltimbanco, she chooses an image that maps neatly onto her representations of migrant identity: a performer and a fake. Furthermore, Beyala's resistance to being positioned as a writer who wants to please is made with a certain degree of bad faith, as this book has demonstrated. In many ways, she is precisely the saltimbanco she is so keen to criticize here, twisting and turning herself to meet her audience's demands, presenting different, 'fake' versions of herself in response to different stimuli and contexts, and producing novels that correspond to the latest literary trend. While she admits, in the same interview, that she often says things that will displease others, the controversial nature of her discourse is also staged and is, I would suggest, part of the phenomenon she has created, another version of a saltimbanco. Like Loukoum, Beyala plays with the stereotypes within with others try to contain her. She chooses when to give the audience what they are expecting (the stereotype of the exotic-erotic woman) and when to subvert those expectations by playing a different role. In other words, by choosing not to please, Beyala is again simply repeating a performance, one that she has established and that her audience has come to expect.

While Beyala's strategic play is undoubtedly individualistic, such performances are to an extent inevitable in our market-driven, post-exotic world. As this book has shown, Beyala is well aware of her value as a saleable commodity and it is her understanding of the marketplace that has, to a large part, generated her success. France needs Calixthe Beyala not only to satisfy readers' desire for consumption of 'the Other' but also to promote the benefits of 'la Francophonie'. Paradoxically, despite Beyala's criticisms of the former Senegalese President, Mongo Beti suggests that Beyala might, in fact, be the new Senghor, not least because both have been the darlings of the Académie Française.[36] While this may indeed be the case as far as the French are concerned, Beyala's agenda suggests more than a desire for assimilation. Rather, she is both a product of, and a participant in, the post(colonial) exotic. In this respect, she and her fiction fit Huggan's definition of a 'transculturated product', a term he applies to the carved African statue of Tintin that features on the cover of his book. Transculturated products, Huggan writes, are produced in an awareness of their commercial viability.[37] He explains that:

> Cultural products operating under the sign of this [postcolonial] 'exotic' are likely to raise the challenging question: what is really is exotic about me? My 'Tintin' asks that question, eyebrows raised in obvious mischief: 'so you find me exotic; and what does that say, my friend, about *you*?'[38]

Huggan's Tintin is a well-chosen metaphor since it is a copy of an image that, on one level, epitomizes the West, and on the other is a symbol of the 'exotic'. One of Hergé's most notorious Tintin tales is *Tintin au Congo* in which the eponymous blonde hero and his little white dog, Milou, have adventures among African peoples who are represented as wild savages with bones through their noses, speaking pidgin and often looking ridiculous.[39] Huggan's statue thus connotes the colonial explorer – particularly as Tintin's hair resembles a pith helmet – and is, to a Western reader, both familiar and exotic. Tintin is both recognizable and unfamiliar in this carved 'fake' version of his image. A useful connection can be made here with Alvim's painting that I discussed at the beginning of this chapter. As Alvim and Huggan suggest, we are all post-exotic in so far as we are all positioned in and by discourses of the exotic, whether as observed or observer, native or tourist, migrant or indigene. What Beyala and her fiction demonstrate is on the one hand the inescapability of the (post)exotic, but on the other the migrant's potential to turn the (post)exotic against itself and adapt it to her own ends.

Of course, this can be a very dangerous game for a writer to play since it is one that relies on Beyala keeping her readers on her side. In the 1997 article we have already discussed, Mongo Beti painted Beyala as a writer of cynical ambition who saw herself becoming a member of the Académie Française within the next five years but who was, at the same time, a writer whose success would not last.[40] Eight years after this pessimistic assessment of Beyala's future as a writer, she continues to experience phenomenal success in terms of book sales in France, but her reputation remains blighted by both the allegations of 1996 and her controversial appearances on TV and radio. Furthermore, with the publication of *La Plantation* in 2005, Beyala appears to have begun to fulfil Beti's claim that she lacks the talent as a writer to fully realize her ambition. This novel confirms the fact that Beyala is now treading a very fine line between reappropriating exoticism and selling out to an exoticist readership. *La Plantation* presents us with a version of Beyala that now appears ready to turn out books that are badly written and poorly edited in order to maintain a gruelling publishing schedule of at least one novel every two years and to keep up with the latest literary trends. Over 450 pages long, *La Plantation* is the least compelling of Beyala's novels, and contains a number of mistakes that should have been picked up by her editors: errors are made over characters' names and geographical place names are misspelled.[41] Such sloppy presentation in a novel that claims to be a fictional commentary on Mugabe's land reforms discredits Beyala as a serious writer.[42] I think it highly unlikely that this latest novel will generate the critical debate that surrounded novels such as *C'est le soleil qui m'a brûlée* and even *Les Honneurs perdus*. Although the novel's subject is topical, the writing lacks the innovation of Beyala's earlier works and demonstrates a disappointing lack of political engagement. The mediocrity of *La Plantation* combined with the contentious nature of her previous novel, *Femme nue, femme noire*, suggests that Beyala is beginning to test the limits of her self-constructed politics of performance. Perhaps like the 'cochon pendu' she so often refers to in her writing, Beyala has played a dangerous game too long and ended up losing her grip.

That said, Beyala's performances continue to maintain her readers' interest: despite its weaknesses, *La Plantation* was ranked as a bestselling novel in France. By constantly revising her script both in terms of her public performances and her identification as a writer (feminist, migrant author, erotic novelist, etc.), Beyala prevents the literary tourists who enjoy her fiction from becoming over-familiar with her product and seeking their exotic thrills elsewhere. Ultimately, she plays the search for exoticism against itself, deliberately positioning herself and her writing as both familiar and unpredictable, thus forever out of reach. This constant play in Beyala's role as author and public figure mirrors the ways in which her migrant novels celebrate the unlocatability of migrant subjectivies. That is not to suggest that migrant subjectivities do not exist but rather that they are constantly repositioning themselves in relation to their ever-shifting 'points de repère' [points of reference]. Like Philomène Tralala, Beyala overcomes all attempts to dismiss her as a bad writer, a loudmouth or a plagiarist by appropriating such criticisms into her game plan. In Gloria Anzaldúa's terms, Beyala is a francophone version of 'the new *mestiza*':

> The new *mestiza* copes by developing a tolerance for contradictions, a tolerance for ambiguity. [...] She learns to juggle cultures. She has a plural personality, she operates in a pluralistic mode – nothing is thrust out, the good, the bad and the ugly, nothing rejected, nothing abandoned. Not only does she sustain contradictions, she turns the ambivalence into something else.[43]

Ambivalence is part of the performance of Calixthe Beyala in what has become a kind of postcolonial game. In this respect, Harrow is right to suggest that she represents a contemporary version of the African trickster. Although this kind of play, as Mongo Beti so convincingly argues, can be politically problematic, it has nevertheless proved a useful strategy for a migrant African women writer seeking commercial success in postcolonial France.

Notes

Introduction

1 Dominique Mataillet, 'Le cas Beyala', *Jeune Afrique*, 1876–1877, December 1996.

2 Figure for 21–27 March 2005 taken from Albin Michel's website: http://www.albinmichel.fr/pages/20best/1.htm *La Plantation* was also ranked twenth-fifth by *Livres-hebdo/Le Nouvel Observateur*.

3 Sennen Andriamirado and Emmanuelle Pontié, '"Je reste révoltée mais je cherche à comprendre"', *Jeune Afrique*, 1876–1877, 18–31 December 1996.

4 Emmanuelle Pontié, 'Belleville à l'honneur', *Afrique Magazine*, May 1999.

5 Indigenous African editions are generally expensive to buy and reinforce the French readership's perception of African women's writing as marginal and foreign. Metropolitan African editions such as L'Harmattan are also more expensive than mass-produced paperbacks and suffer from low prestige and a lack of distribution networks.

6 These are *The Sun Hath Looked Upon Me*, trans. Marjolijn de Jager (Oxford: Heinemann,1996); *Your Name Shall be Tanga*, trans. Marjolijn de Jager (Oxford: Heinemann,1996); and *Loukoum: The 'Little Prince of Belleville'*, trans. Marjolijn de Jager (Oxford: Heinemann, 1995). Wherever possible, I have supplied quotations from the published translations. All other translations are my own.

7 Mataillet, 'Le cas Beyala'.

8 Rangira Béatrice Gallimore, *L'Oeuvre romanesque de Calixthe Beyala: le renouveau de l'écriture féminine en Afrique francophone sub-saharienne* (Paris: L'Harmattan, 1997).

9 Irène Assiba d'Almeida, *Francophone Women Writers: Destroying the Emptiness of Silence* (Gainesville, FL: Florida University Press, 1994); Juliana Makuchi Nfah-Abbenyi, *Gender in African Women's Writing: Identity, Sexuality, and Difference* (Bloomington, IN: Indiana University Press, 1997).

10 Odile Cazenave, *Femmes rebelles: naissance d'un nouveau roman africain au féminin* (Paris: L'Harmattan, 1996); Kenneth W. Harrow, *Less than One and Double: a Feminist Reading of African Women's Writing* (Portsmouth, NH: Heinemann, 2002)

11 Elleke Boehmer, *Colonial and Postcolonial Literature* (Oxford: Oxford University Press, 1995), p. 236.

12 Gayatri Spivak, 'Poststructuralism, Marginality, Postcoloniality and Value', in Peter Collier and Helga Geyer-Ryan (eds), *Literary Theory Today* (Ithaca, NY: Cornell University Press, 1990), pp. 219–44 (p. 228).

13 Paul Gilroy, *The Black Atlantic: Modernity and Double Consciousness* (London: Verso 1993), p. 3.

14 The 'Loukoum' diptych consists of *Le petit prince de Belleville* (1992) and *Maman a un amant* (1993).

15 Boehmer, *Colonial and Postcolonial*, p. 24. This goes part of the way to explaining the relative lack of success in France of women writers based in Africa such as Aminata Sow Fall.

16 Russell King, John Connell and Paul White, 'Preface', in King, Connell and White (eds), *Writing across Worlds: Literature and Migration* (London: Routledge, 1995), p. xiii.

17 Françoise Lionnet, *Postcolonial Representations* (Ithaca, NY: Cornell University Press, 1995), p. 3

18 Graham Huggan, *The Postcolonial Exotic: Marketing the Margins* (London: Routledge, 2001), p. 7.

19 For an engaging critique of postcolonial theory, see Stuart Hall, 'When was "the Post-colonial"? Thinking at the Limit', in Iain Chambers and Lidia Curtis (eds), *The Post-Colonial Question: Common Skies, Divided Horizons* (London and New York: Routledge, 1996), pp. 242–60 For a discussion of the relationship between postcolonial and francophone studies, see Charles Forsdick and David Murphy, 'The Case for Francophone Postcolonial Studies', in Forsdick and Murphy (eds), *Francophone Postcolonial Studies: an Introduction* (London: Arnold, 2003), pp. 3–14. See also David Murphy's excellent article, 'De-centring French Studies: Towards a Postcolonial Theory of Francophone Cultures', *French Cultural Studies*, 13.2 (2002), pp. 163–85.

20 Nicholas Harrison, *Postcolonial Criticism* (Cambridge: Polity Press, 2003), p. 9. Celia Britton and Michael Syrotinski also make a case for resisting the containment of postcolonial theory. See Britton and Syrotinski, 'Introduction', *Paragraph*, 24.3 (2001), pp. 1–9.

21 Carole Boyce Davies, *Black Women, Writing and Identity: Migrations of the Subject* (London: Routledge, 1994), p. 46.

22 H. Adlai Murdoch and Anne Donadey, 'Introduction: Productive Intersections', in Murdoch and Donadey (eds), *Postcolonial Theory and Francophone Literary Studies* (Gainesville, FL: University of Florida Press, 2005), pp. 1–17 (p. 9).

23 Michel Laronde, *L'Ecriture décentrée: la langue de l'Autre dans le roman contemporain* (Paris: L'Harmattan, 1996), p. 8 (capitalization in the text). Laronde's use of the term 'décalage' is interesting here as it also suggests a time difference or lag. In other words, he suggests that decentred writing is, to use my own term, 'out of sync' (see Chapter 4).

24 See Emily Apter, *Continental Drift: From National Characters to Virtual Subjects* (Chicago: University of Chicago Press, 1999); Britton and Syrotinski, 'Introduction'; Forsdick and Murphy, 'The Case for Francophone Postcolonial Studies'.

25 Michel Laronde, 'Displaced Discourses: Post(-)coloniality, Francophone Space(s) and the Literature(s) of Immigration in France', in Murdoch and Donadey (eds), *Postcolonial Theory and Francophone Literary Studies*, pp. 175–92.

26 The debate over the hyphen has long exercised critics in Britain and the US. See for example, Kwame Anthony Appiah, 'Is the Post- in Postmodernism the Post-

in Postcolonial?', *Critical Inquiry*, 17.2 (1991), pp. 336–57; Anne McClintock, 'The Angels of Progress: Pitfalls of the Term "Postcolonialism"', *Social Text*, 10.2–3 (1992), pp. 84–98; and Hall, 'When was "the Post-colonial"?'.

27 Jean-Marc Moura, *Littératures francophones et théorie postcoloniale* (Paris: PUF, 1999).

28 Britton and Syrotinski, 'Introduction', p. 3.

29 James Procter, 'Cultural Studies into Francophone Postcolonial Studies: Towards a "Disciplined" Interdisciplinarity', *Francophone Postcolonial Studies*, 1.2 (2004), pp. 47–52 (p. 48)

30 Stuart Hall, 'Cultural Identity and Diaspora', in Jonathan Rutherford (ed.), *Identity, Community, Culture, Difference* (London: Lawrence and Wishart, 1990), pp. 222–37 (p. 222).

31 Developed in the 1930s by African and Caribbean writers in Paris including Léopold Sédar Senghor and Aimé Césaire, Negritude promoted the distinctive nature of blackness. This included what was vaguely described as a 'black soul' whose roots were in Africa and whose traits were shared by all black people in the world. See Léopold Sédar Senghor, *Liberté I: Négritude et humanisme* (Paris: Seuil, 1964).

32 Edward W. Said, ' Introduction', in *Reflections on Exile and Other Literary and Cultural Essays* (London: Granta, 2001), pp. xi–xxxv (p. xv).

33 Charles Forsdick, 'Challenging the Monolingual, Subverting the Monocultural: the Strategic Purposes of Francophone Postcolonial Studies', *Francophone Postcolonial Studies*, 1.1 (2003), pp. 33–41 (p. 33).

34 Huggan, *The Postcolonial Exotic*, p. vii.

35 Mongo Beti, 'L'Affaire Calixthe Beyala ou comment sortir du néocolonialisme en littérature', *Palabres: Revue Culturelle Africaine*, 1.3-4 (1997), pp. 39–48 (pp. 45–46).

36 Huggan, *The Postcolonial Exotic*, p. 277, n. 11. Huggan himself uses Butler's work as a springboard for his reading of queer performativity in Hanif Kureishi's work (pp. 95–103).

37 The only critic to deploy Butler's work as a tool for analysing some of Beyala's novels is US-based academic Kenneth Harrow in *Less than One and Double*. Although Harrow's fascinating study is largely limited to a feminist psychoanalytical reading of Beyala through Butler, his chapter on *Assèze l'Africaine* raises points about performance and representation with which I engage in my own reading in Chapter 5. Drawing on the writings of Bhabha and Irigaray, Harrow focuses on the metaphors of masquerade and mime which, I argue, are central to an understanding of Beyala's oeuvre,

38 Judith Butler, 'Performative Acts and Gender Constitution: an Essay in Phenomenology and Feminist Theory', in Henry Bial (ed.), *The Performance Studies Reader* (London: Routledge, 2004), pp. 154–66 (p. 160).

39 Judith Butler, *Bodies that Matter* (London: Routledge, 1993), p. 2.

40 Paul White, 'Geography, Literature and Migration', in King, Connell and White (eds), *Writing across Worlds*, pp. 1–19 (p. 3).

41 Ayo Abiétou Coly, 'Neither Here nor There: Calixthe Beyala's Collapsing Homes', *Research in African Literatures*, 33.2 (2002), pp. 34–45. Despite claiming to discuss Beyala's first four novels, Coly ignores the lesser-known novel, *Seul le diable le savait*, published in 1990 (i.e. between *Tu t'appelleras Tanga* and *Le petit prince de Belleville*) and republished by J'ai Lu as *La Négresse rousse* in 1997.

42 King, Connell and White (eds), *Writing across Worlds*, 'Preface', p. xiv.
43 Denise Brahimi, 'Calixthe Beyala', *Notre Librairie*, 125 (1996), p. 63.
44 Andriamirado and Pontié, 'Je reste révoltée'.
45 Members of the Collectif include Manu Dibango, Princesse Erika, Dieudonné, Luc Saint-Eloi, and le Secteur A (Passy, Doc Gynéco and Stommy Bugsy).
46 The CSA review also commissioned the second major study of French television's representation of ethnic minorities. The project, entitled *Présence et representation des 'minorités visibles' à la télévision française*, was co-ordinated by Marie-France Malonga, and focused on the number and types of representation of people of black African, Maghrebian or Asian descent in one week of programmes (11–17 October 1999) on five French terrestrial channels (TF1, France 2, France 3, Canal + and M6) between 5pm and midnight. For further discussion of the CSA study, see Nicki Hitchcott, 'Calixthe Beyala: Black Face(s) on French TV', *Modern and Contemporary France*, 12.4 (2004), pp. 473–82.
47 'La 25ème nuit des César', Canal +, 19 February 2000.

Chapter One

1 Calixthe Beyala in Narcisse Mouellé-Kombi, 'Calixthe Beyala et son petit prince de Belleville', *Amina*, 268 (August 1992).
2 Assouline made the accusation on the radio programme 'Lire-RTL' on 24 November 1996. Okri's editors, Julliard, chose not to pursue the allegation. *Les Honneurs perdus* was also shortlisted for the Prix Goncourt in 1996.
3 Huggan, *The Postcolonial Exotic*.
4 Huggan, *The Postcolonial Exotic*, p. 37.
5 Jean-Marie Volet, 'Calixthe Beyala, or the Literary Success of a Cameroonian Woman Living in Paris', *World Literature Today*, 67.2 (1993), pp. 309–14.
6 Sylvie Genevoix, 'Portrait: Calixthe Beyala', *Madame Figaro*, 22 July 1993.
7 This was not the first time Beyala had been awarded a prize by the Academy: *Assèze l'Africaine* was awarded the Prix François Mauriac in 1994.
8 Pierre Bourdieu, *The Field of Cultural Production* (Cambridge: Polity Press, 1993), p. 42.
9 In terms of marketing, the alleged plagiarism in *Les Honneurs perdus* has now become less important than the prize. The allegations of plagiarism are discussed in more detail later in this chapter.
10 Choga Regina Egbeme, *Je suis née au harem* (Paris: L'Archipel, 2003), originally published in German as *Hinter goldenen Glittern* (Munich: Econ Ullstein, 2001).
11 Timothy Brennan, *At Home in the World: Cosmopolitanism Now* (Cambridge, MA: Harvard University Press, 1997), p. 38.
12 Beti, 'L'Affaire Calixthe Beyala', p. 43. Beti is referring to the Alain Juppé/Jacques Chirac leadership of France. Although Beti implies that Beyala's book sales fell as a result of the plagiarism allegations, in fact they were unaffected.
13 Beti, 'L'Affaire Calixthe Beyala', p. 43. Mongo Beti is ignoring Beyala's brief parody of Cameroon's political history in *Les Honneurs perdus*, pp. 122–23.
14 Emmanuel Matateyou, 'Calixthe Beyala: entre le terroir et l'exil', *The French*

Review, 69.4 (1996), pp. 605–15 (p. 613).

15 Quoted in Mataillet, 'Le cas Beyala'.

16 Matateyou, 'Calixthe Beyala', p. 606. See Chapter 4 for further discussion of Beyala's 'Afro-pessimism'.

17 Quoted in Mataillet, 'Le cas Beyala'.

18 http:\\www.albinmichel.fr

19 Bennetta Jules-Rosette, *Black Paris: the African Writers' Landscape* (Urbana and Chicago: University of Illinois Press, 1998), p. 7.

20 Becky Clarke, 'The African Writers Series – Celebrating Forty Years of Publishing Distinction', *Research in African Literatures*, 34.2 (2003), pp. 163–74.

21 The other francophone African authors in the series are Cheikh Hamidou Kane, Ferdinand Oyono, Ousmane Sembene and Sony Labou Tansi.

22 Huggan, *The Postcolonial Exotic*, p. 51.

23 Huggan, *The Postcolonial Exotic*, pp. 50–57.

24 Quoted in Clarke, 'The African Writers Series', p. 172.

25 Clarke, 'The African Writers Series', pp. 168–69.

26 Mariama Bâ's *Une si longue lettre* featured in the top twelve; Véronique Tadjo's title is a book for children, *Mamy Wata et le monstre*. The full list can be viewed at: http://www.columbia.edu/cu/lweb/indiv/africa/cuvl/Afbks.html#list

27 Ambroise Kom, 'L'univers zombifié de Calixthe Beyala', *Notre Librairie*, 125 (1996), pp. 63–71 (p. 63).

28 Although it should be pointed out that French hypermarkets generally stock an impressive range of both popular and canonical texts.

29 Huggan, *The Postcolonial Exotic*, p. 50.

30 Beti, 'L'Affaire Calixthe Beyala', p. 45.

31 Sonja Darlington, 'Calixthe Beyala's Manifesto and Fictional Theory', *Research in African Literatures*, 34.2 (2003), pp. 41–52 (p. 51).

32 Brahimi, 'Calixthe Beyala', p. 63.

33 Andriamirado and Pontié, '"Je reste révoltée mais je cherche à comprendre"'.

34 Madeleine Borgomano, 'Calixthe Beyala: une écriture déplacée', *Notre Librairie*, 125 (1996), pp. 72–74 (p. 74)

35 Francesca Canadé Sautman, 'The Race for Globalization: Modernity, Resistance, and the Unspeakable in Three African Francophone Texts', in Farid Laroussi and Christopher L. Miller (eds), *Yale French Studies* 103, *French and Francophone* (2003), pp. 106–22 (p. 110).

36 Ambroise Têko-Agbo, 'Werewere Liking et Calixthe Beyala: le discours féministe et la fiction', *Cahiers d'études africaines*, 37.1 (1997), pp. 39–58 (p. 41).

37 See Chandra Mohanty, 'Under Western Eyes: Feminist Scholarship and Colonial Discourse', *Feminist Review*, 30 (1988), pp. 61–88 and Trinh T. Minh-ha, *Woman, Native, Other* (Bloomington: Indiana University Press, 1989). For an interesting critique of Mohanty and Trinh, see Leela Gandhi, *Postcolonial Theory: a Critical Introduction* (Edinburgh: Edinburgh University Press, 1998), pp. 82–88.

38 Têko-Agbo, 'Werewere Liking', p. 53. In Têko-Agbo's view, the subtlety of Beyala's less explicitly feminist novel, *Les Honneurs perdus*, makes it a more successful work of fiction. The quotation is from *TTT*, p. 27 (In *YNT*, de Jager mistranslates this as the 'free-thinking, free-flying woman'. An 'homme de plume' is a writer, or man of letters).

39 Adèle King, 'Calixthe Beyala et le roman féministe africain', in Régis Antoine (ed.), *Carrefour de Cultures: Mélanges offerts à Jacqueline Leiner* (Tübingen: Gunter Narr Verlag, 1993), pp. 101–07 (p. 101).
40 Borgomano, 'Calixthe Beyala', p. 74.
41 Beyala, *Lettre d'une Africaine à ses soeurs occidentales*, p. 20.
42 Jean-Bernard Gervais, 'Calixthe Beyala, Africaine et rebelle', *Amina*, 304 (1995).
43 Nfah-Abbenyi, *Gender in African Women's Writing*, pp. 93–94.
44 See Daniel Atchebro, 'Beyala: trop "brûlante" pour les mecs!', *Regards Africains*, 8 (1988), p. 29; David Ndachi Tagne's review of *C'est le soleil qui m'a brûlée*, *Notre Librairie*, 100 (1990), pp. 96–97; Joseph Ndinda, 'Ecriture et discours féminin au Cameroun: trois générations de romancières', *Notre Librairie*, 118 (1994), pp. 6–12.
45 Calixthe Beyala quoted in Gallimore, *L'Oeuvre romanesque de Calixthe Beyala*, p. 199. These remarks were made before the publication of *Femme nue, femme noire* (2003) which contains explicit descriptions of sexual acts between women.
46 Tunde Fatunde, 'Calixthe Beyala Rebels Against Female Oppression', *African Literature Today*, 24 (2004), pp. 69–76 (p. 75).
47 Kom, 'L'Univers zombifié', p. 67.
48 Kom, 'L'Univers zombifié', p. 67. It should be noted that Kom's remarks were made before the publication of *Femme nue, femme noire* (see below).
49 Calixthe Beyala, 'La Sonnette', in Marc Dolisi (ed.), *Troubles de femmes* (Paris: Spengler, 1994), pp. 11–21.
50 Dominique Mataillet, 'Radis noirs et autres crudités', *Jeune Afrique*, 18 May 2003
http://www.Lintelligent.com/articleImp.asp?art_cle=LIN18053radisstiduro.
51 Catherine Millet, *La Vie sexuelle de Catherine M* (Paris: Seuil, 2002). Millet is a well-known figure in the art world in Paris and is the editor of Art Press publishing house.
52 http://www.afrik.com/forum.php3?id_article=6389&retour=article6389.html.
53 See Marie-France Etchegoin, 'Sexe: quand les femmes disent tout', *Le Nouvel Observateur*, 24–31 May 2001.
54 Beyala, *C'est le soleil qui m'a brûlée*, back cover (Stock edition)
55 Quoted in Philippe Cusin, 'Les Inspirations de Calixthe Beyala', *Le Figaro*, 25 November 1996.
56 Of course, Beyala's words are also chosen to win the sympathy of the readers of *Le Figaro*. Mongo Beti points out the illogical nature of a black writer condemning the left in 'L'affaire Calixthe Beyala', p. 43.
57 Quoted in Pierre Assouline, 'L'Affaire Beyala rebondit', *Lire*, February 1997.
58 Assouline, 'L'Affaire Beyala rebondit'.
59 Matt Seaton, Dan Glaister and Alex Duval Smith, 'Famished Road Feeds French Book Fever', *The Guardian*, 26 November 1996.
60 Véronique Porra, '"Moi, Calixthe Beyala, la plagiaire!" ou ambiguïtés d'une "défense et illustration" du plagiat', *Palabres*, 1.3-4 (1997), pp. 23–37.
61 Seaton et al., 'Famished Road'.
62 Seaton et al., 'Famished Road'.

63 Ironically, Beyala implicitly condemns immigrants who cry racism rather than taking responsibility for their actions in *Lettre d'une Afro-française* (p. 18)
64 Calixthe Beyala, 'Moi, Calixthe Beyala, la plagiaire!', *Le Figaro*, 25 January 1997.
65 'Ben Okri répond à Calixthe Beyala', *Libération*, 28 November 1996.
66 Assouline claims that the members of the Academy were made aware of the judgment against Beyala in a fax sent by a rival publisher ('L'Affaire Beyala rebondit').
67 Assouline, 'L'Affaire Beyala rebondit'. Beyala also makes this point in 'Moi, Calixthe Beyala, la plagiaire!'
68 In Assouline, 'L'Affaire Beyala rebondit'.
69 Marilyn Randall, *Pragmatic Plagiarism: Authorship, Profit, and Power* (Toronto: University of Toronto Press, 2001), p. 187.
70 Ouologuem consistently claimed that any plagiarism in *Le Devoir de violence* was the result of his publisher's omission of quotation marks. For further discussion of the Ouologuem controversy, see Christopher Miller, *Blank Darkness: Africanist Discourse in French* (Chicago: University of Chicago Press, 1985), pp. 216–45, Christopher Wise, 'In Search of Yambo Ouologuem', *Research in African Literatures*, 29.2 (1998), pp. 159–82 and Eric Sellin, 'The Unknown Voice of Yambo Ouologuem', *Yale French Studies*, 53 (1976), pp. 137–62.
71 *Le Devoir de violence* was finally republished by Le Serpent à Plumes in 2003.
72 Mataillet, 'Le cas Beyala'.
73 Quoted in Mataillet, 'Le cas Beyala'.
74 Andriamirado and Pontié, '"Je reste révoltée mais je cherche à comprendre"'.
75 Mouellé-Kombi, 'Calixthe Beyala et son petit prince de Belleville'.
76 Quoted in Mataillet, 'Le cas Beyala'.
77 *La Lettre du CSA*, 129, (juin 2000), p. 13.
78 Frédéric Beigbeder, 'La case de tante Beyala', *Elle*, 14 October 1996.
79 There are twelve recorded appearances for this year in the copyright archives of the Institut National de l'Audiovisuel (INA) in Paris
80 See, for example, Thierry Beccaro in 'Matin Bonheur', Antenne 2, 8 December 1987. Much of Beccaro's interview with Beyala consists of whole-screen close-up shots of her face. See also Serge Moati in 'Ripostes', La Cinquième, 28 May 2000 and Patrick Poivre d'Arvor in 'A la Folie', 25 October 1987.
81 'Matin Bonheur', Antenne 2, 20 September 1988
82 Homi K. Bhabha, 'The Other Question... Homi K. Bhabha Reconsiders the Stereotype and Colonial Discourse', *Screen*, 24.6 (1983), pp. 18–36 (p. 18).
83 Nicolas Blanchard and Pascal Bancel, *De l'indigène à l'immigré* (Paris: Gallimard, 1998), p. 83.
84 Huggan, *The Postcolonial Exotic*, p. 28.
85 Huggan, *The Postcolonial Exotic*, p. 214.
86 Huggan, *The Postcolonial Exotic*, p. 215
87 Edward Said, *Representations of the Intellectual* (New York: Vintage, 1994), p. xi.

Chapter Two

1 Beyala, *Tu t'appelleras Tanga*, p. 150 ('Elle' here is Anna-Claude).
2 Beyala, *Your Name Will be Tanga*, p. 101 ('She' here is Anna-Claude).
3 This term is taken from Yambo Ouologuem, *Le Devoir de violence* (1968; Paris: Le Serpent à Plumes, 2003), p. 153..
4 Sellin, 'The Unknown Voice', p. 143. Sellin stresses the fact that he has never accused Ouologuem of plagiarism, but rather of hypocrisy and literary 'mauvaise foi' (p. 147). It could be argued that such a protest underlines the importance of this issue in the context in which Sellin was writing: a direct accusation would have provided ammunition for those intent on proving that African literature was not 'Literature'.
5 For further discussion of Ouologuem's 'authenticity', see Seth Wolitz, 'L'Art du plagiat', *Research in African Literatures*, 4.1 (1973), pp. 130–34.
6 The 'petit-nègre' [pidgin] word 'Missié' [Mister] is a more loaded term that its English translation suggests. By referring to Assouline in this way, Beyala reduces her critic to the status of a 'savage' and thus reverses the power dynamic. For a discussion of Beyala's admiration for Dumas as a model of cultural integration, see Eloise A. Brière, 'Quebec and France: *La Francophonie* in a Comparative Postcolonial Frame', in H. Adlai Murdoch and Anne Donadey (eds), *Postcolonial Theory and Francophone Literary Studies* (Gainesville, FL: University Press of Florida, 2005), pp. 151–74 (p. 159).
7 Iain Chambers, *Migrancy, Culture, Identity* (London: Routledge, 1994) p. 74.
8 Jules-Rosette, *Black Paris*, pp. 8–9.
9 Jules-Rosette, *Black Paris*, p. 11.
10 Elizabeth Ezra, 'Empire on Film: from Exoticism to "Cinéma Colonial"', in Charles Forsdick and David Murphy (eds), *Francophone Postcolonial Studies: a Critical Introduction* (London: Arnold, 2003), pp. 56–65 (pp. 56–57).
11 See Charles Forsdick, 'Revisiting Exoticism: from Colonialism to Postcolonialism', in Forsdick and Murphy (eds), *Francophone Postcolonial Studies*, pp. 46–55.
12 Jules-Rosette, *Black Paris*, pp. 8–14.
13 James Clifford, *The Predicament of Culture: Twentieth-Century Ethnography, Literature, and Art* (Cambridge, MA: Harvard University Press, 1988), p. 12.
14 Clifford, *The Predicament of Culture*, p. 59.
15 Graham Huggan, 'Anthropologists and Other Frauds', *Comparative Literature*, 46.2 (1994), pp. 113–28 (p. 125). For further discussion of 'salvage ethnography', see James Clifford, 'On Ethnographic Allegory', in James Clifford and George E. Marcus (eds), *Writing Culture: the Poetics and Politics of Ethnography* (Berkeley and Los Angeles: University of California Press, 1986), pp. 98–121 (pp. 112–13).
16 Senghor was a great admirer of Frobenius. Indeed, his theory of Negritude was partly inspired by Frobenius's work.
17 Huggan, 'Anthropologists and other Frauds', p. 117.
18 Mataillet, 'Le cas Beyala'. In her early career, Beyala claimed to have grown up alone with only her older sister for company. See Assiatou Bah Diallo, 'Un nouveau roman de Calixthe Beyala', *Amina*, 223 (November 1988).
19 Gallimore, *L'Oeuvre romanesque de Calixthe Beyala*, pp. 35–61. Indeed, as David Murphy notes, 'romans de la désillusion' were common among the post-

independence generation of African writers. See David Murphy, 'Will the Real Africa Please Stand Up? Resistance and Representation in African Literature', in David Murphy and Aedín Ní Loingsigh (eds), *Thresholds of Otherness/Autrement Mêmes: Identity and Alterity in French-Language Literatures* (London: Grant and Cutler, 2002), pp. 305–22 (p. 316).

20 Paul Biya took over the presidency of Cameroon in 1982 succeeding long-term President Ahmadou Ahidjo who retired on health grounds. Although former Prime Minister Biya was Ahidjo's chosen successor, conflicts soon emerged between them and led to a coup plot headed by Ahidjo which Biya suppressed. Ahidjo then left Cameroon and died in exile.

21 Coly, 'Neither Here nor There', p. 34. Coly is referring to Andrew Gurr, *Writers in Exile: the Identity of Home in Modern Literature* (Brighton: Atlantic Highlands, 1981).

22 Coly, 'Neither Here nor There', p. 34.

23 De Jager varies the translation of 'fesse'/'fesses' as 'backside', 'fanny' and even 'tongue-waggers' (*SHL*, p. 56), lessening the impact of Beyala's substitution of 'fesses' for 'femmes' in French.

24 In a press release issued by Amnesty International on 29 February 2000, UN Special Rapporteur, Sir Nigel Rodley, confirmed that torture and ill-treatment of prisoners and detainees in Cameroon are 'systematic and widespread'. See <http://www.amnesty.org.uk/news/press/14086.shtml>.

25 Awa Thiam, *La Parole aux Négresses* (Paris: Denoël, 1978), translated as *Speak out Black Sisters* in 1986.

26 Kesso Barry's autobiographical text, *Kesso, Princess peulhe* (Paris: Seghers, 1988) is another rare exception to this silence.

27 For a discussion of inertia and tradition in Beyala's first novel, see Christiane Ndiaye, 'Mouvances: Du féminin à l'africanité dans *C'est le soleil qui m'a brûlée*', *Etudes Francophones*, 14.1 (1999), pp. 43–64.

28 Christiane Ndiaye, 'Beyala et Kamanda: comment fatiguer le malheur par paroles interposées', *Etudes Francophones*, 18.1 (2003), pp. 73–88 (78).

29 Many of Beyala's female characters dream of 'ailleurs' [elsewhere].

30 Nancy Arenberg, 'Body Subversion in Calixthe Beyala's *Tu t'appelleras Tanga*', *Dalhousie French Studies*, 45 (1998), pp. 111–20 (p. 111).

31 See the Child Rights Information Network (CRIN) for further information on the abuse and exploitation of children in Africa <http://www.crin.org>.

32 Harrow, *Less than One and Double*, p. 76. Harrow offers a Kristevan reading of *Tu t'appelleras Tanga* which focuses on the African abject. Later in his book, he argues that Beyala's later novels present a far less subversive picture. While the more recent novels are certainly less explicitly negative, I would suggest that what I identify later in this chapter as Beyala's strategy of recuperation and rejection nevertheless has an element of subversion.

33 Odile Cazenave, 'Calixthe Beyala's "Parisian Novels": an Example of Globalization and Transculturation in French Society', *Sites*, 4.1 (2000), pp. 119–27 (pp. 121–22). Harrow similarly condemns *Les Honneurs perdus*, claiming that 'it is little wonder that it was this totally nonsubversive version of a picturesque "rocambolesque" Africa that the Académie Française chose to honor with their Grand Prix, rather than Beyala's more disconcerting early novels of abjection', in *Less than One*

and Double, p. 328, n. 5.

34 Cazenave, 'Calixthe Beyala's "Parisian Novels"', p. 123.
35 Cazenave, 'Calixthe Beyala's "Parisian Novels"', p. 124.
36 Cazenave, 'Calixthe Beyala's "Parisian Novels"', p. 123. Eloise Brière makes a similar point in her reading of *Les Arbres en parlent encore* when she claims that 'Beyala's use of stereotypes supports France's old binary view of the world, still sitting squarely at the center of "la francophonie"', in 'Quebec and France', p. 162.
37 Fatunde, 'Calixthe Beyala Rebels Against Female Oppression', p. 74.
38 Boehmer, *Colonial and Postcolonial Literature*, p. 237.
39 Appiah, 'Is the Post- in Postmodernism the Post- in Postcolonial?, p. 354.
40 Kom, 'L'Univers zombifié', p. 64.
41 In Stéphane Tchakam, 'Calixthe Beyala en toute franchise', *Cameroon Tribune*, 8 January 2004. The problems of book distribution in francophone Africa are not to be underestimated.
42 Kom, 'L'Univers zombifié', p. 65.
43 Calixthe Beyala, *The Sun Hath Looked Upon Me*, trans. Marjolijn de Jager (Oxford: Heinemann, 1996), back cover.
44 See Séwanou Dabla, *Nouvelles écritures africaines: romanciers de la seconde génération* (Paris: L'Harmattan, 2000).
45 For further discussion of gender in Bâ's novels, see Nicki Hitchcott, *Women Writers in Francophone Africa* (Oxford: Berg, 2000), pp. 71–88.
46 Claudia Martinek, Review of *Femme nue, femme noire* http://www.apela-asso.net/Publications/1602.htm
47 On her way back to New Bell, Irène meets Jean-Claude who tells her that a fellow thief had been killed by having a burning rubber tyre placed around his neck. This form of torture, known as 'necklacing', was common in South Africa in the 1980s.
48 Ayo Abiétou Coly, 'Court Poet and Wild Child: Two Readings of Calixthe Beyala's *Les honneurs perdus*', *Nottingham French Studies*, 43.3 (2004), pp. 46–59 (p. 48).
49 Coly, 'Court Poet and Wild Child', p. 49.
50 Murphy, 'Will the Real Africa Please Stand Up?', p. 310.
51 Murphy, 'Will the Real Africa Please Stand Up?', p. 307.
52 Aimé Césaire, *Cahier d'un retour au pays natal* (1939; Paris: Présence Africaine, 1983).
53 Jean-Paul Sartre, 'Orphée noir', preface to L. S. Senghor, *Anthologie de la nouvelle poésie nègre et malgache de langue française* (Paris: PUF, 1948), pp. ix–xliv.
54 Chambers, *Migrancy, Culture, Identity*, p. 74
55 A longer version of this discussion of *Comment cuisiner son mari à l'africaine* appears as Nicki Hitchcott, '*Comment cuisiner son mari à l'africaine*: Calixthe Beyala's Recipes for Migrant Identity', *French Cultural Studies*, 14.2 (2003), pp. 211–20. I am grateful to the editors for permission to reprint some of the material here.
56 David Bell and Gill Valentine, *Consuming Geographies: We are Where we Eat* (London: Routledge, 1997), p. 116.
57 Drawing on the work of Arjun Appadurai, Ian Cook and Philip Crang write that 'regional cuisines are invented traditions (inventions in which the genre of cookery books often seem to have played a particularly important role)', in 'The

World on a Plate: Culinary Culture, Displacement and Geographical Knowledges', *Journal of Material Culture*, 1.2 (1996), pp. 131–53 (p. 139). See also Arjun Appadurai, 'How to Make a National Cuisine: Cookbooks in Contemporary India', *Comparative Studies in Society and History*, 30 (1988), pp. 3–24.

58 Igor Cusack, 'African Cuisines: Recipes for Nation-Building?', *Journal of African Cultural Studies*, 13.2 (2000), pp. 207–25 (p. 208).

59 Of course, the price of an imported novel from France would also exclude a large number of literate Cameroonians. In other words, Cusack's conclusion that African cookbooks 'are generally aimed at the Western cook, but perhaps also at African nationals living in the West' (p. 213) could equally apply to texts published in French in France by prestigious Parisian publishers such as Albin Michel.

60 Tchakam, 'Calixthe Beyala en toute franchise'.

61 Mildred Mortimer, 'Transforming the Word: the Storyteller in the Works of Calixthe Beyala, Malika Mokeddem and Assia Djebar', *Nottingham French Studies*, 40.1 (2001), pp. 86–92.

62 Trinh, *Woman, Native, Other*, p. 121.

63 A longer version of this discussion of *Les Arbres en parlent encore* appears as Nicki Hitchcott, 'Telling Tales: Calixthe Beyala's *Les Arbres en parlent encore*', *Dalhousie French Studies*, 68 (2004), pp. 17–25. I am grateful to the editors of *Dalhousie French Studies* for permission to republish a short section of this article here.

64 Florence Dini, 'Calixthe Beyala: "Mes personnages féminins sont rebelles et frondeurs…"' Interview published in *Amina* (March 2002), http://www.arts.uwa.edu.au/AFLIT/AMINABeyala2002.html. In this interview, Beyala also comments on the animistic belief that trees have spirits, and on the archetypal associations of trees with memory, roots and culture.

65 This call-and-response is repeated at the end of the novel (*APE*, p. 393), stressing the cyclical nature of the story. (An identical call-and-response is found in *La petite fille du réverbère* (*PFR*, p. 164)).

66 As narrator, Edène admits that she was a liar when she was younger and that she will be again when she faces death (*APE*, p. 71).

67 The nvet or mvet is a five-stringed instrument, a bit like a harp or sitar.

68 Alioune Tine, 'Pour une théorie de la littérature écrite', *Présence Africaine*, 133–34 (1984), pp. 99–121 (p. 104).

69 Tine, 'Pour une théorie de la littérature écrite', p. 106.

70 Trinh, *Woman, Native, Other*, p. 123.

71 Clifford, 'On Ethnographic Allegory', p. 113.

72 Beyala is herself a practising Christian.

73 Bernard B. Dadié, 'Authenticité de la littérature africaine écrite dans les langues européennes et sa fonction de reintroduction de la littérature orale dans la littérature mondiale', in Institut Culturel Africain, *La Tradition orale, source de la littérature contemporaine* (Dakar: Nouvelles Editions Africaines, 1984), pp. 55–62 (pp. 56–57). Beyala's text makes an interesting conflation of anthropologist and storyteller when the villagers try to comprehend the story of Edène's brother, Gatama, transformed into a 'mamiwater' (*APE*, p. 175).

74 Trinh, *Woman, Native, Other*, p. 126.

75 Huggan, *The Postcolonial Exotic*, p. 158.

76 Clifford, *The Predicament of Culture*, p. 11

Chapter Three

1 Abdou in *Le petit prince de Belleville*, p. 48.
2 Abdou in *Loukoum: the Little Prince of Belleville*, p. 29.
3 Although not explicitly named in *CCMA*, the twentieth 'arrondissement' is clearly located by mentions of rue de la Tourtille and rue Jean-Pierre Timbaud, as well as references to the surrounding topography of the east of Paris, notably Stalingrad and Père Lachaise cemetery. We learn that Bolobolo and Aïssatou both went to school in the rue Jean-Pierre Timbaud, a reference to the private Catholic Ecole Saint-Joseph (p. 44). Calixthe Beyala herself spent several years living in Belleville.
4 Stuart Hall, 'Signification, Representation, Ideology: Althusser and the Post-Structuralist Debates', *Critical Theories of Mass Communication*, 2.2 (1985), pp. 91–114 (p.109).
5 Susan Ireland and Patrice J. Proulx, 'Introduction', in *Immigrant Narratives in Contemporary France* (Westport, CT: Greenwood Press, 2001), pp. 1–4 (p. 1).
6 In *Les Honneurs perdus*, Saïda finds all doors closed (*HP*, p. 188)
7 Jane Freedman, 'Immigrant and Ethnic Minority Women', in Abigail Gregory and Ursula Tidd (eds), *Women in Contemporary France* (Oxford: Berg, 2000), pp. 153–70 (p. 155).
8 Before 1993, co-wives of immigrants from former colonies were granted residence provided that they bore children while in France.
9 Stuart Hall, 'Introduction: Who Needs Identity?', in Stuart Hall and Paul du Gay (eds), *Questions of Cultural Identity* (London: Sage, 1996), pp. 1–17 (pp. 2–3).
10 Hall, 'Introduction', p. 2.
11 Aedín Ní Loingsigh, 'Immigration, Tourism and Postcolonial Reinventions of Travel', in Forsdick and Murphy (eds), *Francophone Postcolonial Studies*, pp. 155–65 (p. 164).
12 Ní Loingsigh, 'Immigration, Tourism and Postcolonial Reinventions of Travel', p. 164.
13 Claire Dwyer, '"Where are you from?" Young British Muslim Women and the Making of "Home"', in Alison Blunt and Cheryl McEwan (eds), *Postcolonial Geographies* (New York: Continuum, 2002), pp. 184–99 (p. 198).
14 Dwyer, '"Where are you from?"', p. 191.
15 Among women migrants from sub-Saharan Africa this search has led to the development of African women's associations in France which by their very existence challenge the Republican model of integration rather than multiculturalism. See Catherine Quiminal, 'The Associative Movement of African Women and New Forms of Citizenship', in Jane Freedman and Carrie Tarr (eds), *Women, Immigration and Identities in France* (Oxford: Berg, 2000), pp. 39–56.
16 Kevin Robins, 'Tradition and Translation: National Culture in its Global

Context', in John Corner and Sylvia Harvey (eds), *Enterprise and Heritage: Crosscurrents of National Culture* (London: Routledge, 1991), pp. 21–44 (p. 41).

17 Robins, 'Tradition and Translation', p. 41.

18 Quoted in Robins, 'Tradition and Translation', pp. 42–43.

19 Salman Rushdie, *Imaginary Homelands* (London: Granta, 1991), p. 17

20 Pius Adesanmi, 'Anti-Manichean Aesthetics: the Economy of Space in Maryse Condé's *Crossing the Mangrove* and Calixthe Beyala's *Loukoum*', *English in Africa*, 29.1 (2002), pp. 73–83 (p. 79).

21 Adesanmi, 'Anti-Manichean Aesthetics', p. 76. In particular, Adesanmi considers the role of Madame Saddock which, as I argue in Chapter 4, represents the incompatibility of Western feminism with African 'Tradition'. See also Nicki Hitchcott, 'Calixthe Beyala and the Post-colonial Woman', in Alec G. Hargreaves and Mark McKinney (eds), *Post-colonial Cultures in France* (London: Routledge, 1997), pp. 211–25 (p. 218).

22 Mouellé-Kombi, 'Calixthe Beyala'.

23 For an interesting discussion of the parenthesis in Beyala's fiction, see Coly, 'Court Poet and Wild Child', pp. 54–58.

24 Boehmer, *Colonial and Postcolonial Literature*, p. 227 (see also Gayatri Chakravorty Spivak, *In Other Worlds: Essays in Cultural Politics* (London: Routledge, 1988), p. 13).

25 Eloise Brière, *Le roman camerounais et ses discours* (Paris: Nouvelles du Sud, 1993), p. 10.

26 Françoise Lionnet, 'Narrative Strategies and Postcolonial Identity in Contemporary France: Leïla Sebbar's *Les Carnets de Shérazade*', in Gisela Brinker-Gabler and Sidonie Smith (eds), *Writing New Identities: Gender, Nation and Immigration in Contemporary Europe* (Minneapolis, MN: University of Minnesota Press, 1997), pp. 62–77 (p. 63).

27 For an interesting discussion of Beyala's use of Eton, see Matateyou, 'Calixthe Beyala', pp. 607–08. See also Clément Mbom, 'Nouvelles tendances de la création romanesque chez Calixthe Beyala', in Daniel Delas and Danielle Deltel (eds), *Voix nouvelles du roman africain* (Paris: RITM, 1994), pp. 49–72 (pp. 61–64) for an analysis of her language.

28 Boehmer, *Colonial and Postcolonial Literature*, p. 227.

29 See Chapter 5 for further discussion of gender as performance.

30 Alec G. Hargreaves, *Immigration, 'Race' and Ethnicity in Contemporary France* (London: Routledge, 1995), p. 108.

31 For a discussion of the legal maze facing polygamous immigrant families in France, see Hargreaves, *Immigration, 'Race' and Ethnicity*, pp. 114–16.

32 Sotteria suggests that the girl is stupid ('sotte' in French).

33 These 'memoirs' take the form of musings addressed to an anonymous French friend. For further discussion of M'am's memoirs, see Hitchcott, 'Calixthe Beyala and the Post-colonial Woman', pp. 222–23. It is significant that, although Abdou is illiterate, his musings in *Le petit prince de Belleville* are not presented as translated by Loukoum.

34 Homi K. Bhabha, 'The Third Space', in Jonathan Rutherford (ed.), *Identity, Community, Culture* (London: Lawrence and Wishart, 1990), pp. 207–21 (p. 210)

35 Bhabha, 'The Third Space', p. 211.

36 Although M'am is technically not a virgin when she has sex with Tichit, he tells her that she is because she has never had an orgasm (*MAA*, p. 78).

37 Alain-Philippe Durand, 'Le côté de Belleville: négociation de l'espace migratoire chez Calixthe Beyala', *Etudes Francophones*, 14.2 (1999), pp. 53–65 (p. 62).

38 Durand, 'Le côté de Belleville', p. 60.

39 Hall, 'Introduction', p. 4.

40 Emphasis in the text.

41 White, 'Geography, Literature and Migration', p. 15.

Chapter Four

1 Loukoum in *Maman a un amant*, p. 81.

2 Calixthe Beyala, *Lettre d'une Afro-française à ses compatriotes* (Paris: Mango, 2000); *Lettre d'une Africaine à ses soeurs occidentales* (Paris: Spengler, 1995).

3 Calixthe Beyala, *Lettre d'une Africaine à ses soeurs occidentales*.

4 Beyala adds that immigrants of European extraction are not labelled in the same way (*LAFC*, pp. 40–41).

5 'Bouvard des succès', France 2, 26 August 2000

6 Homi K. Bhabha, *The Location of Culture* (London: Routledge, 1994), p. 219

7 Bhabha, *The Location of Culture*, p. 219.

8 Bhabha, *The Location of Culture*, p. 211

9 Bhabha, *The Location of Culture*, p. 211.

10 Jane Ifekwunigwe, 'Old Whine, New Vassals: Are Diaspora and Hybridity Postmodern Inventions?', in Phil Cohen (ed.), *New Ethnicities, Old Racisms* (London: Zed Books, 1999), pp. 180–204.

11 Robert Young, *Colonial Desire: Hybridity in Theory, Culture and Race* (London: Routledge, 1995), pp. 7–8.

12 Young, *Colonial Desire*, p. 18.

13 See Senghor, 'De la liberté de l'âme ou éloge du métissage', pp. 98–103.

14 In *Amours sauvages*, Océan is initially presented as a gay African busker whose former lover was Alexandre. Here Beyala creates an intertextual echo with *Assèze l'Africaine* where Océan is a mixed-race musician who has relationships with both Sorraya and Assèze. Alexandre is Sorraya's husband and becomes Assèze's lover.

15 One of the best-known and most easily accessible is *The Congo Cookbook* [http://www.geocities.com/congocookbook/]. Others websites include *The African Studies Cookbook* [http://www.sas.upen.edu/African_Studies/cookbook/about_cb_wh.html] and *Sally's Place* [http://sallys-place.com/food/ethnic_cusine/Africa.htm [sic]. For printed recipes, see Jean Grimaldi and Alexandrine Bikia, *Le grand livre de la cuisine camerounaise* (Yaoundé: SOPECAM, 1985), Dorinda Hafner, *A Taste of Africa* (London: Headline, 1993) and Inquai Tebereh, *A Taste of Africa: an African Cookbook* (Trenton, NJ: Africa World Press, 1998).

16 My emphasis.

17 Bell and Valentine, *Consuming Geographies*, p. 41.

18 The use of the adjective 'impure' is interesting here because of its connotations of racial impurity.

19 'The development of a national cuisine will involve the summoning of a variety of dishes into the ambit of the discourse of the nation, and the very mention then of some national dish will quietly flag the nation', Cusack, 'African Cuisines', p. 209.

20 cf. Robin Cook's widely reported remark in 2000 that chicken tikka masala is now Britain's national dish.

21 Bell and Valentine, *Consuming Geographies*, p. 113.

22 Writing about migrant foodways in the USA, Kalčik concludes that 'Americans must eat the foods of all their ethnic groups, Americanizing them in some ways, because by this act we perform the sense of our national ethnic identity. By ingesting the foods of each new group, we symbolize the acceptance of each group and its culture', in Susan Kalčik, 'Ethnic Foodways in America: Symbol and the Performance of Identity', in Linda Keller Brown and Kay Mussell (eds), *Ethnic and Regional Foodways in the United States* (Knoxville, TN: University of Tennessee Press, 1984), pp. 37–65 (p. 61). Kalčik's comment has interesting implications for France, a country in which integration remains a problematic issue.

23 Doreen Massey re-examines the idea of time-space compression in 'A Global Sense of Place', *Marxism Today*, June 1991.

24 Alec G. Hargreaves and Marc McKinney, 'Introduction', in Hargreaves and McKinney, *Post-colonial Cultures in France*, pp. 1–25 (p. 11)

25 Young, *Colonial Desire*, p. 28.

26 Gloria Anzaldúa defines a borderland as 'a vague and undetermined place created by the emotional residue of an unnatural boundary. It is in a constant state of transition. The prohibited and forbidden are its inhabitants', in *Borderlands/La Frontera* (San Francisco: Aunt Lute, 1987), p. 3.

27 Anzaldúa, *Borderlands*, p. 63.

28 White, 'Geography, Literature and Migration', pp. 3–4.

29 In spite of her decision to sleep with Ibrahim, Saïda still demonstrates the extent to which she has internalized patriarchal gender roles when she insists that Ibrahim cannot be impotent since only women have sexual problems (*HP*, p. 350).

30 Freedman, 'Immigrant and Ethic Minority Women', p. 157,

31 Gallimore, *L'Oeuvre romanesque de Calixthe Beyala*, p. 88. It should be pointed out that Gallimore's discussion is limited to the early novels as it was published in 1997.

32 Gill Allwood, 'Gender, Class and Ethnicity in French Public Policy Debates', paper presented at 'Gender and Power in the New Europe, the Fifth European Feminist Research Conference', 20–24 August, 2003, Lund University, Sweden. www.5thfeminist.lu.se/filer/paper_648.pdf.

33 While she dreams of being a Hollywood actress, Soumana's only possible option would be to work illegally in the sex industry, as she unwittingly remarks: 'J'suis pas plus mal que celles qui montrent leur derrière au cinéma' (*PPB*, p. 91) [I'm no worse than those who show their arse in the films] (*LPPB*, p. 60).

34 Tasker analyses the way in which Stallone's star image has consciously shifted in his attempt to be taken seriously. See Yvonne Tasker, *Spectacular Bodies: Gender, Genre and the Action Cinema* (London: Routledge, 1993), pp. 83–87.

35 Maffé is a type of stew which combines meat, vegetable and a peanut sauce. Nfoufou (or foufou) is a staple made from some kind of flour (e.g. yam or cassava) and water.

36 Mireille Rosello, *Declining the Stereotype: Ethnicity and Representation in French Cultures* (Hanover, NH: University Press of New England, 1998), p. 133.

37 Rosello, *Declining the Stereotype*, p. 133.

38 See Rosello, *Declining the Stereotype*, pp. 134–36 for a slightly different reading of this passage.

39 Said, 'Introduction', in *Reflections on Exile*, p. xv.

40 Gallimore, *L'Oeuvre romanesque de Calixthe Beyala*, p. 203.

41 A balafon is a traditional African musical instrument, a bit like a xylophone. Claude François was a well-known French pop star in the 1970s. Soukouss is rooted in Cuban rumba in the 1950s and was very popular in Paris in the 1980s when it was generally performed by migrants from Congo and Democratic Republic of Congo.

42 Of course, the lines between stereotype and authenticity are often difficult to draw (see Chapter 2).

43 Bill Ashcroft, Gareth Griffiths and Helen Tiffin, *Post-Colonial Studies: the Key Concepts* (London: Routledge, 2000), p. 139.

44 Bhabha, *The Location of Culture*, p. 86.

45 Said, 'Reflections on Exile', in Said, *Reflections on Exile*, pp. 173–86 (p. 186).

46 Durand, 'Le côté de Belleville, p. 54.

47 Odile Cazenave, 'Writing New Identities: the African Diaspora in Paris', in Susan Ireland and Patrice J. Proulx (eds), *Immigrant Narratives in Contemporary France* (Westport, CT: Greenwood Press), pp. 153–63 (p. 160). In an earlier article, Cazenave highlights the ambiguity of Beyala's personal positioning. See 'Calixthe Beyala: l'exemple d'une écriture décentrée dans le roman africain au féminin', in Michel Laronde (ed.), *L'Ecriture décentrée: la langue de l'Autre dans le roman contemporain* (Paris: L'Harmattan, 1996), pp. 123–47.

48 Dominic Thomas, 'Daniel Biyaoula: Exile, Immigration and Transnational Cultural Productions', in Ireland and Proulx (eds), *Immigrant Narratives in Contemporary France*, pp. 165–76 (p. 166).

49 Thomas, 'Daniel Biyaoula', p. 167.

50 Bhabha, *The Location of Culture*, p. 86.

51 See Mireille Rosello, *Postcolonial Hospitality: the Immigrant as Guest* (Stanford, CA: Stanford University Press, 2001).

52 See Thomas, 'Daniel Biyaoula', p. 167 for an interesting discussion of this epigraph.

53 Said, 'Reflections on Exile', p. 186 (my emphasis).

Chapter Five

1 Aïssatou in *Comment cuisiner son mari à l'africaine*, p. 117.

2 Roger Bromley, *Narratives for a New Belonging: Diasporic Cultural Fictions* (Edinburgh: Edinburgh University Press, 2000), p. 105.

3 See also Mégri's description of her wedding photos (*SDS*, pp. 250–51).

4 John Picton, 'West Africa and the Guinea Coast', in Tom Phillips (ed.), *Africa: the Art of a Continent* (Munich/New York: Prestel, 1996), pp. 327–477 (p. 342),

5 The renaming of this novel as *La Négresse rousse* for the J'ai Lu edition confirms this emphasis on corporeality.

6 Kom, 'L'univers zombifié', p. 71.

7 For further discussion, see Chapter 8 of Hitchcott, *Women Writers in Francophone Africa*.

8 Butler is used by Boyce Davies to read Ama Ata Aidoo, and by Huggan to read Hanif Kureishi. See Boyce Davies, *Black Women, Writing and Identity*, pp. 8 and 74; and Huggan, *The Postcolonial Exotic*, p. 95.

9 Butler, 'Performative Acts', p. 154 (emphasis in the text).

10 Judith Butler, 'Critically Queer', in Erin Striff (ed.), *Performance Studies* (Basingstoke: Palgrave Macmillan, 2003), pp. 142–65 (p. 155).

11 Susan Leigh Foster, 'Choreographies of Gender', in Striff (ed.), *Performance Studies*, pp. 166–77 (p. 168). See also J. L. Austin, *How to Do Things with Words* (Oxford: Clarendon Press, 1962).

12 Butler, 'Performative Acts', p. 155.

13 Butler, 'Critically Queer', pp. 160–62.

14 Mary Ann Doane, 'Film and the Masquerade: Theorising the Female Spectator', in E. Ann Kaplan (ed.), *Feminism and Film* (Oxford: Oxford University Press, 2000), pp. 418–36 (p. 427).

15 Judith Butler, *Gender Trouble* (London: Routledge, 1990), p. 137.

16 De Jager translates 'c'est pas une vraie nana' as 'I think that woman isn't very nice'.

17 Frantz Fanon, *Peau noire, masques blancs* (Paris: Seuil, 1952).

18 Harrow, *Less than One and Double*, p. 190.

19 Doane, 'Film and the Masquerade', p. 427.

20 Harrow, *Less than One and* Double, p. 285.

21 Bhabha, *The Location of Culture*, p. 88.

22 The lines, 'Belle marquise, vos beaux yeux me font mourir d'amour', 'Mourir d'amour me font belle marquise vos beaux yeux' [Lovely Marquess, your beautiful eyes make me die of love, Die of love make me, lovely Marquess, your beautiful eyes] are taken from Act II, scene IV of Molière's play.

23 Such moments also add weight to Beyala's debunking of the myth of the oral tradition (see Chapter 2).

24 I have not cited the published translation as the sentence 'les immigrés raffolent de la chose' is translated as 'immigrants are keen on that [saying vulgar things about women]' (*LPPB*, p. 138), whereas in Loukoum's narration, 'faire la chose' means to have sex.

25 Rosello, *Declining the Stereotype*, p. 11.

26 Rosello, *Declining the Stereotype*, p. 1.

27 Butler, *Gender Trouble*, p. 137.

28 Huggan, *The Postcolonial Exotic*, p. 87. See also Dean MacCannell, *The Tourist: a New Theory of the Leisure Class* (1976; New York: Schocken Books, 1989).

29 Huggan, *The Postcolonial Exotic*, p. 88.

30 Hall, 'Cultural Identity and Diaspora', p. 225.

31 Butler, 'Critically Queer', p. 159.

32 Harrow, *Less than One and Double*, p. 235.

33 See Nicki Hitchcott, 'Calixthe Beyala: Prizes, Plagiarism and "Authenticity"',

Research in African Literatures (forthcoming, 2006).

34 Brière, 'Quebec and France', p. 160. See also Chapter 2 for further discussion of the lies in *Les Arbres en parlent encore*.

35 Harrow, *Less than One and Double*, p. 104. Harrow expresses reservations about using this term.

36 Henry Louis Gates, Jr, 'The Blackness of Blackness: a Critique of the Sign and the Signifying Monkey', in Henry Louis Gates, Jr (ed.), *Black Literature and Literary Theory* (New York: Routledge, 1990), pp. 285–321 (pp. 286–87).

37 Gates, 'The Blackness of Blackness', p. 285.

38 Gates, 'The Blackness of Blackness', p. 289. Gates is paraphrasing Thomas Kochman here.

39 Harrow, *Less than One and Double*, p. 23.

40 Gates, 'The Blackness of Blackness', p. 291.

41 Unlike the angst-ridden philosopher of Kane's novel, this version is now working in Paris as a bouncer. He left Mali to provide for his materialistic wife who is now cheating on him (*HP*, p. 215).

42 Sunday O. Anozie, 'Negritude, Structuralism, Deconstruction', in Henry Louis Gates, Jr (ed.), *Black Literature and Literary Theory* (New York: Routledge, 1990), pp. 105–25 (p. 121).

43 Rey Chow, *Writing Diaspora: Tactics of Intervention in Cultural Studies* (Bloomington, IN: Indiana University Press, 1993), p. 25.

44 Calixte [sic] Beyala, 'Jouons au cochon pendu', *Etudes Francophones*, 12.1 (1997), pp. 7–9.

45 Aijaz Ahmad, 'The Politics of Literary Postcoloniality', *Race and Class*, 36.3 (1995), pp. 1–20.

46 In some respects, Beyala's ambiguity echoes that of a more famous postmodern icon and performer: the pop singer Madonna. Like Beyala, Madonna performs a range of identities, challenges received ideas about gender, flirts with political activity and divides critics who see her, in Pamela Robertson's terms, as either 'glamorized fuckdoll or the queen of parodic critique'. See Pamela Robertson, *Guilty Pleasures: Feminist Camp from Mae West to Madonna* (London: I.B. Taurus, 1996), p. 118. Madonna's ambivalent reception reflects the fact that, like Beyala, she blurs the line between hyperbolic display and subversive parody.

47 Hall, 'Cultural Identity and Diaspora', p. 235.

48 Helen Gilbert, 'De-scribing Orality: Performance and the Recuperation of Voice', in Chris Tiffin and Alan Lawson (eds), *De-scribing Empire: Post-colonialism and Textuality* (London: Routledge, 1994), pp. 98–111 (p. 105).

49 Butler, *Gender Trouble*, p. 146.

50 Clifford, *The Predicament of Culture*, p. 13.

51 Bill Ashcroft, *Post-Colonial Transformation* (London: Routledge, 2001), p. 4.

52 Ashcroft, *Post-Colonial Transformation*, p. 4.

53 Tchakam, 'Calixthe Beyala en toute franchise'.

54 This, he argues, is the price that African francophone writers pay for literary success in France. See Beti, 'L'Affaire Calixthe Beyala', p. 42.

55 Butler, 'Performative Acts', p. 162.

56 Clifford, *The Predicament of Culture*, pp. 223–24.

57 Assouline writes that 'Pour des raisons qui ne paraissent pas très littéraires, il

fallait que ce fût Beyala et nulle autre. En tout cas, certains académiciens déployèrent tout leur talent et leur entregent afin d'entraîner le reste de la Compagnie sur cette pente savoureuse' [For reasons which do not appear very literary, it had to be Beyala and no other. In any case, some members of the Academy used all their talent and their networking skills to lead the rest of the Company on this slippery slope], in Assouline, 'L'Affaire Beyala rebondit', p. 10.

58 Bhabha, *The Location of Culture*, p. 86.
59 Ashcroft et al., *Post-Colonial Studies: the Key Concepts*, p. 139.

Conclusion

1 See exhibition catalogue, *Africa Remix: Contemporary Art of a Continent* (London: Hayward Gallery, 2005), p. 58 for a photograph of the canvas.
2 Huggan, *The Postcolonial Exotic*, p. 32.
3 Huggan, *The Postcolonial Exotic*, p. 33.
4 Butler, *Gender Trouble*, p. 93.
5 Harrow, *Less than One and Double*, pp. 15–16.
6 Butler, *Gender Trouble*, p. 93. Harrow does include this quotation from Butler in his book, but not in his analyses of Beyala.
7 Winifred Woodhull, 'Ethnicity on the French Frontier', in Gisela Brinker-Gabler and Sidonie Smith (eds), *Writing New Identities: Gender, Nation, and Immigration in Contemporary Europe* (Minneapolis, MN: University of Minnesota Press, 1997), pp. 31–61 (p. 49).
8 Huggan, *The Postcolonial Exotic*, p. 91.
9 Fouad Laroui, *La Fin tragique de Philomène Tralala* (Paris: Julliard, 2003). I am grateful to Mireille Rosello for alerting me to the existence of this text.
10 It is surprising that reviews of Laroui's novel appear to have failed to spot the similarities. See, for example, Annie Devergnas's review for *Limag*, http://www.limag.refer.org/Textes/Devergnas/LarouiPhilomeneTralala.htm and Virginie Labetoulle writing for *L'Idéaliste*, http://www.librairing.com/pdf.php/id/2748
11 'Il en va de l'identité d'un être comme de n'importe quelle matière: elle se recycle' (Laroui, *La fin tragique*, p. 51) and the quotation from Maupassant, 'Que peut se vanter, parmi nous, d'avoir écrit une page, une phrase qui ne se trouve déjà, à peu près pareille, quelque part?' (Laroui, *La fin tragique*, p. 57).
12 Laroui, *La fin tragique*, p. 136. The quotation is impossible to translate into English.
13 Laroui, *La fin tragique*, p. 17.
14 Laroui, *La fin tragique*, p. 96.
15 Laroui, *La fin tragique*, p. 100.
16 Laroui, *La fin tragique*, p. 20.
17 Brière, 'Quebec and France', p. 161.
18 Brière, 'Quebec and France', p. 161.
19 In February 2005, the French parliament passed a new law which demands that the school curriculum recognizes the positive effects of French colonization, particularly in North Africa.
20 See Hitchcott, 'Calixthe Beyala: Black Face(s) on French TV' for further dis-

cussion of the Collectif's campaign.

21 Former Senegalese President, Abdou Diouf, was elected to the post in October 2002. As David Murphy explains, Beyala's 'ideas for *la Francophonie* are extremely idealistic and aspirational without any concrete plan for putting them into practice'. See Murphy, 'De-centring French Studies', p. 167, n. 4.

22 Renée Mendy-Ongoundou, 'Calixthe Beyala', *Amina*, 378 (October 2001).

23 See, for example, Beti, 'L'Affaire Calixthe Beyala'. David Murphy presents a succinct analysis of the neocolonial implications of 'La Francophonie' in 'De-centring French Studies'.

24 Beti, 'L'Affaire Calixthe Beyala', p. 44.

25 See Harrison, *Postcolonial Criticism*, pp. 92–111, for a useful discussion of the representativity of the minority writer.

26 Beti, 'L'Affaire Calixthe Beyala', p. 44.

27 Françoise Cévaër, 'Interview de Calixthe Beyala (Romancière camerounaise)', *Revue de Littérature Comparée*, 265 (1993), pp. 161–64 (p. 162).

28 Durand, 'Le côté de Belleville', p. 60.

29 White, 'Geography, Literature and Migration', p. 2.

30 Durand, 'Le côté de Belleville', p. 53.

31 Quoted in Gallimore, *L'Oeuvre romanesque de Calixthe Beyala*, p. 24.

32 Boyce Davies, *Black Women: Writing and Identity*, p. 36.

33 Gilroy, *The Black Atlantic*, p. 29.

34 Sidonie Smith and Gisela Brinker-Gabler, 'Introduction: Gender, Nation, and Immigration in New Europe', in Brinker-Gabler and Smith (eds), *Writing New Identities: Gender, Nation, and Immigration in Contemporary Europe* (Minneapolis, MN: University of Minnesota Press, 1997), pp. 1–27 (p. 16).

35 In Tchakam, 'Calixthe Beyala en toute franchise'.

36 Beti, 'L'Affaire Calixthe Beyala', p. 47. Senghor was seen by many, including Beti, as a hypocritical emblem of French colonial policy. As the first black member of the Académie Française, he was vaunted by the French as a symbol of successful assimilation.

37 Huggan, *The Postcolonial Exotic*, pp. 263–64.

38 Huggan, *The Postcolonial Exotic*, p. 264.

39 Hergé, *Tintin au Congo* (1946; Paris: Casterman, 1974).

40 Beti, 'L'Affaire Calixthe Beyala', p. 44. The Algerian woman writer, Assia Djebar, was elected to the Académie Française in 2005.

41 For example, in a conversation with Franck, a young mixed-race woman explains that Franck (rather than Ernest) is being hounded out of his home (*LP*, p. 137). The Ethiopian capital is named as 'Addis Abeba' (p. 82).

42 In July 2000 Zimbabwean President Robert Mugabe announced a controversial series of land reforms which allowed for the redistribution of white-owned land to landless black 'war veterans' who had fought for independence. At the time, white farmers controlled around 70% of the land. This led to widespread occupations of white-owned farms, large-scale violence and economic crisis. In November 2001 the Land Acquisitions Act was amended to allow the immediate eviction of white farmers from their land. Of the 4500 large-scale white farmers in Zimbabwe at the beginning of the programme, there are now around 600 left. Many have fled the country.

43 Anzaldúa, *Borderlands*, p. 101.

Bibliography of Works Cited

1. Works by Calixthe Beyala

Beyala, Calixthe, *C'est le soleil qui m'a brûlée* (Paris: Stock, 1987).
——, *Tu t'appelleras Tanga* (Paris: Stock, 1988).
——, *Seul le diable le savait* (Paris: Le Pré aux Clercs, 1990; republished as *La Négresse rousse*).
——, *Le petit prince de Belleville* (Paris: J'ai Lu, 1992).
——, *Maman a un amant* (Paris: J'ai Lu, 1993).
——, *Assèze l'Africaine* (Paris: Albin Michel, 1994).
——, 'La Sonnette', in Marc Dolisi (ed.), *Troubles de femmes* (Paris: Spengler, 1994), pp. 11-21.
——, *Lettre d'une Africaine à ses soeurs occidentales* (Paris: Spengler, 1995).
——, *Les Honneurs perdus* (Paris: Albin Michel, 1996).
——, 'Moi, Calixthe Beyala, la plagiaire!', *Le Figaro*, 25 January 1997.
——, *La petite fille du réverbère* (Paris: Albin Michel, 1998).
——, *Amours sauvages* (Paris: Albin Michel, 1999).
——, *Comment cuisiner son mari à l'africaine* (Paris: Albin Michel, 2000).
——, *Lettre d'une Afro-française à ses compatriotes* (Paris: Mango, 2000).
——, *Les Arbres en parlent encore* (Paris: Albin Michel, 2002).
——, *Femme nue femme noire* (Paris: Albin Michel, 2003).
——, *La Plantation* (Paris: Albin Michel, 2005).
Beyala, Calixte [sic], 'Jouons au cochon pendu', *Etudes Francophones*, 12.1 (1997), 7-9.

2. English Translations of Works by Calixthe Beyala

Beyala, Calixthe, *The Sun Hath Looked Upon Me*, trans. Marjolijn de Jager (Oxford: Heinemann, 1996).
——, *Your Name Shall be Tanga*, trans. Marjolijn de Jager (Oxford: Heinemann, 1996).
——, *Loukoum: The 'Little Prince of Belleville*, trans. Marjolijn de Jager (Oxford: Heinemann, 1995).

3. Critical Works on Calixthe Beyala

Adesanmi, Pius, 'Anti-Manichean Aesthetics: the Economy of Space in Maryse Condé's *Crossing the Mangrove* and Calixthe Beyala's *Loukoum*', *English in Africa*, 29.1 (2002), pp. 73–83.
Andriamirado, Sennen and Emmanuelle Pontié, '"Je reste révoltée mais je cherche à comprendre"', *Jeune Afrique*, 1876–1877, December 1996.
Arenberg, Nancy, 'Body Subversion in Calixthe Beyala's *Tu t'appelleras Tanga*', *Dalhousie French Studies*, 45 (1998), pp. 111–20.
Assouline, Pierre, 'L'Affaire Beyala rebondit', *Lire*, February 1997.
Atchebro, Daniel, 'Beyala: trop "brûlante" pour les mecs!', *Regards Africains*, 8 (1988), p. 29.
Beigbeder, Frédéric, 'La case de tante Beyala', *Elle*, 14 October 1996.
'Ben Okri répond à Calixthe Beyala', *Libération*, 28 November 1996.
Beti, Mongo, 'L'Affaire Calixthe Beyala ou comment sortir du néocolonialisme en littérature', *Palabres: Revue Culturelle Africaine*, 1.3-4 (1997), pp. 39–48.
Borgomano, Madeleine, 'Calixthe Beyala: une écriture déplacée', *Notre Librairie*, 125 (1996), pp. 72–74
Brahimi, Denise, 'Calixthe Beyala', *Notre Librairie*, 125 (1996), p. 63.
Cazenave, Odile, 'Calixthe Beyala's "Parisian Novels": an Example of Globalization and Transculturation in French Society', *Sites*, 4.1 (2000), pp. 119–27.
——, 'Calixthe Beyala: l'exemple d'une écriture décentrée dans le roman africain au féminin' in Michel Laronde (ed.), *L'Ecriture décentrée: la langue de l'Autre dans le roman contemporain* (Paris: L'Harmattan, 1996), pp.123–47.
Cévaër, Françoise, 'Interview de Calixthe Beyala (Romancière camerounaise)', *Revue de Littérature Comparée*, 265 (1993), pp. 161–64.
Coly, Ayo Abiétou, 'Court Poet and Wild Child: Two Readings of Calixthe Beyala's *Les honneurs perdus*', *Nottingham French Studies*, 43.3 (2004), pp. 46–59.
——, 'Neither Here nor There: Calixthe Beyala's Collapsing Homes', *Research in African Literatures*, 33.2 (2002), pp. 34–45.
Cusin, Philippe Cusin, 'Les Inspirations de Calixthe Beyala', *Le Figaro*, 25 November 1996.
Darlington, Sonja, 'Calixthe Beyala's Manifesto and Fictional Theory,' *Research in African Literatures*, 34.2 (2003), pp. 41–52.
Diallo, Assiatou Bah, 'Un nouveau roman de Calixthe Beyala', *Amina*, 223 (November 1988).
Dini, Florence, 'Calixthe Beyala: "Mes personnages féminins sont rebelles et frondeurs..."', Interview published in *Amina* (March 2002), http://www.arts.uwa.edu.au/AFLIT/AMINABeyala2002.html.
Durand, Alain-Philippe, 'Le côté de Belleville: négociation de l'espace migratoire chez Calixthe Beyala', *Etudes Francophones*, 14.2 (1999), pp. 53–65.
Fatunde, Tunde, 'Calixthe Beyala Rebels Against Female Oppression', *African Literature Today*, 24 (2004), pp. 69–76.
Gallimore, Rangira Béatrice, *L'Oeuvre romanesque de Calixthe Beyala: le renouveau de l'écriture féminine en Afrique francophone sub-saharienne* (Paris: L'Harmattan, 1997).
Genevoix, Sylvie, 'Portrait: Calixthe Beyala', *Madame Figaro*, 22 July 1993.

Gervais, Jean-Bernard, 'Calixthe Beyala, Africaine et rebelle', *Amina*, 304 (1995).
Hitchcott, Nicki, 'Calixthe Beyala: Black Face(s) on French TV', *Modern and Contemporary France*, 12.4 (2004), pp. 473–82.
——, 'Calixthe Beyala and the Post-colonial Woman', in Alec G. Hargreaves and Mark McKinney (eds), *Post-colonial Cultures in France* (London: Routledge, 1997), pp. 211–25.
——, 'Calixthe Beyala: Prizes, Plagiarism and "Authenticity"', *Research in African Literatures* (forthcoming, 2006).
——, '*Comment cuisiner son mari à l'africaine*: Calixthe Beyala's Recipes for Migrant Identity', *French Cultural Studies*, 14.2 (2003), pp. 211–30.
——, 'Telling Tales: Calixthe Beyala's *Les Arbres en parlent encore*', *Dalhousie French Studies*, 68 (2004), pp. 17–25.
King, Adèle, 'Calixthe Beyala et le roman féministe africain', in Régis Antoine (ed.), *Carrefour de Cultures: Mélanges offerts à Jacqueline Leiner* (Tübingen: Gunter Narr Verlag, 1993), pp. 101–07.
Kom, Ambroise, 'L'univers zombifié de Calixthe Beyala', *Notre Librairie*, 125 (1996), pp. 63–71.
Martinek, Claudia, Review of *Femme nue, femme noire* http://www.apela-asso.net/Publications/1602.htm.
Mataillet, Dominique, 'Le cas Beyala', *Jeune Afrique*, 1876–1877, December 1996.
——, 'Radis noirs et autres crudités', *Jeune Afrique*, 18 May 2003 http://www.Lintelligent.com/articleImp.asp?art_cle=LIN18053radisstiduro
Matateyou, Emmanuel, 'Calixthe Beyala: entre le terroir et l'exil', *The French Review*, 69.4 (1996), pp. 605–15.
Mbom, Clément, 'Nouvelles tendances de la création romanesque chez Calixthe Beyala', in Daniel Delas and Danielle Deltel (eds), *Voix nouvelles du roman africain* (Paris: RITM, 1994), pp. 49–72.
Mendy-Ongoundou, Renée, 'Calixthe Beyala', *Amina*, 378, October 2001.
Mortimer, Mildred, 'Transforming the Word: the Storyteller in the Works of Calixthe Beyala, Malika Mokeddem and Assia Djebar', *Nottingham French Studies*, 40.1 (2001), pp. 86–92.
Mouellé-Kombi, Narcisse, 'Calixthe Beyala et son petit prince de Belleville', *Amina*, 268, August 1992.
Ndachi Tagne, David, Review of *C'est le soleil qui m'a brûlée*, *Notre Librairie*, 100 (1990), pp. 96–97.
Ndiaye, Christiane, 'Beyala et Kamanda: comment fatiguer le malheur par paroles interposées', *Etudes Francophones*, 18.1 (2003), pp. 73–88.
——, 'Mouvances: Du féminin à l'africanité dans *C'est le soleil qui m'a brûlée*', *Etudes Francophones*, 14.1 (1999), pp. 43–64.
Ndinda, Joseph, 'Ecriture et discours féminin au Cameroun: trois générations de romancières', *Notre Librairie*, 118 (1994), pp. 6–12.
Pontié, Emmanuelle, 'Belleville à l'honneur', *Afrique Magazine*, May 1999.
Porra, Véronique, '"Moi, Calixthe Beyala, la plagiaire!" ou ambiguïtés d'une "défense et illustration" du plagiat', *Palabres*, 1.3-4 (1997), pp. 23–37.
Seaton, Matt, Dan Glaister and Alex Duval Smith, 'Famished Road Feeds French Book Fever', *The Guardian*, 26 November 1996.
Tchakam, Stéphane, 'Calixthe Beyala en toute franchise', *Cameroon Tribune*, 8 January 2004.

Têko-Agbo, Ambroise, 'Werewere Liking et Calixthe Beyala: le discours féministe et la fiction', *Cahiers d'études africaines*, 37.1 (1997), pp. 39–58.

Jean-Marie Volet, 'Calixthe Beyala, or the Literary Success of a Cameroonian Woman Living in Paris', *World Literature Today*, 67.2 (1993), pp. 309–14.

4. Other Works Cited

Africa Remix: Contemporary Art of a Continent (London: Hayward Gallery, 2005).

Ahmad, Aijaz, 'The Politics of Literary Postcoloniality', *Race and Class*, 36.3 (1995), pp. 1–20.

Allwood, Gill, 'Gender, Class and Ethnicity in French Public Policy Debates', paper presented at 'Gender and Power in the New Europe, the Fifth European Feminist Research Conference', 20–24 August, 2003, Lund University, Sweden. www.5thfeminist.lu.se/filer/paper_648.pdf

Anozie, Sunday O., 'Negritude, Structuralism, Deconstruction', in Henry Louis Gates, Jr (ed.), *Black Literature and Literary Theory* (New York: Routledge, 1990), pp. 105–25.

Anzaldúa, Gloria, *Borderlands/La Frontera: The New Mestiza* (San Francisco: Aunt Lute, 1987).

Appadurai, Arjun, 'How to Make a National Cuisine: Cookbooks in Contemporary India', *Comparative Studies in Society and History*, 30 (1988), pp. 3–24.

Appiah, Kwame Anthony, 'Is the Post- in Postmodernism the Post- in Postcolonial?', *Critical Inquiry*, 17.2 (1991), pp. 336–57.

Apter, Emily, *Continental Drift: From National Characters to Virtual Subjects* (Chicago: University of Chicago Press, 1999).

Ashcroft, Bill, *Post-Colonial Transformation* (London: Routledge, 2001).

Ashcroft, Bill, Gareth Griffiths and Helen Tiffin, *Post-Colonial Studies: the Key Concepts* (London: Routledge, 2000).

Austin, J. L., *How to Do Things with Words* (Oxford: Clarendon Press, 1962).

Barry, Kesso, *Kesso, Princess peulhe* (Paris: Seghers, 1988).

Bell, David and Gill Valentine, *Consuming Geographies: We are Where we Eat* (London: Routledge, 1997).

Bhabha, Homi K., *The Location of Culture* (London: Routledge, 1994).

——, 'The Other Question... Homi K. Bhabha Reconsiders the Stereotype and Colonial Discourse', *Screen*, 24.6 (1983), pp. 18–36.

——, 'The Third Space', Interview with Jonathan Rutherford, in Jonathan Rutherford (ed.), *Identity, Community, Culture, Difference* (London: Lawrence and Wishart, 1990), pp. 207–21.

Blanchard, Nicolas and Pascal Bancel, *De l'indigène à l'immigré* (Paris: Gallimard, 1998).

Blunt, Alison and Cheryl McEwan, 'Introduction', in Alison Blunt and Cheryl McEwan (eds), *Postcolonial Geographies* (London: Continuum, 2002), pp. 1–6.

Boehmer, Elleke, *Colonial and Postcolonial Literature* (Oxford: Oxford University Press, 1995).

Bourdieu, Pierre, *The Field of Cultural Production* (Cambridge: Polity Press, 1993).
Boyce Davies, Carole, *Black Women, Writing and Identity: Migrations of the Subject* (London: Routledge, 1994).
Brennan, Timothy, *At Home in the World: Cosmopolitanism Now* (Cambridge, MA: Harvard University Press, 1997).
Brière, Eloise A., 'Quebec and France: *La Francophonie* in a Comparative Postcolonial Frame', in H. Adlai Murdoch and Anne Donadey (eds), *Postcolonial Theory and Francophone Literary Studies* (Gainesville, FL: University Press of Florida, 2005), pp. 151–74.
——, *Le roman camerounais et ses discours* (Paris: Nouvelles du Sud, 1993).
Britton, Celia and Michael Syrotinski, 'Introduction', *Paragraph*, 24.3 (2001), pp. 1–9.
Bromley, Roger, *Narratives for a New Belonging: Diasporic Cultural Fictions* (Edinburgh: Edinburgh University Press, 2000).
Butler, Judith, *Bodies that Matter* (London: Routledge, 1993).
——, 'Critically Queer', in Erin Striff (ed.), *Performance Studies* (Basingstoke: Palgrave Macmillan, 2003).
——, *Gender Trouble* (London: Routledge, 1990).
——, 'Performative Acts and Gender Constitution: an Essay in Phenomenology and Feminist Theory', in Henry Bial (ed.), *The Performance Studies Reader* (London: Routledge, 2004), pp. 154–66.
Cazenave, Odile, *Femmes rebelles: naissance d'un nouveau roman africain au féminin* (Paris: L'Harmattan, 1996).
——, 'Writing New Identities: the African Diaspora in Paris', in Susan Ireland and Patrice J. Proulx (eds), *Immigrant Narratives in Contemporary France* (Westport, CT: Greenwood Press, 2001), pp. 153–63.
Césaire, Aimé, *Cahier d'un retour au pays natal* (1939; Paris: Présence Africaine, 1983).
Chambers, Iain, *Migrancy, Culture, Identity* (London: Routledge, 1994).
Chow, Rey, *Writing Diaspora: Tactics of Intervention in Contemporary Cultural Studies* (Bloomington, IN: Indiana University Press, 1993).
Clarke, Becky, 'The African Writers Series – Celebrating Forty Years of Publishing Distinction', *Research in African Literatures*, 34.2 (2003), pp. 163–74.
Clifford, James, 'On Ethnographic Allegory', in James Clifford and George E. Marcus (eds), *Writing Culture: the Poetics and Politics of Ethnography* (Berkeley and Los Angeles: University of California Press, 1986), pp. 98–121.
——, *The Predicament of Culture: Twentieth-Century Ethnography, Literature, and Art* (Cambridge, MA: Harvard University Press, 1988).
Cook, Ian and Philip Crang, 'The World on a Plate: Culinary Culture, Displacement and Geographical Knowledges', *Journal of Material Culture*, 1.2 (1996), pp. 131–53.
Cusack, Igor, 'African Cuisines: Recipes for Nation-Building?', *Journal of African Cultural Studies*, 13.2 (2000), pp. 207–25.
Dabla, Séwanou, *Nouvelles écritures africaines: romanciers de la seconde génération* (Paris: L'Harmattan, 2000).
Dadié, Bernard B., 'Authenticité de la littérature africaine écrite dans les langues européennes et sa fonction de reintroduction de la littérature orale dans la

littérature mondiale', in Institut Culturel Africain, *La Tradition orale, source de la littérature contemporaine* (Dakar: Nouvelles Editions Africaines, 1984), pp. 55–62.

D'Almeida, Irène Assiba, *Francophone Women Writers: Destroying the Emptiness of Silence* (Gainesville, FL: Florida University Press, 1994).

Doane, Mary Ann, 'Film and the Masquerade: Theorising the Female Spectator', in E. Ann Kaplan (ed.), *Feminism and Film* (Oxford: Oxford University Press, 2000), pp. 418–36.

Donadey, Anne, *Recasting Postcolonialism: Women Writing between Worlds* (Portsmouth, NH: Heinemann, 2001).

Dwyer, Claire, '"Where are you from?" Young British Muslim Women and the Making of "Home"', in Alison Blunt and Cheryl McEwan (eds), *Postcolonial Geographies* (London: Continuum, 2002), pp. 184–99.

Egbeme, Choga Regina, *Je suis née au harem* (Paris: L'Archipel, 2003).

Etchegoin, Marie-France, 'Sexe: quand les femmes disent tout', *Le Nouvel Observateur*, 24–31 May 2001.

Ezra, Elizabeth, 'Empire on Film: from Exoticism to "Cinéma Colonial"', in Charles Forsdick and David Murphy (eds), *Francophone Postcolonial Studies: a Critical Introduction* (London: Arnold, 2003), pp. 56–65.

Fanon, Frantz, *Peau noire, masques blancs* (Paris: Seuil, 1952).

Forsdick, Charles, 'Challenging the Monolingual, Subverting the Monocultural: the Strategic Purposes of Francophone Postcolonial Studies', *Francophone Postcolonial Studies*, 1.1 (2003), pp. 33–41.

——, 'Revisiting Exoticism: from Colonialism to Postcolonialism', in Charles Forsdick and David Murphy (eds), *Francophone Postcolonial Studies* (London: Arnold, 2003), pp. 46–55.

Forsdick, Charles and David Murphy, 'The Case for Francophone Postcolonial Studies', in Forsdick and Murphy (eds), *Francophone Postcolonial Studies: an Introduction* (London: Arnold, 2003), pp. 3–14.

Foster, Susan Leigh, 'Choreographies of Gender', in Erin Striff (ed.), *Performance Studies* (Basingstoke: Palgrave Macmillan, 2003), pp. 166–77.

Freedman, Jane, 'Immigrant and Ethnic Minority Women', in Abigail Gregory and Ursula Tidd (eds), *Women in Contemporary France* (Oxford: Berg, 2000), pp. 153–70.

Gandhi, Leela, *Postcolonial Theory: a Critical Introduction* (Edinburgh: Edinburgh University Press, 1998).

Gates, Jr, Henry Louis, 'The Blackness of Blackness: a Critique of the Sign and the Signifying Monkey', in Henry Louis Gates, Jr (ed.), *Black Literature and Literary Theory* (New York: Routledge, 1990), pp. 285–321.

Gilbert, Helen, 'De-scribing Orality: Performance and the Recuperation of Voice', in Chris Tiffin and Alan Lawson (eds), *De-scribing Empire: Post-colonialism and Textuality* (London: Routledge, 1994), pp. 98–111.

Gilroy, Paul, *The Black Atlantic: Modernity and Double Consciousness* (London: Verso, 1993).

Griffiths, Gareth, 'The Myth of Authenticity', in Chris Tiffin and Alan Lawson (eds), *De-scribing Empire: Post-colonialism and Textuality* (London: Routledge, 1994), pp. 70–85.

Grimaldi, Jean, and Alexandrine Bikia, *Le grand livre de la cuisine camerounaise* (Yaoundé: SOPECAM, 1985).
Gurr, Andrew, *Writers in Exile: the Identity of Home in Modern Literature* (Brighton: Atlantic Highlands, 1981).
Hafner, Dorinda, *A Taste of Africa* (London: Headline, 1993).
Hall, Stuart, 'Cultural Identity and Diaspora', in Jonathan Rutherford (ed), *Identity: Community, Culture, Difference* (London: Lawrence and Wishart, 1990), pp. 222–37.
——, 'Introduction: Who Needs Identity?', in Stuart Hall and Paul du Gay (eds), *Questions of Cultural Identity* (London: Sage, 1996), pp. 1–17.
——, 'Signification, Representation, Ideology: Althusser and the Post-Structuralist Debates', *Critical Theories of Mass Communication*, 2.2 (1985), pp. 91–114.
——, 'When was "the Post-colonial"? Thinking at the Limit', in Iain Chambers and Lidia Curtis (eds), *The Post-Colonial Question: Common Skies, Divided Horizons* (London and New York: Routledge, 1996), pp. 242–60.
Hargreaves, Alec G., *Immigration, 'Race' and Ethnicity in Contemporary France* (London: Routledge, 1995).
Hargreaves, Alec G. and Marc McKinney, 'Introduction', in Hargreaves and McKinney, *Post-colonial Cultures in France* (London: Routledge, 1997), pp. 1–25.
Harrison, Nicholas, *Postcolonial Criticism* (Cambridge: Polity Press, 2003).
Harrow, Kenneth W., *Less than One and Double: a Feminist Reading of African Women's Writing* (Portsmouth, NH: Heinemann, 2002).
Hergé, *Tintin au Congo* (1946; Paris: Casterman, 1974).
Hitchcott, Nicki, *Women Writers in Francophone Africa* (Oxford: Berg, 2000).
Huggan, Graham, 'Anthropologists and Other Frauds', *Comparative Literature*, 46.2 (1994), pp. 113–28.
——, *The Postcolonial Exotic: Marketing the Margins* (London: Routledge, 2001).
Ifekwunigwe, Jane, 'Old Whine, New Vassals: Are Diaspora and Hybridity Postmodern Inventions?', in Phil Cohen (ed.), *New Ethnicities, Old Racisms* (London: Zed Books, 1999), pp. 180–204.
Ireland, Susan and Patrice J. Proulx, 'Introduction', in Ireland and Proulx (eds), *Immigrant Narratives in Contemporary France* (Westport, CT: Greenwood Press, 2001), pp. 1–4.
Jules-Rosette, Bennetta, *Black Paris: the African Writers' Landscape* (Urbana and Chicago: University of Illinois Press, 1998).
Kalčik, Susan, 'Ethnic Foodways in America: Symbol and the Performance of Identity', in Linda Keller Brown and Kay Mussell (eds), *Ethnic and Regional Foodways in the United States* (Knoxville, TN: University of Tennessee Press, 1984), pp. 37–65.
King, Russell, John Connell and Paul White (eds), *Writing across Worlds: Literature and Migration* (London: Routledge, 1995).
La Lettre du CSA, 129, June 2000.
Laronde Michel, 'Displaced Discourses: Post(-)coloniality, Francophone Space(s) and the Literature(s) of Immigration in France', in H. Adlai Murdoch and Anne Donadey (eds), *Postcolonial Theory and Francophone Literary Studies* (Gainesville, FL: University Press of Florida, 2005), pp. 175–92.

——, *L'Ecriture décentrée: la langue de l'Autre dans le roman contemporain* (Paris: L'Harmattan, 1996).
Laroui, Fouad, *La fin tragique de Philomène Tralala* (Paris: Julliard, 2003).
Lionnet, Françoise, '"Logiques Métisses": Cultural Appropriation and Postcolonial Representations', in Mary Jane Green et al. (eds), *Postcolonial Subjects: Francophone Women Writers* (Minneapolis, MN: University of Minnesota Press, 1996), pp. 321–43.
——, 'Narrative Strategies and Postcolonial Identity in Contemporary France: Leïla Sebbar's *Les Carnets de Shérazade*', in Gisela Brinker-Gabler and Sidonie Smith (eds), *Writing New Identities: Gender, Nation and Immigration in Contemporary Europe* (Minneapolis, MN: University of Minnesota Press, 1997), pp. 62–77.
——, *Postcolonial Representations* (Ithaca, NY: Cornell University Press, 1995).
MacCannell, Dean, *The Tourist: a New Theory of the Leisure Class* (1976; New York: Schocken Books, 1989).
Massey, Doreen, 'A Global Sense of Place', *Marxism Today*, June 1991.
McClintock, Anne, 'The Angels of Progress: Pitfalls of the Term "Postcolonialism"', *Social Text*, 10.2–3 (1992), pp. 84–98.
Miller, Christopher, *Blank Darkness: Africanist Discourse in French* (Chicago: University of Chicago Press, 1985).
Millet, Catherine, *La Vie sexuelle de Catherine M* (Paris: Seuil, 2002).
Mohanty, Chandra, 'Under Western Eyes: Feminist Scholarship and Colonial Discourse', *Feminist Review*, 30 (1988), pp. 61–88.
Moura, Jean-Marc, *Littératures francophones et théorie postcoloniale* (Paris: PUF, 1999).
Murdoch, H. Adlai and Anne Donadey, 'Introduction: Productive Intersections', in Murdoch and Donadey (eds), *Postcolonial Theory and Francophone Literary Studies* (Gainesville, FL: University of Florida Press, 2005), pp. 1–17.
Murphy, David, 'De-centring French Studies: Towards a Postcolonial Theory of Francophone Cultures', *French Cultural Studies*, 13.2 (2002), pp. 163–85.
——, 'Will the Real Africa Please Stand Up? Resistance and Representation in African Literature', in David Murphy and Aedín Ní Loingsigh (eds), *Thresholds of Otherness/Autrement Mêmes: Identity and Alterity in French-Language Literatures* (London: Grant and Cutler, 2002), pp. 305–22.
Nfah-Abbenyi, Juliana Makuchi, *Gender in African Women's Writing: Identity, Sexuality, and Difference* (Bloomington, IN: Indiana University Press, 1997).
Ní Loingsigh, Aedín, 'Immigration, Tourism and Postcolonial Reinventions of Travel', in Forsdick and Murphy (eds), *Francophone Postcolonial Studies: a Critical Introduction* (London: Arnold, 2003), pp. 155–65.
Ouologuem, Yambo, *Le Devoir de violence* (1968; Paris: Le Serpent à Plumes, 2003).
Picton, John, 'West Africa and the Guinea Coast', in Tom Phillips (ed.), *Africa: the Art of a Continent* (Munich/New York: Prestel, 1996), pp. 327–477.
Procter, James, 'Cultural Studies into Francophone Postcolonial Studies: Towards a "Disciplined" Interdisciplinarity', *Francophone Postcolonial Studies*, 1.2 (2004), pp. 47–52.
Quiminal, Catherine, 'The Associative Movement of African Women and New Forms

of Citizenship', in Jane Freedman and Carrie Tarr (eds), *Women, Immigration and Identities in France* (Oxford: Berg, 2000), pp. 39–56.

Randall, Marilyn, *Pragmatic Plagiarism: Authorship, Profit, and Power* (Toronto: University of Toronto Press, 2001).

Robertson, Pamela, *Guilty Pleasures: Feminist Camp from Mae West to Madonna* (London: I.B. Taurus, 1996).

Robins, Kevin, 'Tradition and Translation: National Culture in its Global Context', in John Corner and Sylvia Harvey (eds), *Enterprise and Heritage: Crosscurrents of National Culture* (London: Routledge, 1991), pp. 21–44.

Rosello, Mireille, *Declining the Stereotype: Ethnicity and Representation in French Cultures* (Hanover, NH: University Press of New England, 1998).

——, *Postcolonial Hospitality: the Immigrant as Guest* (Stanford, CA: Stanford University Press, 2001).

Rushdie, Salman, *Imaginary Homelands* (London: Granta, 1991).

Said, Edward W., 'Introduction', in *Reflections on Exile and Other Literary and Cultural Essays* (London: Granta, 2001), pp. xi–xxxv.

——, 'Reflections on Exile', in *Reflections on Exile and Other Literary and Cultural Essays* (London: Granta, 2001), pp. 173–86.

——, *Representations of the Intellectual* (New York: Vintage, 1994).

Sartre, Jean-Paul, 'Orphée noir', preface to L.S. Senghor, *Anthologie de la nouvelle poésie nègre et malgache de langue française* (Paris: PUF, 1948), pp. ix–xliv.

Sautman, Francesca Canadé, 'The Race for Globalization: Modernity, Resistance, and the Unspeakable in Three African Francophone Texts', in Farid Laroussi and Christopher L. Miller (eds), *Yale French Studies 103, French and Francophone* (2003), pp. 106–22.

Sellin, Eric, 'The Unknown Voice of Yambo Ouologuem', *Yale French Studies*, 53 (1976), pp. 137–62.

Senghor, Léopold Sédar, *Liberté I: Négritude et humanisme* (Paris: Seuil, 1964).

Smith, Sidonie and Gisela Brinker-Gabler, 'Introduction: Gender, Nation, and Immigration in New Europe', in Gisela Brinker-Gabler and Sidonie Smith (eds), *Writing New Identities: Gender, Nation, and Immigration in Contemporary Europe* (Minneapolis, MN: University of Minnesota Press, 1997), pp. 1–27.

Spivak, Gayatri Chakravorty, *In Other Worlds: Essays in Cultural Politics* (London: Routledge, 1988).

——, 'Poststructuralism, Marginality, Postcoloniality and Value', in Peter Collier and Helga Geyer-Ryan (eds), *Literary Theory Today* (Ithaca, NY: Cornell University Press, 1990), pp. 219–44.

Tasker, Yvonne, *Spectacular Bodies: Gender, Genre and the Action Cinema* (London: Routledge, 1993).

Tebereh, Inquai, *A Taste of Africa: an African Cookbook* (Trenton, NJ: Africa World Press, 1998).

Thiam, Awa, *La Parole aux Négresses* (Paris: Denoël, 1978).

Thomas, Dominic, 'Daniel Biyaoula: Exile, Immigration and Transnational Cultural Productions', in Susan Ireland and Patrice J. Proulx (eds), *Immigrant Narratives in Contemporary France* (Westport, CT: Greenwood Press), pp. 165–76.

Tine, Alioune, 'Pour une théorie de la littérature écrite', *Présence Africaine*, 133–34 (1984), pp. 99–121.

Trinh, T. Minh-ha, *Woman, Native, Other* (Bloomington, IN: Indiana University Press, 1989).
White, Paul, 'Geography, Literature and Migration', in Russell King, John Connell and Paul White (eds), *Writing across Worlds: Literature and Migration* (London: Routledge, 1995), pp. 1–19.
Wise, Christopher, 'In Search of Yambo Ouologuem', *Research in African Literatures*, 29.2 (1998), pp. 159–82.
Wolitz, Seth, 'L'Art du plagiat', *Research in African Literatures* 4.1 (1973), pp. 130–34.
Woodhull, Winifred, 'Ethnicity on the French Frontier', in Gisela Brinker-Gabler and Sidonie Smith (eds), *Writing New Identities: Gender, Nation, and Immigration in Contemporary Europe* (Minneapolis, MN: University of Minnesota Press, 1997), pp. 31–61
Young, Robert, *Colonial Desire: Hybridity in Theory, Culture and Race* (London: Routledge, 1995).

Index

Académie Française 17, 32, 79, 135–6, 141, 148, 149
acculturation 79–80, 85–6, 87, 93, 94, 99
Achebe, Chinua 21
Adesanmi, Pius 76
Africa 1–4, 7, 9–11, 14–16, 18–22, 25, 27, 141, 143
   Beyala's fictitious 10–11, 44–51, 52–61, 116–17, 121, 123, 132
   Beyala's reception in 50–1, 143–5
   colonial constructions of 123
   in combat 41
   contempt for 93–4
   corruption of 44–8
   diversity of 53–5
   eurocentric views of 50, 53
   exoticist representations of 41, 53
   fictitious images of 41
   homogenizing approach to 53–4
   horror of postcolonial 45–50, 52–3, 55–6
   invented authenticities surrounding 41, 43–61, 62
   lack of an authentic 28, 41, 54–9
   magic and mystery of 58–9
   migrant relationships with 68, 108
   migration from 66–88, 95, 113
   myths surrounding 28, 41, 123–5
   natural/untouched 41
   reductionist approach to 53–4
   scientific 41, 57
   squalor/poverty of 45
African art 137
African authenticity 28, 30, 32, 41, 43–61, 54–9, 62
African cuisine 57, 95, 97
African identity 7, 8, 124
African music 54
African Publishers' Network 22
African trickster figure 128–30, 138, 150
African Writers Series (AWS) (Heinemann) 2, 21–2, 51
'Africa's 100 Best Books' project 21–2
Afro-française 10, 89–111
   hybrid hyphenations 91
Afro-pessimism 19, 50
Ahmad, Aijaz 130
AIDS 143
Albin Michel (publisher) 1, 11, 20, 21, 30, 134, 140
alienation 56, 84, 94–5, 98–9, 115
Allwood, Gill 103–4
Alvim, Fernando 137, 149
'amalgamation' thesis 92
ambivalence
   Beyala's towards Africa 10
   and gender identity 101
   migrant 68, 72, 87–8, 99–101, 108–10, 120, 131
   postcolonial 91
   regarding Beyala 3–4, 7–8, 15, 20, 23, 28, 30, 131, 137–8, 145, 149–50
Amina magazine 34, 60
Amours sauvages 13–14, 101–2, 103, 133
   black-white sexual relationships 94–5
   gender identity 85
   migration 68, 69, 70, 77, 113
Anglo-Saxon theoretical frameworks 6
Anozie, Sunday 129

Antenne 2 34–5
anthropological exotic 16, 21
anti-colonialism 59
anti-feminism 25–6
anti-racist groups 13
Anzaldúa, Gloria 98–9, 150
Appadurai, Arjun 76
Appiah, Kwame Anthony 50, 54
Arabization 100
Arbres en parlent encore, Les 9, 57–8, 59–64, 116, 128, 133
  metaphorical masks 114
  narrative layering 61–2
Arenberg, Nancy 48
art-culture system 134
Ashcroft, Bill 109, 132–3, 136
Assèze l'Africaine 1, 32–3, 91, 92–3, 107–8, 133, 145
  'faking it' 114, 127–8
  gender identity 85, 87
  migration 68, 69–70, 71–2, 73–4, 77, 79, 80, 85, 87
  portrayal of heterosexuality 46
  racial stereotypes 123–4
  setting 44, 55
assimilation 72, 79, 87, 95, 100, 107, 120, 127, 148
Assouline, Pierre 3, 15, 30, 31–3, 39, 40, 134, 135–6, 140, 141
Atwood, Margaret 37
Audouard, Yvan 59
Austin, J. L. 117, 118
Australian Aboriginals
  texts 65
  theatre 131
authenticity 7, 9, 129
  African 28, 30, 32, 41, 43–61, 54–9, 62
  French readers' desire for 39–40
  invented 7, 28, 39–65, 76, 145
  manufacture of 134
  meaninglessness of 40–1, 84, 112
  staged 124
authority 7, 117–18

Bâ, Mariama 22, 24, 51–2
Baartman, Saartje 35

Bancel, Pascal 36
Bardot, Brigitte 34
beauty, cultural conventions of 95–6, 97
Becarro, Thierry 35
becoming, process of 87
Bell, David 95–6, 97
belonging 12, 73–5
  counter-narratives of 41
Benjamin, Walter 84
Beti, Mongo 7, 18, 19, 20, 23, 26, 134, 143–4, 148, 149, 150
'Beyala Affair' ('l'Affaire Beyala') 3, 31–3, 39–40, 108, 135, 140
Beyala, Calixthe
  absence of a desire to please 147–8
  African reception of 22, 50–1, 143–5
  African settings 10–11, 44–51, 52–61, 116–17, 121, 123, 132
  Afro-française identity 89–111
  ambivalent status 3–4, 7–8, 15, 20, 23, 28, 30, 131, 137–8, 140–5, 149–50
  ambivalent feelings towards Africa 10
  American reception 22, 23
  authenticity of 32–3, 134–5
  autobiographical work 40, 44
  beauty 34
  Belleville setting (Afro-Paris) 76–7, 83, 86, 101, 113
  as both Parisian self and African other 16
  childhood 44
  colonial representations of 35–8
  commerciality of 1–2, 141, 149, 150
  commodification 7–8, 141, 148
    complicity in 20
    as symptom of postcolonial exotic 15–16, 22–3, 25, 27, 36–7, 148
  controversial media appearances 13, 14, 18, 19–20, 34–6, 141–2, 149, 150
  as cultural celebrity 37–8
  distancing of herself from her African roots 18–19
  in exile in France 18–19, 45
  exoticism 3, 7, 11, 15–16, 134, 136–9, 141, 143, 148–50

erotic-exotic object 28–30, 34–8, 53, 65, 141
reinvention of 137
feminism 12, 25–6
féminitude 26–7, 52
as fictional construct 142
as francophone author 20, 31, 37, 110–11, 142
and the French language 1, 23–4, 78–9
French readership 49–50, 90, 95, 139
French settings 10–11, 76–7, 83, 86, 101, 113
gallicization of her writing 49–50
and gender issues 24–7
geographical dislocation 4, 9–10, 12
as icon of black femininity 15, 34
identification with France 18–19, 20–1, 49–50, 89–90, 110
as inauthentic/fake 134–5
individualistic self-interest/opportunism of 143–5
as innovator/pioneer 51, 133–4
and invented authenticities 39–65
literacy legitimacy of 17–18
as literary ambassador for Africa 50
literary prizes 1, 11, 15, 17, 18, 32–3, 135–6, 141
migrant writing of 2–5, 10, 14, 16–18
and migrating subjectivities 66–88
and Negritude 7, 26, 51–2
orphan work 144
otherness of 16, 37–8, 148
and the performance of migrant identity 112–36
plagiarism convictions 1, 3, 9, 15, 30–3, 39–40, 43, 128–9, 134–6, 140, 144, 149, 150
political interests 13–14, 23, 89–90, 143
pornographic material 9, 28–30
portrayal of sexual acts 9, 11, 23, 27, 28–30, 42–3, 46, 47, 48, 52–3, 96
and positive racial discrimination 90, 109

as postcolonial icon 139
as postcolonial puppet 138
and racism 13, 30–2, 33–4, 35–6, 37, 53, 89, 108–9
reductive stereotyping of African women 52–3
resistance of 136, 147
self-positioning 4, 89, 137, 138, 146, 150
self-representation 10, 128
on social injustice 11–12
strategic pattern of self-defence 24
subversive nature 137–8, 139, 148
as transculturated product 148
works, *see individual titles*
writing/narrative style 23–4, 78–9
Bhabha, Homi 35, 76, 84, 91, 92, 94, 109, 110, 120–1, 124, 136
Bible 64
Biya, Paul 18, 44, 144
black inferiority 119–20
black rights movement 13
black superiority 27
Blanchard, Nicolas 36
Boehmer, Elleke 3, 50, 78
borderland 98–9, 112
Borgomano, Madeleine 24–6
Bourdieu, Pierre 17
Bourges, Hervé 13
Bouvard, Philippe 90
Brahimi, Denise 10–11, 23
Brennan, Timothy 17–18
Brière, Eloise 78, 128, 142–3
Brinker-Gabler, Gisela 147
Britton, Celia 6
Bromley, Roger 112
Bugul, Ken 22
Buten, Howard 15, 31, 129
Butler, Judith 8, 117–18, 119, 120, 124, 126, 132, 134, 138

Cabiria 103–4
Cameroon 1, 18–19, 24, 44–5, 49, 51–3, 55, 57, 68–70, 72–4, 79–80, 82, 95, 113, 135, 144
Cameroon Tribune (newspaper) 147
Cameroonian literary tradition 26

Canard enchaîné, Le (magazine) 3, 31
Cazenave, Odile 2, 49–50, 53, 110
Césaire, Aimé 42, 56, 107, 132
César ceremony 2000 13
C'est le soleil qui m'a brûlée 2, 10–11, 51, 133, 138, 141–2, 149
   gender issues 115, 116, 121–2
   mimicry 121
   photography 113–14
   portrayal of sexual acts 30, 46, 48, 96
   setting 44, 45, 47, 48
Cévaër, Françoise 144–5
Chambers, Iain 40–1, 56
Chicanos 99
child abuse 47, 48–9
Chow, Rey 130
Christianity 64
cinematic terminology 122–3
Clarke, Becky 21, 22
Clifford, James 42, 43, 63, 65, 132, 134
code switching 105, 108–9
Collectif Egalité 13–14, 35, 89–90, 143
colonial discourses 35–8, 119–20, 136
colonial ideology 131
colonial mimicry 119–21, 124
colonialism 59, 119–20, 123, 143
   French 107
Coly, Ayo Abiétou 9, 45, 53
Comment cuisiner son mari à l'africaine 13–14, 35, 56–7, 68, 80, 95–9, 108, 126, 133
community 75
Connell, John 4, 10
Conrad, Joseph 53
Conseil Supérieur de l'Audiovisuel (CSA) 13, 143
Constant, Paule 31, 32–3, 129
cookery
   African 57, 95, 97
   French 96–7
cosmopolitanism 17–18
cultural hybridity 91–5, 100–1, 106–10, 130
   faking it 112
   negative 93–4
cultural identity 6–9

cultural mixing 92
cultural mobility 82–3
cultural norms
   instability of 84
   subversion 138
cultural Otherness 37–8
cultural studies 5, 6–7
cultural synthesis 91
cultural translation 75–6, 84, 91
cultural transsexualism 79, 80, 81–2, 92
cultural values 86
culture
   dominant 124, 139
   host 3, 9, 12, 68–9, 72–3, 75, 78–9, 90, 95–7, 99, 118, 130
   'making strange' of French 77–9
Cusack, Igor 57
Cusin, Philippe 30–1

Dadié, Bernard 21, 64
D'Almeida, Irène Assiba 2
Dangaremba 129
Darlington, Sonja 23
Davies, Carole Boyce 5, 117, 146
de Beauvoir, Simone 117
De Gaulle, Charles 104
de-centred writing 5–6
death 45, 48, 52–3, 55, 86, 92–4, 98, 122, 145–6
defeminization 82
Delafosse 64
Delon, Alain 104
dependency 55
diaspora 130, 131
disguise 114, 116–17
displacement 12
djellabas 105
Doane, Mary Anne 118–19, 120
dominant cultures 124, 139
   see also host cultures
dominant discourses 65, 136, 146
Donadey, Anne 5, 6
Douala, Cameroon 1, 24, 44, 55, 69–70, 73–4, 79, 80, 82, 85, 123, 135, 144
dowry system 46
drag 118–19, 120, 124, 126

see also transvestism
Dumas, Alexandre 40
Durand, Alain-Philippe 86, 110, 145, 146
Dwyer, Claire 73

eating disorders 95–6
economic freedom 69, 75, 102–4, 130–1
Eden 63
Editions de Minuit 30
Editions J'ai Lu 2
education, African women and 82–3, 84
Egbeme, Choga Regina 17
Elle (magazine) 34
emasculation 82
essentialism
  cultural 77, 84, 91, 92–4
  ethnic 42–3, 56–7, 73, 77, 92–3, 98, 106, 108–9, 132–3
  gender 42–3, 52, 134
ethnic identity 17–18
ethno-texts 62
ethnography 43, 63–4
  'salvage ethnography' 43, 58
ethnoscapes 76–7
Etudes Francophones 130
eurocentrism 50, 53
Eve 64
exoticism 3, 7, 11, 15–16, 28–30, 34–8, 53, 65, 120, 134, 136–41, 143, 148–50
  performance of 127–8
  strategic 137, 138
  see also anthropological exotic
L'Express (magazine) 1
Ezra, Elizabeth 41

fakery 112, 113–14, 117, 119, 127–8, 134–5, 147
Fall, Aminata Sow 19, 22
Fanon, Frantz 120
Fatunde, Tunde 28, 50
female genital mutilation 46
femininity
  alternative 83, 99, 116
  black 15, 34, 146–7
  crisis of 80
  performance of 115, 118–19, 120, 122
  renegotiated 84–6
  social construction of 117
feminism 12, 25–6
  African rejection of 25
  French 102
féminitude 26–7, 52
feminization 81
femme fatale 118–19, 120, 122, 126
Femme nue, femme noire 9, 52, 133, 134, 150
  commerciality 141
  female homosexuality 27, 42–3
  invented authenticities 42–3
  performativity 122
  portrayal of sex in 29–30, 47, 52–3
Figaro, Le (newspaper) 30–1, 32
Forsdick, Charles 7
Foster, Susan Leigh 118
France 1–4, 7–11, 13–21, 27–32, 36–8, 45, 49, 55–6, 135, 142–3, 148, 150
  migration to 66–88, 95, 113, 127
  and scientific Africa 41
francophone authors 20–2, 24, 30–1, 37, 46, 50–1, 110–11, 142
Francophonie 20, 33, 37, 111, 142, 143
Freedman, Jane 70, 101
freedom
  economic 69, 75, 102–4, 130–1
  of movement 69, 82–3, 101–2
  sexual 83
French Africans 16–17
French colonialism 107
French culture, 'making strange' of 77–9
French Republic 110
French universalism 89–90
Freud, Sigmund 116
Frobenius, Leo 43, 64
'frontier style' 78
fundamentalism, Islamic 74

Gallimore, Rangira Béatrice 2, 44, 47, 104, 106–7

Gary, Romain 31
Gates, Henry Louis 128–9
gender 116–17
   and experiences of migration 100–6
   and tradition 46–7, 79–83, 86–7, 97–8
gender identity
   ambivalent 101
   and migration 79–83, 84–7, 97–8, 99, 104–6, 146–7
   performance of 8, 115, 117–20, 121–2, 124, 125, 126–7, 134
   performativity 8, 118, 122
   socially constructed nature of 117
gender norms 116–17, 118–19, 132, 134, 147
gender roles 115–16
   and migration 80–3, 97–8
   normative 118
   performance of 115, 117–20, 121–2, 125, 126–7
gender stereotypes 52–3, 115–16
Genevoix, Sylvie 16
Gervais, Jean-Bernard 26–7
Gilbert, Helen 131–2
Gilroy, Paul 3, 146–7
'global commodity culture' 4
Gomez-Peña, Guillermo 91
Grand Prix du Roman de l'Académie Française 1, 15, 17, 18, 33, 138, 141
Griaule, Marcel 41
Griffiths, Gareth 65
Guardian, The (newspaper) 31, 32
Gurr, Andrew 45

Hall, Stuart 6–7, 68, 72, 73, 76, 87, 125–6, 131
Hargreaves, Alec 80, 98
L'Harmattan 2
Harrison, Nicholas 5
Harrow, Kenneth 2, 49, 120, 124, 128–9, 138, 150
Heinemann, African Writers Series (AWS) 2, 21–2, 51
Hergé 148
heterosexual relationships
   black–white 84–6, 91–2, 94–5, 105
   characterised as abusive 46, 47
   performativity of 122–3
   renegotiation of femininity through black–white encounters 84–6, 91
High Court, Paris 1, 32
Hollywood 104
home, migrant conceptions of 68–9, 74, 84, 101, 109, 111
homosexuality
   female 27, 141
   male 101
Honneurs perdus, Les 11, 15, 17, 20, 53, 91, 96, 98, 100–1, 109, 110–11, 115, 129, 132, 133, 145–6, 149
   accusations of plagiarism 31, 32, 33
   female homosexuality 27
   gender identity 84–5
   migration 68, 69, 70, 71, 78, 83, 86
   sales 33
   setting 44–5, 47
host cultures 3, 9, 12, 68–9, 72–3, 75, 78–9, 90, 95–7, 99, 118, 130
   see also dominant cultures
Huggan, Graham 4, 7, 8, 15, 21, 22, 36–7, 43, 64, 117, 124, 125, 137, 138, 139, 148–9
human rights 45–6
hybrid hyphenations 91

identification 71–2, 75, 115
identity
   African 7, 8, 124
   Afro-française 89–111
   cultural 6–9
   essentialized 132
   ethnic 17–18
   fluid nature of 87–8
   postcolonial 7, 65, 118, 131–2, 138
   racial 117, 125–6
   social construction of 117
   and transculturation 75–6
   see also gender identity; migrant identity
Ifekwunigwe, Jayne 91, 92
illegal immigrants 69, 70–1, 82, 102

improvisation 132, 147
in-betweenness 54, 77, 91, 98–9, 101,
    108–9
incorporation, fantasy of 72
individualism 145
insanity 94
insider/outsider dichotomy 73–4, 91
integration 79, 83, 96
Intégration France 13
intertextuality 31–2
Ireland, Susan 68
Islamic fundamentalism 74

'Jouons au cochon pendu' (article) 130
Jules-Rosette, Bennetta 20–1, 41
Julliard 32

Kelly, Grace 104
King, Adèle 25–6
King, Martin Luther 104
King, Russell 4, 10
Kom, Ambroise 22, 28–9, 30, 53,
    115–16, 124
Kombi, Narcisse Mouellé 34
Koran 64

lactification 80, 95, 96, 119–20
Laronde, Michel 5–6
Laroui, Fouad 140–3, 145
Legitimus, Darling 13
lesbianism 27, 141
*Lettre d'une Africaine à ses soeurs
    occidentales* 11–12, 44, 46, 89,
    90, 145
*Lettre d'une Afro-française à ses
    compatriotes* 11–12, 13, 89–90,
    108–9
'Loukoum' novels 3, 20, 67–8, 70,
    72–3, 74–6, 77, 78, 81–4, 102–3,
    104–6, 108, 109–10, 111, 119,
    121, 123–7, 133, 136, 139, 148
    see also *Le petit prince de Belleville*;
    Maman a un amant
Lionnet, Françoise 4, 78, 79
Lire (magazine) 15, 31
literacy 82–3
longing, narratives of 41

MacCannell, Dean 124
magic 58–9
Makhélé, Caya 34
Maman a un amant 2, 46, 91, 92–3,
    103, 125, 133, 139
    gender roles 81–3, 84
    migration 68, 70, 72–3, 81–4, 87
Mango 11
Manicheanism 116
marginality 103–4, 143
    staged 124–5
marginalization 3–4, 72, 77, 127
Martinek, Claudia 52–3
masculinity
    constructions of 104–5, 116
    crisis of 80, 81–2, 99
    normative 116–17
masks, metaphorical 114, 116–17, 122,
    126
masquerade 114, 116–17, 118–22, 126,
    131
Mataillet, Dominique 29
Matateyou, Emmanuel 18–19, 21
Matin Bonheur (TV programme) 35
Maupassant 40
McKinney, Marc 98
media
    Beyala's controversial appearances in
        13, 14, 18, 19–20, 34–6, 141–2,
        149, 150
    racism in 13, 35–6, 143
'melting-pot' notion 92
migrant identity 68, 71–3, 75–6, 79,
    87–8, 93, 146–7
    and choice/volition 8
    in-between 91
    'making it up' 112, 132
    performance of 4, 8–9, 14, 77, 111,
        112–36, 139
    performativity 4
migrant texts 3–4
migrant writing 2–5, 10, 14, 16–18
migrants
    and 'faking it' 112, 113–14, 147
    illegal 69, 70–1, 82, 102
    and improvisation 132, 147
    losing their way 74–5

and the 'making strange' of French culture 77–9
opportunistic nature 126, 130, 139, 145
'out of sync' experiences of 88, 90–1, 98–9, 112, 126–7
see also Afro-française
migrating subjectivities 66–88, 146–7, 150
migration 9
causes of 69–70
evidence of successful 112–13
as lasting force 88
as space of possibility 87–8
transformative nature 4, 81–2, 126–7, 131–3, 145–6, 150
Millet, Catherine 29
mimicry 109, 110, 119–22, 124, 135
Mitterrand, François 104
mixed-race characters, negative presentation 107–8
modernity, reconciliation with tradition 132
Mohanty, Chandra 25
Molière 121
Monénembo, Tierno 20
mongrelization 98
Mortimer, Mildred 58
Moura, Jean-Marc 6
Mugabe, Robert 9, 149
Murdoch, H. Adlai 5, 6
Murphy, David 54
music 54, 107
Muslims 54, 75, 100, 104–5
British Muslim women 73, 74

narrative layering 61–2
nationalism 144
Ndiaye, Marie 30
Negritude 7, 26, 42–3, 51–2, 56, 106–7, 129, 132–3
neocolonial knowledge industry 21
Nfah-Abbenyi, Juliana Makuchi 2, 27
Ní Loingsigh, Aedín 72
Niven, Alastair 21–2
normativity 118
postcolonial French 136
norms
conformity to and the loss of self 116–17, 122
cultural 84, 138
gender 116–17, 118–19, 132, 134, 147
North America, publishing hegemony 20
Nouvelles Editions Africaines, Les 2

Okri, Ben 15, 31, 32, 129
'On a tout essayé!' (TV programme) 35
opportunism 126, 130, 139, 143–5
oppression 12
oral tradition 60, 64, 78, 129, 133
'oralité feinte' (feigned orality) 62
orality 31–2
Organisation Internationale de la Francophonie 143
Other
African woman as seductive sensual 52
authentic 64–5
immigrant women as 147
pre-civilized 41
Otherness 53
of Beyala 16, 37–8, 148
cultural 37–8
migrant 73
objects of 91
Ouologuem, Yambo 33, 39, 43
'out of sync' experiences 88, 90–1, 98–9, 112, 126–7

Palcy, Euzhan 13
Pan-African Booksellers Association 22
Paris 1–4, 9, 16, 20–1, 56
migration to 66–8, 71, 73–4, 76–7, 80
Parisianism movement 20–1
patriarchy 46–7, 64, 80–1, 147
performance 138–9
distinction from performativity 126
of gender 8, 115, 117–20, 121–2, 124, 125, 126–7, 134
of migrant identity 4, 8–9, 14, 77, 111, 112–36, 139

of racist stereotypes 124, 125
and repetition 117–18
of whiteness 119–20
performativity 116, 131–2
distinction from performance 126
of gender identity 8, 118, 122
of heterosexual relationships 122–3
of migrant identity 4
Petit prince de Belleville, Le 9, 14, 94, 103–6, 108, 131, 133, 140, 145
gender norms 119, 126–7
gender roles 80, 81, 82
migration 67–8, 72, 74–6, 77, 78, 80, 81, 82, 86
mimicry 121
plagiarism accusations 31, 32
racial stereotypes 123, 125
Petite fille du réverbère, La 9, 14, 40, 44, 58–9, 113, 119–20, 122–3, 133, 135
photography 113–14
Picton, John 114
Plantation, La 1, 9, 133, 134, 141, 149–50
pluralist approaches 5
Poivre d'Arvor, Patrick 34
polygamy 46, 70, 86
porn 9, 28–30
Porra, Véronique 31–2
postcolonial ambivalence 91
postcolonial authors 43
postcolonial criticism 4–6
postcolonial dependency 55
postcolonial identity 118, 138
and global market forces 7
inauthenticity of 65
resistance to 131–2
postcolonial literature 7
postcolonial subject
identity 118
paradigmatic 78
postcolonial theory 117
post-exotic age 137, 147, 149
Présence Africaine 2
Prix Femina 30
Prix Renaudot 33
Prix Tropique 32

Procter, James 6
prostitution 46, 47, 48
by migrant females 69, 71, 103–4, 113, 119–20
child 47, 49
transsexual 119
Proulx, Patrice J. 68
publishers 2, 11, 16, 17, 18, 20, 21, 30, 51, 142

racial contamination 91–2
racial identity
fluctuating nature of 125–6
social construction of 117
racism 13, 30–2, 33–4, 35–6, 37, 53, 89, 94, 98, 108–9
scientific 119
racist stereotypes 52–3, 72–3, 81, 106, 108–9, 123–5
Randall, Marilyn 33
rape 47, 52
Rastafarians 56, 133
recognition 71, 74
resistance 136, 147
to the corruption of neocolonialism 47–8
to postcolonial criticism 6
to postcolonial identity 131–2
Riviere, Joan 118
Robins, Kevin 75–6
Rosello, Mireille 105, 109, 123, 124
Rushdie, Salman 76, 98, 139

Said, Edward 7, 37, 106, 109, 110, 111
Saint-Eloi, Luc 13
'salvage ethnography' 43, 58
Sartre, Jean-Paul 56
self, loss of 117, 122
Sellin, Eric 39
Senghor, Léopold Sédar 7, 26, 42–3, 52, 92, 104, 106, 107, 148
Seul le diable le savait 9, 10, 28–9, 44, 59, 115, 116–17, 133
sexual acts 9, 11, 23, 27–30, 42–3, 46–8, 52–3, 96
political agenda of 28–9
see also heterosexual relationships

sexual freedom 83
'Signifying Monkey' figure 128–9
Sinatra, Frank 104
Smith, Sidonie 147
social mobility 82–3
social positioning 4, 73, 89, 104, 137, 138, 146, 150
'Sonnette, La' (short story) 29
Spengler 11
Spivak, Gayatri Chakravorty 3, 78
stage terminology 122–3
Stallone, Sylvester 104
stereotypes 148
    African 28, 41, 123–5
    gender 52–3, 115–16
    racist 52–3, 72–3, 81, 106, 108–9, 123–5
storytelling 58–64
    tradition of 58–61
    unreliability of 61–2
    and writing 58
subjectivities
    alternative 146
    migrating 66–88, 146–7, 150
    shifting 131–2
subversion 137–8, 139, 148
supernatural 58–9
Syrotinski, Michael 6

Tadjo, Véronique 22
Tansi, Sony Labou 24, 47
Tchakam, Stéphane 133
Têko-Agbo, Ambrose 25–6
television 13, 143
Thiam, Awa 46
Thiong'o, Ngugi Wa 21
'third space' 91, 92, 94
Thomas, Dominic 110
Tine, Alioune 62
Tintin 148–9
tourist–native dichotomy 139
tourists, literary 139, 150
tradition
    Belleville setting as refuge for 101
    disregarding of 25
    and gender 46–7, 79–83, 86–7, 97–8
    and individualism 145
    and migrant identities 75–6, 86
    oppression of 12
    patriarchal 46–7
    reconciliation of modernity with 132
    of storytelling 58–61
transculturated products 148
transculturation 75–6, 86
translated peoples 76
transvestism 95
    see also drag
Trautmann, Catherine 13
Trinh, Minh-ha T. 25, 63, 64
Tu t'appelleras Tanga 2, 10, 11, 23, 117, 133, 138
    fictionalized Africa of 55–6
    gender performance 115
    migration 66–7, 113
    setting 44, 45–6, 47, 48–9, 54

universalism 89–90
University of Missouri 146

Valentine, Gill 95–6, 97
virginity 84–5, 100, 131
virginity testing 46
'visitor theory' approach 5
Volet, Jean-Marie 16

Wah, Fred 112
Walker, Alice 31
White, Paul 4, 8–9, 10, 87–8, 99, 146
white supremacy 119–20
whiteness
    performance of 119–20
    see also lactification
Woodhull, Winifred 139

Yaoundé 144
Young, Robert 92, 98

Zimbabwe International Book Fair 2000 22